AF600306

POETRY AND CRISIS

Cultural Politics and Citizenship in the Wake of the Madrid Bombings

JILL ROBBINS

Poetry and Crisis

Cultural Politics and Citizenship in the Wake of the Madrid Bombings

UNIVERSITY OF TORONTO PRESS
Toronto Buffalo London

ISBN 978-1-4875-0473-1 (cloth)
ISBN 978-1-4875-3079-2 (EPUB)
ISBN 978-1-4875-3078-5 (UPDF)

Toronto Iberic

Library and Archives Canada Cataloguing in Publication

Title: Poetry and crisis : cultural politics and citizenship in the wake of the Madrid bombings / Jill Robbins.
Names: Robbins, Jill, 1962– author.
Description: Series statement: Toronto Iberic series ; 47 | Includes bibliographical references and index.
Identifiers: Canadiana 20190188057 | ISBN 9781487504731 (hardcover)
Subjects: LCSH: Madrid Train Bombings, Madrid, Spain, 2004. | LCSH: Madrid Train Bombings, Madrid, Spain, 2004 – Social aspects. | LCSH: Madrid (Spain) – In literature. | LCSH: Poetry – Social aspects – Spain – Madrid. | LCSH: Poetry – Therapeutic use.
Classification: LCC PN1081 .R63 2020 | DDC 809.1/93584641083–dc23

This book has been published with the assistance of the University of California, Merced.

Permission to use citations from the anthology *11-M: Palabras para el recuerdo*, published by the Asociación de Vecinos y Amigos del Pozo del Tío Raimundo, are thanks to the generosity and good will of the Asociación 11-M Afectados del Terrorismo

IIM Asociación 11-M
Afectados Terrorismo

University of Toronto Press acknowledges the financial assistance to its publishing program of the Canada Council for the Arts and the Ontario Arts Council, an agency of the Government of Ontario.

Canada Council for the Arts
Conseil des Arts du Canada

Funded by the Government of Canada
Financé par le gouvernement du Canada

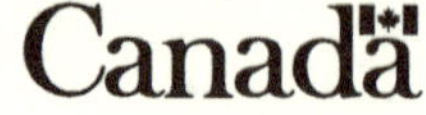

For all those affected by violence

Son flores pedazos de tu cuerpo.
Ana Rossetti

[N]o puedo dejar de oír estas voces que me cantan aquí dentro.
Jaime Gil de Biedma

Contents

Illustrations

Acknowledgments

This project was enriched immeasurably by conversations with a broad range of people over the past eight years, including fellow scholars and artists in the United States, Madrid, and Barcelona; graduate students and colleagues at the University of Texas at Austin; poets; a nurse who tended to the wounded; family and friends; and the librarians at the Railroad Museum in Madrid. Special thanks, in alphabetical order, to Eugenia Afinoguénova, Sam Amago, Miguel Amoraga, Montse Armengou, Jossianna Arroyo, Darcy Baxter, Silvia Bermúdez, Limam Boicha, Noni Benegas, Paul Cahill, Ann Cvetkovich, Olga Diego, Cecilia Enjuto Rangel, Tina Escaja, Debra Faszer-McMahon, Domingo Flores, Jessica Folkart, Concha García, Pedro García Caro, Anthony Geist, Sabine Hake, Catalina Iannone, Roberta Johnson, Victoria Ketz, Héctor Lara, Lorraine Leu, Ana Luengo, Steve Marsh, Jonathan Mayhew, Ramón Mayrata, Raquel Medina, Diana Norton, Fred Nutt, Tatiana Pavlovic, Jorge Pérez, Gema Pérez-Sánchez, Lucas Platero, Pedro Provencio, Sonia Roncador, Ana Rossetti, Joana Sabadell-Nieto, Gabriele Schwab, Shelly Smartt, Jon Snyder, Stuart Spencer, Julie Stephens, and Barbara Zecchi.

I am deeply grateful for the institutional support I received to conduct the research for this project and to write this book. In addition to fostering the intellectual environment that allowed me to flourish as a scholar, the College of Liberal Arts at the University of Texas at Austin provided material support in the form of research funds, a travel grant from the Center for European Studies, and a year-long grant-writing workshop funded by Dean Randy Diehl and overseen by Wayne Rebhorn, in which I elaborated the narrative for my successful National Endowment for the Humanities fellowship application. Without that fellowship, bolstered by sabbatical leave and research funds from the

University of California, Merced, I would not have been able to complete the book.

Many thanks as well to the University of Toronto Press for selecting gifted and dedicated readers for the manuscript. Attuned to the nuances of both contemporary poetry and Spanish cultural studies, they inspired the final version of the manuscript, which brought the detailed analysis of lyrical texts together more seamlessly with reflections about performance, affect, and formal mechanisms of cultural preservation.

Two previously published essays about the spontaneous shrines and public monuments inform the first chapter: "Institutional Sites of Remembrance: Monuments and Archives of the 11-M Train Bombings," which appeared in a special volume of *Hispanic Issues*, "Madrid: Cartographies of [a] Capital," edited by Silvia Bermúdez and Anthony Geist; and "¿Quién ha sido? Perpetradores, política y poesía después del 11-M," in a special Issue of *Hispanic Issues Online*, "Perpetradores y memoria democrática en España," edited by Ana Luengo and Katherine Stafford. Versions of these articles appear with permission from the editor, Nicholas Spadaccini.

I am grateful to the Archivo Histórico Ferroviario del Museo del Ferrocarril de Madrid – Fundación de los Ferrocarriles Españoles (AHF–MFM) for permission to cite texts and reproduce images from the Archivo del Duelo (the Archive of Mourning). Although images from the archive that were not available in high-resolution format could not be included in this book, the reader can find some samples in *El Archivo del Duelo: Análisis de la respuesta ciudadana ante los atentados del 11 de marzo en Madrid*, edited by Cristina Sánchez-Carretero.

I cite texts from the anthology *11-M: Palabras para el recuerdo*, published by the Asociación de Vecinos y Amigos del Pozo del Tío Raimundo, thanks to the generosity and good will of the Asociación 11-M Afectados del Terrorismo. All other lyrical texts are cited with permission from the authors and, in the case of Angelina Gatell, from her heirs.

I can never adequately acknowledge the myriad ways in which Arturo Arias has enriched my life and my scholarship. For more than twenty years, he has been my confidant, inspiration, sounding board, editor, cheerleader, co-parent, friend, and love. I could not have written this book without him.

POETRY AND CRISIS

Cultural Politics and Citizenship in the Wake of the Madrid Bombings

Introduction

On Thursday 11 March 2004, between 7:37 and 7:40 in the morning, Islamist terrorists[1] carried out massive bombings on Madrid's largely working-class commuter trains that left 191 dead[2] and more than 1,500 others wounded. This event, the second of three highly visible jihadist attacks on the West between 2001 and 2005, and the first in Europe, occurred days before national elections in Spain, and it exposed the contradictory cultural forces that underlay notions of national identity, violence, economic transformation, the role of the media, and the social contract in that country. The tension became apparent in the conflicting accounts of the attacks in Spanish media and in the patently false official statements by government leaders, who attributed responsibility for the bombings to the Basque separatist organization Euskadi Ta Askatasuna (Basque Country and Freedom, ETA), even after they knew that the culprits were Islamists. All of this undermined public faith in organized political parties and in the media. Meanwhile, the massive demonstrations in the ensuing days that led to the political defeat of the ruling Partido Popular (Popular Party, PP) revealed the ability of the populace to organize in a networked fashion outside the bounds of traditional social and political structures. The subsequent police investigations and trials have sought to bring closure, but the continued conspiracy theories (for some examples, see Álvarez de Toledo; Arís; Baeza; Burgo; Cardeñosa; Chalvidant; Marlasca and Rendueles; Pino González; among others), the annual commemorative events, and the dedication of monuments, far from healing the rift, have only deepened it, laying bare profound conflicts regarding historical memory, neoliberalism, war, state power, immigration, and national identity in Spain.

As individuals affected by the attacks, and Spanish society as a whole, have struggled to make sense of the events and voice their emotions, poetry has played numerous roles. Poems, both original and canonical, figured prominently in grassroots memorials in all of the train stations – Atocha, El Pozo del Tío Raimundo, and Santa Eugenia – where the bombings occurred. At the behest of workers in the Atocha train station, however, the "spontaneous shrines" (Santino) there were dismantled and replaced by an interactive electronic site, the *Espacio de Palabras* or Space for Words (Sánchez-Carretero, "Madrid Train Bombings" 252), and travellers of all nationalities who passed through the station wrote messages, including poems, at those sites. In a collaborative effort by anthropologists from the Agencia Estatal Consejo Superior de Investigaciones Científicas (the Spanish National Research Council, CSIC) and the Red Nacional de los Ferrocarriles Españoles (the Spanish National Network of Spanish Railways, RENFE), most of these texts and objects were collected and stored in the Archivo del Duelo (Archive of Mourning) within the Archivo Histórico Ferroviario del Museo del Ferrocarril de Madrid–Fundación de los Ferrocarriles Españoles (the Historical Railway Archive of Madrid–Spanish Railroad Foundation, AHF–MFM), located in the Railroad Museum, not far from the Atocha station. Among the archive's approximately seventy thousand items and texts, I found more than eight hundred poems during my research in the summer of 2014. Some of these messages were later inscribed on the inner walls of the crystal cylinder monument to the 11 March (11-M) victims and in other memory sites in the city and on the Web, including a special section of the website of one of the victims' associations. Many poems by Spanish, Latin American, and Moroccan poets, and by countless common citizens, have also been collected into anthologies, and these are ambiguously positioned as memorials, social action, archives, and monuments.[3]

Reading and rereading poetry is a vital exercise in understanding and coming to terms with a catastrophe. Poems provide a space for reflection beyond the parameters of current discourse about an event because they draw on a history of verse about similar events and emotions. This allows their authors and readers to contextualize their pain, anger, and loss, and to reflect upon what has happened in a broader framework of human experience. Poetry can also be especially adept at enacting what Sarah Cole calls the "disenchantment" of violent death: "the active stripping away of idealizing principles, an insistence that the violated body is not a magic site for the production of culture" (1633); nor should the violated body be the justification for an act of violence, an act of terror, an act of war. Poems, like grassroots memorials, can also be "performative events in public space" with "the intention to change" (Margry and Sánchez-Carretero 3) and that invite reading and encourage subsequent writing. And poems can preserve the ephemeral emotions, the vulnerable bodies, and the souls more permanently than a grassroots memorial, more poignantly than an archive, and in a more disinterested manner than a monument. This is also true of song, which is the medium through which most people come into contact with the lyric in their everyday lives.

Thus, although most studies of urban space, trauma, cultural sites, and collective memory in Spain focus on film and fiction, this book will instead make an argument about the unique uses of poetry to reflect a broader and extremely palpable social impulse to make sense of violence, to grieve, to memorialize victims, to expose social rifts, to evoke the sacred, and to encourage social change. Given the variety of sites and uses of poetry related to 11-M, I will take into account a broad range of cultural and collective practices, in accordance with Ann Rigney's astute observation that "the role of literary works in cultural remembrance is a complex one. To understand it fully one needs to go beyond the analysis of individual works to the study of their reception and their interactions with other acts of remembrance in a variety of media and genres" (350). Finally, the poems written, sung, and posted in response to 11-M must be read not only alongside the global literary and personal writings about similar events, but also in the context of Iberian literary and cultural traditions. The variety of lyric texts and performances that respond to 11-M recalls Ann E. Kaplan's caution about discussing traumatic reactions to 9/11 because "how one reacts to a traumatic event depends on one's individual psychic history, on memories inevitably mixed with fantasies of prior catastrophes, and on the particular cultural and political context within which a catastrophe takes place, especially how it is 'managed' by institutional forces" (1). Throughout this study, then, I will work with a broad concept of "poetic or lyric response," one that includes, not only the texts written and published by accomplished and recognized poets, but also the following: the performance and performativity of lyric texts in grassroots memorials, monuments, and archives; popular song; poems written by non-poets; and the institutions (particularly anthologies, concerts, and public schools) that contribute to the constitution and transmission of cultural memory in the poetic field. In this sense, this book is also an investigation into the functions of lyric in construing, contesting, and unravelling the rhetoric of public memory sites and their narratives about the meaning of culture and violent events in the context of contested nationalisms and identities.

Collective Memories and the Emergence of a New Sensibility

The ruling party at the time of the attacks, which occurred three days before national elections in Spain, was the right-wing Popular Party.

Its strategies for addressing the crisis clearly gestured toward concerns regarding national unity in the face of internal separatist terrorists, a legacy of Francoist politics and ideology, as I shall explain in the first section of this book. Even in the face of overwhelming evidence that the perpetrators were jihadist militants, the PP clung to its original story that the terrorists were members of ETA and tried to oblige journalists to do the same. The party had relied heavily on its strong anti-terrorist record in the campaign, touting the support it received from the United States to define ETA as a terrorist group and combat it in the context of the "War on Terror" and portraying the left-wing Partido Socialista Obrero Español (Spanish Socialist Workers' Party, PSOE) as soft on terrorism.[4] For its part, after initially supporting the government's official version, the PSOE quickly seized on the Islamist angle, which was widely reported in articles posted on the Internet by the international media. It then used the PP's insistence on ETA's culpability to discredit the ruling government as both inept and dishonest, willing to ally itself with the United States in a war based on false pretenses and to justify its participation with falsified evidence and thereby sacrifice the needs of the people to narrow business interests underpinned by Francoist ideologies.

In making their arguments, both parties sought to draw on the ghosts of Spain's past to mobilize two opposing elements of the electorate. Spain's democracy had been in place for only about three decades at the time of the attacks – the transition from dictatorship to democracy began in 1975, but the constitution was not approved until 1978. This process in Spain represented part of a trend in democratization during the 1970s, which occurred in countries in Latin America, Asia, and Europe. As Andreas Langenohl explains, the ways in which democracy was secured in this "third wave of democratization" (163) introduced a unique set of problems, including "a possible contradiction between politically pragmatic and juridical-morally just ways of addressing the past, as all three transitions (and especially the Spanish one) were accompanied by impunity for the perpetrators on the part of the democratic regime" (163–4). Langenohl goes on to explain that, although an agreement not to raise the ghosts of the past may help to stabilize democracy in the initial years, "once the democratic institutions have acquired a certain acceptance in society, silence about the past crimes may become dysfunctional and/or result in social conflicts over interpretations" (169). In the German context, Gabriele Schwab writes that "[s]ilencing or covering up violence, refusal to take responsibility, and failure to acknowledge guilt and shame are major factors in sustaining and passing psychic damage on to subsequent generations" (101). Not surprisingly, then, the transition to democracy in Spain after Franco's death, accompanied by a so-called Pacto del Olvido (Pact of Silence) about state crimes under the dictator's regime, did not resolve the conflicts around the history of the Spanish Civil War and its aftermath, because the perpetrators have never been prosecuted, the mass graves of the dictatorship's mortal victims have been only partially exhumed, and no public apology has ever been issued to the victims or the heirs of repression. For these reasons, debates over memory itself – personal and collective, embodied and historical – as well as the identification of perpetrators and victims, rage on in Spanish society and culture, and the meanings attributed to 11-M are imbricated in those disputes.

Despite the persistence of these Civil War and Franco-era memories – and the direct appeals to them in the media by the PP and the PSOE – the truth is that both parties had sought over the preceding decades to promote the image of a modern and democratic Spain, supported by neoliberal projects of urban reconstruction designed to transform Madrid from a third-level European city, or what Neil Brenner has called a "national urban center," into a "global capital" (262).[5] One of the first steps was to eliminate the *chabolas*, or shantytowns, that had sprung up during the dictatorship in the traditionally leftist districts of Villa de Vallecas and Puente de Vallecas, where two neighbourhoods that would be directly impacted by 11-M – Santa Eugenia and El Pozo del Tío Raimundo – are located. The new design elaborated in both the 1985 and 1997 urban plans encouraged the incorporation of these extra-urban districts, often characterized in the press as lawless proto-cities, into the capital proper and the construction of new housing, hospitals, schools, parks, and shopping centres in them. The development of an elaborate network of commuter trains formed a vital element of this project: "La alta velocidad contribuye a la especialización funcional de Madrid como 'ciudad de negocios,' 'ciudad de las compras y de la moda' y 'ciudad del ocio-cultura y turismo.' Dentro de sus objetivos está llevar el tren al centro de la ciudad, lo que en Madrid se ha concretado en la ubicación de sus terminales en Atocha y Chamartín" (The high-velocity train contributes to the functional specialization of Madrid as "a city of business," "a city of shopping and fashion," and "a city of cultural and touristic leisure." Among its objectives are to bring to train to the city centre, which in Madrid is concretely located in the Atocha and Chamartin stations) (*Evaluación del Plan Urbanístico de 1997*, 31).[6]

Unfortunately, the changes in the financial practices associated with property ownership also contributed to the dramatic rise in rent and overall economic precariousness for working-class people in those neighbourhoods (Gonick; Méndez 35; Vives and Rullan 405), developments that arguably represent a form of what Slavoj Žižek calls systemic violence,[7] the result of the catastrophic effects of neoliberal economics. The mortgaging practices and corruption underlying them would be a strong factor in the debilitating economic recession that began in 2008 and led to a crisis in homelessness, with citizens forcibly removed from their homes for their inability to pay ever-increasing mortgages and rents. In effect, these strategies for the physical removal of "the people of the excluded" (Agamben 33) represented part of "the capitalistic-democratic plan to eliminate the poor" (ibid. 35).

The logistical success of the urbanization project facilitated the 11 March attacks, as the extended reach of the urban transportation system allowed the bombs to reach Atocha, the central train station of Madrid and the headquarters of the national railroad company, RENFE. Again, the impact on the suburban poor was disproportionate. The commuter train line that carried the 11-M bombs during the morning rush hour originated in the historic city of Alcalá de Henares and passed through working-class neighbourhoods on its way to the city's historic centre. Of the ten bombs, only three of them exploded in Atocha. Of the remaining seven, four were detonated in a train near Téllez Street, some 800 metres away from Atocha; one went off at the Santa Eugenia station; and two exploded on a train that was just leaving the station of El Pozo del Tío Raimundo, where immigrant workers lived alongside Spanish nationals. The result was that, of the 191 people killed, most were from the working class, and 47 were foreigners, including 16 Romanians and 18 people from Latin American countries. Of the more than 1,500 wounded, the government has recognized at least 334 who were not from Spain and granted them citizenship. Nonetheless, the focus of the national and international press remained on Atocha, in the historic centre of Madrid, and Spain, permitting the construction of a narrative about modern Spanish democracy imperilled by terrorist violence.

President Aznar sought to simply dictate his version of the events to the press, which initially printed the government story without question (Martínez, "El concepto"); information technology, however, generated a civic response that was neither directed nor controlled by party politicians in the days after the bombings (Cañada; Martínez; Aguilera Díaz). Informed simultaneously by non-state posts on the Internet and international cable news, the citizenry did not reach the same conclusion as the government or the opposition party about the authors of the crimes and their motives. On 12 March (12-M), the government organized a massive protest that clogged the public spaces of the city, with a unifying theme about defending the nation and its constitution;

nonetheless, the populace demonstrated against the variety of ills that could have led to the violence and clamoured to know "Quién ha sido?" (Who was responsible?): globalized capital, Spain's participation in the Iraq War, or Basque terrorism? On 13 March, the day before the election, a designated day of reflection when campaigning is forbidden, a political flash mob was organized via text message, a medium not subject to government control (Salido Andrés) – the famous *pásalo* (pass it on). The message rejected traditional party politics and highlighted the fact that the PP itself was "campaigning" through its presentation of the attacks in the media and its organization of the 12-M demonstration. It read: "¿Aznar de rositas? ¿lo llaman jornada de reflexión y Urdazi [*sic*] trabajando? Hoy 13m, a las 18h sede PP c/genova 13, sin partidos. silencio por la verdad. Pásalo" (Aznar sitting pretty? They call it a day of reflection and Urdazi is working? Today, 13 March, at 6 pm at PP headquarters, 13 Genova Street, no political parties, silence for the truth. Pass it on). Alfredo Urdaci was the director of the Spanish broadcaster TVE, which was commonly understood to be controlled by the government. This moment of the *pásalo* marked the breakdown of the government's control of the message and led to the defeat of the PP in the election. Later, the continued public battles over the meaning of the attacks and the definition of the perpetrators, waged in the leading newspapers along strictly ideological lines, put into question both the objectivity of the press and the politicians' dedication to the needs of citizens in a crisis (Partal and Otamendi; Vara Miguel; García Fernández; Artal).

What is more, the protests demonstrated the existence of a politicized populace with a sophisticated sense of the workings of language, technology, and media images; resistant to political commonplaces; and suspicious of the political elite. These people also recognized that the real issues at stake had more to do with globalized capital than with the Spanish Civil War. Their sensibility was not created overnight, but, rather, it evolved along with the mechanisms of what Manuel Castells calls "the network society," which is characterized by ever-increasing flows of information, communication, money, people, and jobs across global networks. This kind of networking mentality was also instrumental in the articulation of a support group for those affected by the bombings, called the Red Ciudadana Tras el 11-M (Citizens' Network Following 11-M).[8] The structure, as the organizers described it, was intentionally informal, non-ideological, and horizontal, and the group was outside the formal mechanisms of politics and journalism (Desdedentro 28) so that it could allow for "un proceso interno de apertura a otras posibilidades de elaboración de lo sucedido no codificadas ni ya instituidas" (an internal process of opening up to other possible ways, not yet codified or institutionalized, to understand the events) (ibid. 21). The Red Ciudadana sought to exemplify the model of interactive, networked politics imagined by Amanda Sey and Manuel Castells, who write that, "an active citizenry may find in the Internet a medium of communication to bypass the filters of mass media and party machines, and to network itself, asserting its collective autonomy" (363–4).

This unofficial form of dialogue beyond the parameters of the traditional media sources or the official monuments and speeches, eventually evolved into an alternative, grassroots social and political organization in the 15-M, or *indignados* (outraged), movement, which originated on 15 May 2011 to protest the government's austerity measures in response to the economic crisis that had begun in 2008. Artists associated with the movement would seek more direct social engagement and advocate for open-source and other alternative publication venues, in protest against the neoliberal multimedia conglomerates that had taken over not only most of the major publishing houses in Spain, but also the large bookstores and the newspapers where literary reviews appeared.[9] Jon Snyder's book *Poetics of Opposition in Contemporary Spain: Politics and the Work of Urban Culture* delves into what he calls the "opposition literacies" of 15-M (70), exploring the ways in which affect coheres around political and social agendas and may be mobilized into actions that counter the dominant discourses – in this case, the discourse surrounding the economic crisis.

Poetry in Memory Sites: Spontaneous Shrines, Archives, Monuments, Anthologies

My study suggests that the seeds of these literacies were sown in the texts at the grassroots memorials and on the website of the Asociación 11-M Afectados del Terrorismo (11-M Association of Those Affected by Terrorism), as well as in performances at the memorial and monument sites. Indeed, much of the struggle to define the past, present, and future of Spain in relation to 11-M – these readings and writings, as it were – took place in the urban and cultural spaces of the capital, and they both exposed and reconfigured the meaning of those sites.

Lyric texts figured prominently in "grassroots memorials" (Margry and Sánchez-Carretero) and "spontaneous shrines" (Santino) in all of the train stations – Atocha, El Pozo del Tío Raimundo, and Santa Eugenia – where the bombings occurred. These types of memory places now regularly "appear if the person who passed away is a personality with a high mass-media status ... or if those who are killed are considered 'victims'" of "'[s]enseless' violence, traffic deaths, and terroristic or natural disasters [which] are human instigated or represent a hazard from outside, beyond personal responsibility, allowing one to blame the 'other'" (Margry and Sánchez-Carretero 33). The Madrid train stations were adorned with objects generally found at such sites – candles, stuffed animals, flowers, religious symbols, and the like (ibid. 25) – but they were also papered with original or copied poems and song lyrics in much the same fashion as Ground Zero after the 9/11 attacks.[10]

Despite the similarities within this global template, each site uses recognizable symbols that can be read rhetorically. In the case of 11-M, media images played an important role in shaping the response to and memory of the attacks, including citizens' poetic response in spontaneous shrines and memorials, as I shall explain in part 1. What is more, some of the rhetoric of the 11-M grassroots memorials is specific not simply to Spain or Madrid, but to the neighbourhoods most directly impacted by the attacks, which have very different histories in relation to many of the symbolic features of the shrines themselves. In order to read the sites, then, one must take into account those different histories, as well as the social narratives about them, the media's framing of them, and politicians' invocation of them. Given the conflicting understandings of the events, it is not surprising that the grassroots memorials became palimpsests with competing or complementary messages (Sánchez-Carretero, "La vida social" 138),[11] sites of public reading and public writing, whose creators were "active producers of meaning and symbolism" (Margry and Sánchez-Carretero 30). Tobin Siebers sees in such collective representations "symbols of community disguised as sacred ideas. They express a desire for social cohesion, creating a form of solidarity without consensus" (106). Béatrice Fraenkel goes a step further, claiming that this process "constitutes a program of action; the result is a new kind of shrine bound up in multiple, cosmopolitan literacies" (231). Paloma Díaz-Mas calls the shrines works of art, developed over the course of many months, that were simultaneously individual and collective, made up of elements from oral and written traditions, with lessons in morality for each person and society in general (123–4).

The easy circulation of oral and written poetry after the bombings allowed it to play a more immediate role in shaping memory, mobilizing social responses, and healing psychological wounds than any other genre. Shorter lyric texts, including songs and prayers, can be – in fact, are often designed to be – easily remembered, and they can therefore be spontaneously reproduced in whole or in part by various sectors of the public. The familiarity of certain poems – those that are taught in schools or incorporated into popular songs (Díaz-Mas 103, 107) – also creates an imagined collective that could unite in a kind of chorus, but the ubiquity of such texts can also fashion what Susan Sontag calls, in the context of photographs, "the illusion of consensus" (6). In the days after the bombings, poems, as well as original compositions, were torn from books, mechanically reproduced, posted on social media, shared via email, hung in windows, reproduced as graffiti, recited, sung, and scribbled on scraps of paper, clothing, and other objects, many of which had belonged to the mourners or the victims before being left at the grassroots memorials. The metonymical relationship between those objects and the dead, the wounded, and the mourning evoked a sense of bodily presence in the mourning sites (Sánchez-Carretero, "La vida social" 144–5). The poems in particular often seem to stand in for the bodies of the departed in a material sense, as the word made flesh (John 1:14), or else they form part of a connective tissue linking the living with the dead, with messages to the departed, or even prayers, scrawled on the same page as the poems themselves. The performance of lyric, including prayers and songs, in public sites also brings bodies to bear on the meanings of the bombings in a more literal way. The lyrics of a song can create awareness of the body; as I explain in chapter 2, this is particularly true in a genre like hip hop, in which the breath and vocal stress of the performer, rather than traditional forms of metre, impose structure on the verses.

Mourners themselves wrote poetic texts in the days and months following the bombings, which they posted at the grassroots memorials and on electronic sites and published in collective volumes. In his book *Poetry as Survival*, Gregory Orr argues that poetry is uniquely suited to the task of helping individuals overcome traumatic experiences. "Perhaps," he writes, "the elaborate and intense patterns of poetry can also make people feel safe. Related to this, it's possible to say that the enormous disordering power of trauma needs or demands an equally powerful ordering to contain it, and poetry offers such an order" (92). Poetry encourages mindfulness, and it allows people to make connections and garner insights through language and to express hidden or repressed emotions from a safe place rather than confronting trauma head-on (Bracegirdle 83). Indeed, several peer-reviewed medical journals address the clinical use of both reading and writing poetry, the theoretical basis for which dates to Freud's "The Relation of the Poet to Daydreaming" (1908)[12] and Jung's 1922 text, "On the Relation of Analytic Psychology to Poetry"[13] (Mazza 46). There is even a journal solely dedicated to the topic: the *Journal of Poetry Therapy*, founded in 1986 by Nicholas Mazza, who has also written extensively on the topic. The therapeutic functions of literary production were clearly understood by the mental health care professionals who were charged with the care of traumatized individuals after the 11-M attacks and who approached their treatment through the production of language (Duque Colino, Mallo Caño, and Álvarez Segura). It is in this context that we can understand many of the poems composed by common citizens grieving their tremendous loss, in shock at the sudden rupture in their lives, eager to help their fellow mourners, and angry at the perpetrators, all experienced with a sense of survivors' guilt.

After the shrines were dismantled, most of the texts and objects were collected and stored in an Archive of Mourning located in the Railroad Museum, not far from the Atocha station. The archive removes objects from circulation, classifying them and then storing them in a place hidden from public view, contributing to a process of "heritagization" and institutionalization of the original structures (Margry and Sánchez-Carretero 17).[14] It has also been argued that the archiving process desacralizes the memorial, in much the same fashion as the display of religious artefacts in museums and libraries re-appropriates them for history by separating them from the context in which they are or were sacred. Thus, Aleida Assmann calls the archive "the unhallowed bureaucratic space of a clean and neatly organized repository" ("Canon" 102). And yet she acknowledges that the objects in the archive can maintain the trace of affect and serve as the "involuntary memory of a past society" (*Cultural Memory* 197). This could be particularly true of the 11-M archive, which had its origins in the traumatic events themselves: as Sánchez-Carretero explains, the anthropologists involved in the project hoped to harness the objective, scientific methodologies of their profession as a therapeutic response to the pain of sudden death (*El Archivo del Duelo* 19).

Not all of the 11-M poems are stored in the Archive of Mourning; many have remained in the public sphere. Some have been included on the website of one of the victims' associations, for example, and others appear in other literary texts, such as the novel *Cosas que brillan cuando están rotas* (Things That Shine When They're Broken), by Nuria Labari. They can also reappear as event, as in the exposition organized by photographer Eduardo Nave at the National Museum of Anthropology from March to May 2016, where the artefacts were accompanied by photos, videos, and an interactive installation titled "Poema de las emociones" (Emotion Poem), which allowed visitors to select and add prefabricated semi-transparent sheets naming their emotions to a collective piece hanging throughout the space.

Other 11-M poems were composed for and incorporated into official monuments and memorials, places of memory that "have a normative quality and are incorporated into a positive self-image and endowed with collective meaning" (A. Assmann, *Cultural Memory* 312). They have a very different affective import than the grassroots memorials, which are places of trauma that "block the path to ... an affirmative interpretation" (ibid.). Official memory sites also confer upon the consecrated, or what Judith Butler calls "grievable," victims the status of heroes, martyrs, and saints, and thereby reveal how "normative frameworks establish in advance what kind of life will be a life worth living, what kind of life will be a life worth preserving, and what life will become worthy of being mourned" (*Frames* 53). This is particularly true when these sites are the location for politically divisive official commemorative events accompanied by media releases and photographs. The ritualized and spontaneous performance of mourning at monuments, however, can provide a means for resisting the incorporation of traumatic sites into institutionalized memory places.

Like monuments, poetry anthologies represent a mechanism for consecrating particular forms of cultural expression, as well as institutional, national, and even local memory, at the same time that they figure strongly in publishers' marketing schemes. The explosion in this genre – Raquel Medina contrasts the 277 published in Spain between 1939 and 1975 with the 1,022 that appeared from 1976 until 2008 (509) – responded to changes in the symbolic and economic value of the book in the consumer culture of post-Franco Spain, and to the role of cultural agents, including poets, in supporting the socio-economic order in an unproblematized and uncritical manner (Medina; Mayhew, *Twilight*). Guillem Martínez and his collaborators in the book *CT o la Cultura de la Transición: Crítica a 35 años de cultura española* (CT or the Culture of the Transition: Criticism of 35 Years of Spanish Culture) name this paradigm simply "CT," which they define as a collusion between the culture industry and politics in which political tolerance, recognition, and subvention of culture depends on the culture class's agreement to toe the party line in politics. It should not be surprising, then, that Spanish poets responded to the 11-M attacks with the creation of anthologies that correspond to a rather conservative notion of cultural intervention, as I shall explain in the introduction to part 2.[15]

Some other 11-M poetry collections, however, function in a counter-hegemonic fashion: eschewing traditional publishing venues, allowing open participation in the poetic enterprise, aligning themselves with groups removed from the PP and the PSOE, and, in two cases, offering poetry at no charge to the public. The first of these was an anthology of poetic texts by witnesses and others directly affected by the bombings, titled *11-M: Palabras para el recuerdo* (11-M: Words for Remembering), edited by the Neighbourhood Association of El Pozo del Tío Raimundo in 2004. Sales of *Palabras* benefited the Asociación 11-M Afectados del Terrorismo, which was legally established three months after the attacks. The Asociación 11-M remains sceptical about victim discourse and the motives of both major political parties, but it reflects leftist values in its demands for social programs to address the problems faced by victims of terrorist attacks.[16] Indeed, Pilar Manjón, who served as its president from 2004 to 2016 and whose son, Daniel Paz Manjón, died in one of the El Pozo trains, earned the ire of the PP, the PSOE, and the media after an accusatory speech on 15 December 2004, about their manipulation of victims for their own political and financial ends.[17] The Associación 11-M maintains a website with a page, "Trazos y Puntadas para el Recuerdo," devoted to artistic responses. Its separate section for poetry includes many original texts from the memorials but remains open to contributions from anyone. With a similar logic, Eulogio Paz Fernández – the ex-husband of Pilar Manjón and the current president of the Asociación 11-M – published an open-source book, *11-M: Palabras para Daniel y cartas al director* (11-M: Words for Daniel and Letters to the Editor, 2006), in which he reproduced poems written by Daniel's friends, himself, and others.[18]

The poems in these collections vary in quality (as, indeed, do the poems in the other anthologies), but they all seek to operate outside of a market logic. They also represent political acts, since "[i]n the modern age, poverty and exclusion are not only economic and social concepts but also eminently political categories" (Agamben 33). Snyder notes that this kind of publishing initiative would assume even greater importance after the financial crisis of 2008, which resulted in substantial cutbacks in state support for the cultural industry (xiii). This meant that, on the one hand, artists could not count on the level of prize monies, grants, or subsidies that they had enjoyed before the crisis; at the same time, cultural products became more expensive for consumers even as their income declined, leading to a significant decrease in sales. This problem was exacerbated by the fact that, while print books were still taxed at a moderate rate of 4 per cent, the tax on electronic books was set at 21 per cent, where it would remain until December 2016. State support for public libraries also declined after the crisis. For these reasons, many in the 15-M movement would also support "the distribution of cultural material as public domain against copyright restrictions, known as the copyleft movement" (Snyder xiv), as well as live artistic performances, interventions, and engagement in accessible spaces in the city that represented innovations in the forms and locations of artistic enunciation (ibid. 67).[19] I see the roots of these changes in the collective responses to 11-M; in this sense, I would argue that the event marks a before and after for Spanish poetics. For this reason, the first part of the present book addresses the ways in which public cultural practices reveal and mobilize emotions in socio-political identifications.

11-M Poetry

The second part of my study focuses on specific poems in the anthologies described above, as well as others published separately, that imply that 11-M represents a critical moment in Spanish poetry. By this, I do not mean that entirely new and unprecedented forms of poetry were suddenly created on or immediately after that date but, rather, that some of the existing tendencies were shown to respond more effectively than others to the violence, its mediatic representations, and the socio-economic conflicts that the events uncovered, as well as to the turn to grassroots organization.

Certainly, a crisis like 11-M can engender what Richard Gray describes in the case of 9/11 as failures of literature, "a desperate retreat into the old sureties" (16) by writers who "dissolve public crisis in the comforts of the personal" or cite "the seductive pieties of home, hearth and family and, related to them, the equally seductive myth of American exceptionalism" (17). In some 11-M poetry, we find evidence of such a retreat – for example, into the falsely progressive style of some men associated with the "poetry of experience" (Mayhew, *Twilight* 18) – as well as the "seductive pieties" of comfortable normality (Villena 24; Mayhew, *Twilight* 19), male friendship (Villena 24), masculine poetic authority (Robbins, "Encuentros" 95–6), expressions of solidarity with the working class that seek to echo the poetry of the Spanish Civil War or social poetry of the 1950s, or lists of objects, including body parts, that recall Tim O'Brien's Vietnam story, "The Things They Carried."

The engaged style of some 11-M poems reflects the broader efforts to elaborate a new social poetry in Spain in the early twenty-first century, as evidenced in a special issue of the journal *Ínsula* in November 2002 dedicated to "Los compromisos de la poesía" (Committed Poetics). One of these efforts is the so-called *poesía de la consciencia* (conscience poetry) or *poesía en resistencia* (resistance poetry), which proposes a new form of poetic realism that resists ideological abstractions and certainties; instead, it is very much imbricated in the physical world, attempting to counter there the algorithmic logic of marketing and opinion polling (see Bray 10). Its precepts were further elaborated in Enrique Falcón's 2007 *Once poéticas críticas* (Eleven Critical Poetics), a collection of texts, some dating from the early 2000s, that present different strategies for making visible and resisting the systemic violence underlying modern Western societies. Falcón's own essay is a series of rhetorical questions that lays bare the contradictions underlying the justifications for war and other forms of violence. Antonio Orihuela writes that these poets believe in "el sentido transformador de la realidad que tienen las palabras, la práctica de la cotidiana resistencia contra esa violencia invisible que permea todos los ámbitos de la vida" (the power that words have to transform reality, the practice of everyday resistance against that invisible violence that permeates every corner of life) ("Voces" 23). For his part, Jorge Riechmann contests the instrumentalization of poetry in the service of ideology, proposing instead a concept of poetry as "práctica de indagación en todos los ámbitos: sin excluir lo social y lo político, por descontado" (a practice of inquiry in every realm, without excluding the social and the political, of course) ("Poesía" 15).[20] Antonio Méndez Rubio calls his own suggestive and evasive form of poetic expression a "guerrilla de la comunicación [en que] se habla de la necesidad de crear espacios libres, de desconcierto y descontrol, resquicios para la emergencia de lo (im)posible ..., una poesía subversiva que no quiera o no pueda limitarse al poder persuasivo del mensaje y de la realidad" (a communicative guerilla that speaks of the need to create free spaces for bewilderment and unregulated disarray, loopholes where the (im)possible can emerge ..., a subversive poetry that doesn't want to or can't limit itself to the persuasive power of messages and reality) ("Des(a)punte" 44–5). Of the eleven poets in Falcón's parallel publication, *Once poetas críticos* (Eleven Critical Poets), six contributed poems to the 11-M anthologies – Falcón, Riechmann, Orihuela, Isabel Pérez Montalbán (the only woman in Falcón's poetry volume, and omitted from the poetics volume), David González, and Méndez Rubio.

Other poets perform critique through an embodied poetics linked to a postsecular or even sacred understanding of the body and the flesh, particularly as they relate to gender, race, and social justice. Mayra Rivera argues in her 2015 book, *Poetics of the Flesh*, that the destroyed human body suggests "the shattering of myths of human progress" (5) but also a sense of vulnerability derived from liberation theology, which "sought models for a corporeal anthropology that avoided the separation between body and soul" (6). Enrique Dussel has dedicated his career to developing this line of inquiry, drawing on the Old and New Testaments, Marx, and Greek literature. Rivera engages with his work, along with that of theologians, phenomenologists (Merleau-Ponty), and other philosophers and writers (particularly Edouard Glissant), to explore the history of theological, philosophical, and political concepts of the body and the flesh, before arriving at a contemporary concept that emphasizes multiplicity and relationality rather than separation and hierarchy (158).

Rivera further claims that "[w]riting flesh requires languages attuned to silences, disruptions, opacity, and to the complex qualities of sensation" (158), and, in this sense, her "poetics of the flesh" reflects Richard Gray's notion of the "prophetic mode" (277) that emerged after 9/11, which he sees as "the end of a bland, desacralized, conversational poetry, whether 'engaged' or not" (279). Jeffrey Gray elaborates on the ways in which what he calls "a precocious mode of witnessing" is "not so much representational as performative, proceeding diachronically and, at times, by blessings, imprecations, rhythms, and curses" (264). For him, it is important that it does not offer explanations – it "does not compromise what happens by pretending to know what happened" – but rather taps "into those archaic modes in order to answer to the missed event of the trauma" (264). Michael Rothberg likewise discusses a "post-secular alternative" in post-9/11 literature, "a vision that integrates private devotion into public space; a rooted cosmopolitanism that establishes a universalist 'fellowship with the dead' at the same time that it finds a place for 'half-dressed foreigners' and headscarfed citizens" ("Seeing Terror" 130). For Rothberg, as for Jeffrey Gray, the poet's renunciation of "knowing" is of paramount importance, as is the temporal delay in responding because the "experience of trauma is thus an experience of accident or surprise" (Rothberg, "There Is No Poetry" 149). This kind of poetry thus registers not the event itself, described in realistic terms, but its belated and stuttering reception, with language that evokes the sacred, including linguistic representations of the body and the grounding of affect in the flesh.[21]

Antony Rowland takes a different approach to the problematics of witnessing terrorist violence, drawing on concepts from Holocaust studies, but he nonetheless arrives at the same kind of truncated, repetitive, stuttering expression that Rivera and Jeffrey Gray describe. For him, the global media spectacle of 9/11 created various degrees of witnessing: what Primo Levi would call the "true witnesses" died in the attack; secondary witnesses would be "survivors of the twin towers, bystanders, rescue workers, and inhabitants of Manhattan" (107); and global witnesses saw the event unfold from a virtual remove. Rowland is concerned by what he sees as the conflation of the latter two categories, which "align themselves with post-9/11 foreign policy in terms of their occlusion of local politics" (121), and he thus advocates for the recuperation of the voices of secondary witnesses in survivor testimonies, much as I do for the poems that were posted in the physical and virtual grassroots memorials. But, contrasting the narrative prose of Primo Levi and Elie Wiesel with the poetry of Raymond Federman, Rowland also notes the unique role that the lyric, as opposed to more "realistic" genres, may play in "performing" testimony, by "conveying the epiphanic moment, truncated traumatic recollections, silences beyond the black print, and the emotive space that need not be repressed behind the supposed objectivity of testimonial facts" (4–5). In this, Rowland builds on the work of Shoshana Felman and Cathy Caruth in distinguishing between seeing trauma and saying trauma, or what Michael Bernard-Donals and Richard Glejzer call the "incommensurability between witness and testimony" (53), which explains why the effects of trauma may become evident less in words than in silences, failures of memory, and missing or suppressed material evidence, including cadavers – "the absent past [that] is also part of reality" (Reyes Mate 22). Paul Ricoeur also discusses "traces that are not 'written testimonies' and that are equally open to historical observation, namely, 'vestiges of the past,'" or "witnesses in spite of themselves" (170). Linda Belau finds such traces in the structure of the linguistic iteration and reiteration of trauma – that is, in the signifier's "repetition of the impossibility that structures both the subject and traumatic experience" (Belau n.p.).

As I explain in chapter 4, among the 11-M poems, several reflect these modes of witnessing and the strength of the affective turn in Spanish poetry. These include: "11 de marzo de 2004" by Angelina Gatell; "La música que oiremos" (The Music We Will Hear) by Antonio Méndez Rubio; "Identificación de cadáveres" (Identifying Bodies) by Isabel Pérez Montalbán; "Todo es muerte en el aire" (All Is Death in the Air) by Clara Janés; "Ciudad profanada" (Profaned City) by Ana Rossetti;[22] "Un día después del 11 de marzo" (One Day after 11 March) by Jorge Riechmann; "Atlas de muerte" (Atlas of Death) by Julia Piera; and "El aliento del cazador" (The Hunter's Breath) by Lola Velasco.

Other 11-M poets dwell on the *mediated* event, how the image on the screen is not real at all. Paul Virilio has argued that our vision is increasingly dependent on computers, which "convert data into an assemblage of pixels, producing a synthesis of information that amounts to nothing more than a 'statistical image,' and thus is a 'rational illusion'" (Bray 4). The distrust of memory and the uncertainty about perceived reality are also an inheritance from 9/11, the paradigmatic globalized media catastrophe, which was watched worldwide and seemed to simultaneously recall Hollywood blockbusters and signal the fall of modernity, the West, and the United States (R. Gray 6). It was a real series of events viewed in real time, but what most people witnessed was a simulation on television or the Internet that distorted place and time because viewers were at a physical remove. What is more, "new media objects" like those digital images are "programmable" and "subject to algorithmic manipulation" (Manovich 27), and they therefore alter the logic of perception and interpretation. They may even come to replace the memory of a witness, as the protagonist of American poet Ben Lerner's first novel, *Leaving the Atocha Station* (2011), suggests: "I went back up to my apartment and refreshed the *Times* ... I could feel the newspaper accounts modifying or replacing my memory of what I'd seen; was there a word for that feeling?" (119). The computer screen also plays a role in this process because, as Lev Manovich explains, in "older, photographic technologies, all parts of an image are exposed simultaneously, whereas now the image is produced through sequential scanning ... Therefore, the different parts of the image correspond to different moments in time" (99).

Richard Gray also points out the viewers' ability to control their experience of witnessing, since "every moment could be replayed, slowed down, speeded up, put in freeze frame or in a wider or narrower perspective: in short, placed under obsessive, compulsive scrutiny" (7). This form of technologically enhanced visualization would become linked to the intensification of government surveillance of individuals and organizations after 9/11, in what Allen Feldman calls the "compulsory visibility" of state antiterrorism, characterized by "the visual staging and technological penetration of the body by cameras, high-velocity bullets, or digitized bombs, which unite both seeing and killing, surveillance and violence, in a unified scopic regime" (30). This "scopic regime" alters the concept of witnessing itself because the emotion of the human witness is replaced by the cold rationality and efficient violence of the algorithm, as the "dominant vision is autonomized and requires no singular authorial eye, only the circuit of visibility and the power relation ignited within this circuit between autonomized technical instruments of visualization and those surveilled and objectified by vision and/or violence" (Feldman 33).[23]

The video cameras in the Atocha station suggest just such a scopic regime, foregrounding the elusiveness of security, which is in itself the justification for ever-increasing state-sponsored surveillance. This technology converts public spaces into a kind of panopticon, subjecting ordinary citizens to vigilance and discipline. It could be interpreted as a visible manifestation of other surveillance technologies that reach into the private spaces as well, monitoring conversations on cellphones and landlines, prying into browser histories, or observing suspects of ETA or Islamist terrorism (but also innocent citizens) at home and work through telephoto lenses. The idea that potential state violence is lurking in digital technologies had appeared previously in Spanish poetry: Jorge Riechmann, for example, wrote in his 1997 book, *El día que dejé de leer "El País"* (The Day I Stopped Reading *El País*), that "el poder / se permite el lujo de la tolerancia / mientras digitaliza los datos por si acaso" (power / allows itself the luxury of tolerance / while it digitizes the data just in case) (33), but this topic appears only tangentially in the 11-M poems, as when Felipe Juaristi, in "Txorien aberria / La patria de los pájaros" (The Homeland of the Birds), links the attacks to the disciplinary structures of statehood – weapons, military camps, insane asylums, and cages – designed to control some forms of nationalist violence and to legitimate others (Jordá and Mateos 82–3).

Though this approach is rare in the 11-M anthologies, some poets do engage the interplays of media, memory, violence, surveillance, marketing, and testimony in their work. Agustín Fernández Mallo's untitled poem, Javier Rodríguez Marcos's "Solo en casa" (Home Alone), Josep M. Rodríguez's "Las semillas del viento" (Seeds of the Wind) and "Frente al televisor" (In Front of the TV), and Tina Escaja's *Código de barras* (Bar Code) all comment on and represent the ways in which digital images and branding have shaped the perception and memory of the attacks and their aftermath. Some eight years after the 11-M bombings, Pedro Provencio published the most sustained and sophisticated poetic response to date, *Onda expansiva* (Shock Wave). The book re-creates the voices of each victim of 11-M, weaving them together with the prophetic voice of the poet and the false pieties of the executioners in a book-length representation and critique of the systemic violence, including misogynistic violence, engendered by the algorithmic logic of neoliberalism, cyber-surveillance, and organized religion in "a regime of market research" (Bray 10). These texts are the focus of chapter 5.

As the discussion above implies, the present study will be divided into two parts. The first, which includes a brief introduction and chapters 1 through 3, examines the ways in which people used poetry in the public sphere after the events, with a focus on the rhetorical functions of poetic texts in memory sites, the relationship of those texts to broader social and political narratives about the meaning of the events, and the emergence of unexpected forms of collectivity as a result of performance and circulation. The second part considers how Spanish poets responded to 11-M. It begins with a discussion of the cultural politics underlying the organizational logic of the two anthologies that they compiled in the months following the attacks, before moving to a study of the poems themselves in the final two chapters, one focusing on a postsecular trend toward embodiment and a poetics of the flesh in response to our vulnerability to violence and death, and the other, on the technologies of the virtual and the post-human. Both of these, I argue, represent an affective turn in poetry that resists the old certainties – the liberal subject, traditional poetic forms, political parties – as well as the new cultural and economic logic based on the mathematization of identity in post-industrial neoliberal capitalism. In this sense, this poetry corresponds to the emerging socio-political consciousness based in affective networks that would lead to the 15-M movement after the 2008 crisis.

PART ONE

Poetry, Politics, Performance

In his 2012 book *Trauma: A Social Theory*, Jeffrey Alexander explains how certain narratives about catastrophic events come to cohere in the construction of what constitutes a collective traumatic experience. "They can become so," Alexander writes, "if they are conceived as wounds to social identity. This is a matter of intense cultural and political work. Suffering collectivities – whether dyads, groups, societies, or civilizations – do not exist simply as material networks. They must be imagined into being. The pivotal question becomes not who did this to me, but what group did this to us?" (2). "Which narrative wins out," he adds, "is a matter of performative power" (2).

On 11 March 2004, that power was exercised by the ruling Partido Popular (PP) largely through the media. The narrative focused relentlessly and exclusively on Euskadi Ta Askatasuna (Basque Country and Freedom, ETA), even though, by the late morning, ETA experts had discounted the theory of the separatists' authorship, and the police had discovered the perpetrators' van, which contained an Islamist tape (Flesher Fominaya, "Madrid Bombings and Popular Protest" 292). Nonetheless, the PP minister of the interior, Ángel Acebes, announced at 1:30 p.m. that same day that there was no doubt that ETA was the culprit, and President José María Aznar called the major newspapers shortly afterwards to confirm the story.[1] At 8 p.m., Acebes repeated the ETA story but mentioned the van and the tape (ibid.). Representatives of the PP repeated some version of this story for three consecutive days on state television and radio, and they still insist that ETA played a role.

In the days after the bombings, several key media images sought to reinforce the government's narrative about the events, which "ineludiblemente interviene[n] condicionando la opinión del espectador" (inevitably intervene, conditioning the spectator's opinion) (López Raso 79). In her seminal book *Regarding the Pain of Others*, Susan Sontag claims that media images help to create a collective memory of events, since "[w]hat is called collective memory is not a remembering but a stipulating: that this is important and this is the story of how it happened" (86). Nonetheless, the interpretation of images is not so easy to control. As I mentioned in the introduction, Sontag notes that what they may actually create is "the illusion of consensus" or a "hypothetical shared experience" (6). Nonetheless, they can also encourage deep ethical thinking, which manifests itself "as involvement or attention – a focused sensory and cognitive effort with limited attention to other things" (Coleman 836). Photographs, then, can also provide a space for reflection, and, as Sontag puts it, "There's nothing wrong with standing back and thinking" (118). Contemplating those images from a different perspective provides distance from their manipulative use; this is precisely what many poets did, as I explain in part 2.

A Barbaric Way of Waging War

The best-known image from the attacks, which appeared on the front page of *El País* on 12 March,[2] portrays a number of victims being tended by their fellow travellers next to one of the devastated trains, emphasizing the compassionate, care-taking function of citizens in crisis. The headline read: "Infierno terrorista en Madrid: 192 muertos y 1400 heridos. Interior investiga la pista de Al Qaeda sin descartar a ETA" (Terrorist hell in Madrid: 192 dead and 1400 wounded. The State Department is investigating an Al Qaeda lead without ruling out ETA). The rhetoric of the photo suggests many readings: shock; the despair of innocent victims; the dehumanizing effect of violence, which turns people and their effects into debris; the arbitrary way in which death visits some and not others; the appeal to a compassionate but outraged citizenry. On the ground in the photo is a blood-red femur, a shocking detail that was photoshopped grey, or out of the picture altogether, in many foreign papers, because photos of the dead raise ethical issues in photojournalism, particularly in the United States, where they are seen as disrespectful or even injurious to the viewer (see Fishman and Marvin) in a way that written descriptions are not.[3] Sontag argues that the first precedent for this iconography of modern warfare comes from Goya's *Disasters of War*, and there is clearly a visual link between the human wreckage in that painting and in the news photo. The photo also strongly recalls both the rhetoric and the intended effect of the images of the Guernica bombings circulated in protest of fascist abuses in the Spanish Civil War, images that, Sontag claims, do not just show war but "a particular way of waging war, a way at that time routinely described as 'barbaric,' in which civilians are the target" (9). Thus, the photo recalls what are arguably the origins of international organizing in response to the Civil War carpet-bombing of civilians on a market day, 26 April 1937, in Guernica, a town deeply tied to Basque identity.

Picasso's artistic rendering of the intertwined human and animal suffering occasioned by the Guernica bombing has, of course, come to dominate the visual imagination with respect to attacks on civilians as a horror that defies the traditional boundaries of landscape and portraiture. An article by Timothy Garton Ash in *El País* on 13 March 2005 called the Atocha monument "our new Guernica," referring not to that monument's aesthetic qualities, but to the desire expressed in it to "end all wars" through myriad contacts between citizens. This rhetoric also appears in the second-most-recognizable image of the 11-M attacks, which shows a derailed train with a gaping hole in the side. It first appeared on 11 March on the 3 p.m. broadcast on TVE, the national, state-owned public television station, along with a report blaming ETA, but it was also on the front page of *La Vanguardia* the next day,[4] with an acknowledgment that Al Qaeda had claimed responsibility, even though the government remained focused on ETA The image brings to mind an injured creature with its entrails exposed, a personification of the violence of the explosion and the absence produced by the dead.

Attacks on a United and Constitutional Spain

The PP stood by the story of ETA's culpability because it fit into its broader narrative about a united, democratic Spain, senselessly and repeatedly besieged by separatist terrorists, and it justified the party's relentless antiterrorist drive, which led to Spain's involvement in the Iraq War. As Aznar put it in his first address following the bombings:

> Estamos del lado de la Constitución. Es el pacto de la inmensa mayoría de los españoles que garantiza las libertades y los derechos de todos. Es también el gran acuerdo sobre nuestro régimen político, y es la expresión de nuestra España unida y plural. No vamos a cambiar de régimen ni porque los terroristas maten ni para que dejen de matar ... No hay negociación posible ni deseable con estos asesinos que tantas veces han sembrado la muerte por toda la geografía de España. (Europa Press)
>
> (We are on the side of the Constitution. It is the pact that represents the vast majority of Spaniards and guarantees the freedoms and rights of all. It is also the great agreement about our political system, and it is the expression of our united and plural Spain. We are not going to change the system because terrorists kill or to stop them from killing ... There is no possible or desirable negotiation with those assassins, who have so often sowed death across the Spanish geography.)

The words "pact" and "agreement" bring to mind the 1977 "Pactos de Moncloa" (Moncloa Pacts), which symbolically represent the compromises between the right and the left that allowed for the transition to a stable democracy after Franco's death. The pacts included two sets of accords, one of which addressed the economic crisis, and the other, juridical and political matters. Among other provisions, the former increased unemployment benefits, but it also placed limits on salary increases and public expenditures.[5] Although the majority of items in the latter accord involved increased liberties, one provision of the public order code called for increased measures to combat terrorism, and, prior to 11-M, those efforts had largely focused on internal separatists and radical leftists. Aznar's reference to repeated attacks on "our united and plural Spain" also recalls the Basques' rejection of the constitution of 1978. Aznar's text, then, implicitly identifies the separatist terrorists of ETA as the perpetrators of the attacks and continued enemies of the democratic state.

This logic would explain the rhetoric of the protest organized by the government for 12 March, in which political leaders carried a banner reading "Con las víctimas, con la Constitución, por la derrota del terrorismo" (With the victims, with the constitution, for the defeat of terrorism). The slogan would make sense only if the perpetrators were ETA operatives, given that Islamists could not be interpreted as attacking the constitution. By including, among others, Ángel Acebes, José Luis Rodríguez Zapatero (the Partido Socialista Obrero Español [PSOE] presidential candidate), José María Aznar, and King Juan Carlos's children, Crown Prince Felipe, Princess Elena, and Princess Cristina, the image of the banner sought to reinforce the message that all political parties and the Crown stood behind that slogan and the government's story about the bombings.

The myth of seamless cohesion in post-Franco democracy crops up in another image of the 12-M protest march, which appeared in all of the major newspapers, showing a colourful sea of umbrellas, as protestors gathered in the rain in what appears to be a harmonious and silent collective mourning. Indeed, one of the most common metaphors for representing the creation of a collective "we" following the attacks is the rain, linked to both the debris falling from the air after the explosion and the tears shed by witnesses to those images. What the photo shows, then, is an aesthetic confirmation of the myth of a unified Spanish identity, which was held up as an ideal by both major political parties in the Culture of the Transition (CT), and is literally being held up by them in this image. As Amador Fernández-Savater puts it, "El objetivo de la CT, su obsesión, es la 'cohesión'" (the objective of the CT, its obsession, is "cohesion"), and it maintains the illusion that it exists through its "monopolio de las palabras, los temas y la memoria" (its monopoly on words, themes, and memory). "Neither silence nor unity," however, "characterised the demonstrations of approximately 11 million Spaniards who marched in the pouring rain that evening. The strong divisions in public opinion, although glossed by the media, were exceedingly clear" (Flesher Fominaya, "Madrid Bombings and Popular Protest" 296). Pablo Ordaz's 13 March article in *El País*, titled "Quién ha sido" (Who was responsible), also emphasizes the noisy disagreement among participants in the demonstration.

The call to unity also appears in the phrase "En ese tren íbamos todos" (We were all on that train) and the myriad images of the Spanish flag, which imply that the victims and the mourners are all identified with the idea of the Spanish nation. In this context, it is important to keep in mind that the Spanish flag has a very different history and symbolic value than the American flag, with origins not in the foundation of a new nation, but in the pragmatic need to distinguish the nationality of ships on the high seas. Originally white and red, the flag's current colours of red and yellow date only to the end of the eighteenth century, and it remained exclusively the flag of the military (the navy and then the army) until the nineteenth century. Since then, it has undergone several transformations: aesthetic changes to the shield of the Catholic monarchs, for example; the addition of a crown over the shield; a change in colour to red, yellow, and purple, and the removal of the crown, replaced by a castle, under the Second Republic (1931–6); a return to the original colours, reinstatement of the crown, and addition of an eagle and a fascio of arrows (symbol of the fascist party, La Falange) under Franco; and the current design, which removes the eagle and the arrows. In its present form, it is a highly contested symbol, representing for the left and many in the working class, not the Spanish nation – they prefer the flag of the Second Republic – but the values of the dictatorship, including the attempted elimination of linguistic and cultural differences in the Basque country, Catalonia, and Galicia, under the rubric of *Hispanidad*, the notion of a single, transnational, Hispanic race united by Catholicism. Another key word for "unproblematic" cultural homogenization that is frequently invoked by the PP in opposition to separatist nationalisms is *convivencia* (living together), which recalls the Franco-era myth of a medieval paradise on the Iberian Peninsula in which people of the three Abrahamic faiths (Christianity, Judaism, and Islam) lived peacefully together.

Who Did It?

Through a detailed analysis of a variety of sources with different ideological bents, including radio and television news, several major newspapers, listservs, and Internet sites, Cristina Flesher Fominaya has demonstrated how, on 12 March, the narrative power began to shift from the PP to alternative sources after foreign newspapers reported on Al Qaeda's authorship of the bombings. Soon afterwards, major Spanish newspapers "remov[ed] ETA from the headlines, but report[ed] the government's insistence that 'all signs point to ETA,'" and then "Cadena SER, the radio station with the largest audience share, ... reported that investigators were claiming that all evidence pointed to a radical Islamic group" (Flesher Fominaya, "Madrid Bombings and Popular Protest" 295). As Flesher Fominaya explains, it was then that grief began to turn to anger against the government "within the autonomous/leftist social movement network" (ibid.). Soon afterwards, a "small nucleus of activists" who worked with a "network of civil disobedience" that had previously organized protests against the 2002 *Prestige* oil spill and the Iraq War (ibid. 302) sent out a text message, a medium not subject to government control (Salido Andrés). This was the famous "*pásalo*" (pass it on) that organized a protest outside PP headquarters on Genova Street for the following day, 13-M. The response exceeded the organizers' expectations, numbers reflecting the widespread use of this medium among youth, which facilitated the rapid circulation of the text (Flesher Fominaya, "Madrid Bombings and Popular Protest" 302). A large crowd gathered, holding signs asking for peace and truth. The visual images of this event in the international press and on the Web presented a very different image of the perpetrators (the government) and the victims (people who wanted peace). The image of armoured vehicles protecting the politicians recalled the heavy-handed tactics of state police under the dictatorship, and the protesters "drew explicit connections between Franco-era censorship and the PP's handling of information during the two days following 11-M, which was seen as a grave attack on civil liberties. Historical memory clearly marked the understanding of the protest" (ibid. 300). Protesters also linked the attacks with Spain's intervention in the Iraq War, which they identified as the motivation for the bombings. This would become the second major narrative about the 11-M attacks, as I explain more fully in chapter 1.

The following three chapters will explore how the lyric first seemed to support and then to unravel these narratives in the months and years after the events, contributing to conflicting processes associated with ideological affirmation, denunciation, affect, and collective memory in grassroots memorials, songs, performance, monuments, and archives.

Chapter One

Rhetoric and Ideology in Grassroots Memorials and Official Monuments

Cristina Sánchez-Carretero believes that media images are decisive in shaping the public response to trauma at grassroots memorials (*Archivo* 15). This perspective is borne out in the 11-M sites, as evidenced by the photos of the sites and the preponderance of archival materials collected from them. Indeed, an analysis of the memorials at the Atocha, Santa Eugenia, and El Pozo train stations reveals what Avery Gordon calls the "blind field and its fundamental imbrication in the visible field" (107) – that is, a haunting that is specific not simply to Spain or Madrid, but to the neighbourhoods most directly impacted by the attacks. Thus, even though the "form and content" of this type of spontaneous shrine has "developed into a seemingly uniform template" (Margry and Sánchez-Carretero 11), each site uses recognizable symbols that can be read rhetorically, as Dickinson, Blair, and Ott have argued in relation to public places in general:

> Rhetorical legibility is predicated in publicly recognizable symbolic activity in context. That is, rhetoric typically understands discourses, events, object, and practices as timely, of the moment, specific, and addressed to – or constitutive of – particular audiences in particular circumstance. The contexts within or against which it interprets discourses, events, objects, and practices are multiple, ranging from the historical accretion of various symbols to immediate political interests, to social norms, to available generic prototypes and cultural predispositions toward symbolicity in general. (4)

Margry and Sánchez-Carretero agree that, "[a]lthough they constitute emblematic places and spaces and show patterns and formats of a structural and global kind, memorials are also indexes to dissatisfactions, values, and ideological opinions in a particular group or in a society as a whole" (36).

Certainly the spontaneous shrine erected at the Atocha station seemed to reinforce many elements of the government's interpretation of events, whereas the grassroots memorials at Santa Eugenia and El Pozo del Tío Raimundo reflected to a larger degree the angry civilian response to the government's attempted manipulation of the events for political advantage. These explanations resonate with opposing histories of the Spanish Civil War and the Franco dictatorship, which bubble up to the surface in many of the symbolic features of the shrines themselves, including the Spanish flag, black ribbons, white hands, prayer cards, hymns, artistic works, and, of course, poetry. These recurring motifs mirror what Sara Ahmed describes in *The Cultural Politics of Emotions* as the articulation of love or hate as political emotions in contemporary society, which

> involve a process of movement or association, *whereby feelings take us across different levels of signification, not all of which can be admitted in the present.* This is what I call the "rippling" effect of emotions: they move sideways (through "sticky" associations between signs, figures and objects) as well as forwards and backwards (repression always leaves its trace in the present – hence "what sticks" is bound up with the absent presence of historicity). (44–5; emphasis in the original)

In the case of 11-M, the rhetorical elements of the memorials, and the sticky associations of key words – "paz," "guerra," "libertad," "democracia," "terrorismo," "solidaridad," "comunidad," "justicia" (peace, war, freedom, democracy, terrorism, solidarity, community, justice) – come together to tell very different stories regarding what happened, to whom it happened, to what broader collective the victims belonged, and who is to blame.

These signs also appear in the official monuments and memorials, and in the commemorative acts that take place there each year. Donald Joralemon argues that the construction of such sites is intended to offer "therapy on a grand scale, a kind of monumental catharsis" (179). Nonetheless, as I mentioned in the introduction to this volume, monuments are normative and "endowed with collective meaning" (A. Assmann, *Cultural Memory* 312). They confer upon the consecrated, or what Judith Butler calls "grievable," victims the status of heroes, martyrs, and saints, and they determine whose life is worth mourning and how (*Frames* 53). In a society that cannot agree about the identity of the perpetrators and the victims, or the meaning of the event, those sites will inevitably stage conflict rather than reconciliation.

ETA Attacks the Spanish Nation

The discourse associated with the PP's 11-M narrative employs "sticky associations" regarding freedom, justice, democracy, peace, terrorism, nation, unity, and class, which have served largely to link ETA with communism and class struggle, as well as anti-clericalism, through the common identification of ETA and far-left organizations like Grupos de Resistencia Antifascistas Primero de Octubre (October 1st Groups of Antifascist Resistance, GRAPO), the military arm of the reconstituted Spanish Communist Party, as internal enemies of the state. The branding of these organizations as "rojos" (Reds) marked them as foreigners, in part through the discourse on *Hispanidad*, the notion of a single, transnational Hispanic race united by Catholicism, which was propagated during the dictatorship as a form of cultural legitimation that justified the persecution of the population associated with those who lost the Civil War: communists, anarchists, republicans, atheists, separatists, feminists, homosexuals, and so on.[1] As Michael Richards explains, this narrative continues to shape the reaction by the political and economic elite to social conflict in relation to neoliberalism because the patriotism of the working poor remains suspect; their religious faith, in doubt; and their resistance to the designs of global capital, criminalized (129).

A point of encounter for travellers from many countries and the headquarters of the national railroad company, RENFE, the Atocha station is now symbolically identified primarily with the internationalism and neoliberal development schemes of the dominant class, even if it also serves as a destination for local commuter trains bringing workers from the periphery to the centre of Madrid. It is the site where Felipe, the prince of Asturias, and his wife, Letizia (now the king and queen of Spain), paid their respects to 11-M victims in the name of the monarchy.

In strong contrast to the displays at the other two stations, a considerable number of texts at Atocha were characterized by a nationalist and Catholic rhetoric that implicitly linked ETA with the rebellious working class. This sentiment was embodied in anti-ETA signs and texts, along with countless images of the iconic white hands and black ribbons that had previously symbolized the pro-peace movement specifically targeted against ETA violence, with the result that these symbols came to imply an identification between the Basque separatists and the perpetrators of the 11-M attacks.[2]

These particular nationalistic and antiterrorist concepts are reproduced in the logic of many poems, as well as in accompanying images. White hands appear above the title of Francisco Moya Romero's

1.1. Outside the Atocha station (Archivo Histórico Ferroviario del Museo del Ferrocarril de Madrid, Francisco M. Gil García).

"Trenes de tragedia" (Trains of Tragedy), along with the words "Basta ya de sangre inocente" (Enough innocent blood). I transcribe two of the stanzas here:

Con estas letras que escribo
va mi corazón pegado
llorando por los difuntos
que el terrorismo ha sembrado

También me siento orgulloso
de ser ciudadano español
porque Madrid era España
en el llanto y el dolor (DP-4466)[3]

(With these letters that I write / my heart goes attached / crying for the dead / that terrorism has sown // I am also proud / to be a Spanish citizen / because Madrid was Spain / in the weeping and the pain)

The speaker of the poem, which is written in ballad form (octosyllabic lines, assonant rhyme in the even verses), insists on his own identity as a Spanish citizen (not a Basque or Catalan one, for example) and proposes the identification of Madrid with all of Spain, a sentiment that would not likely be shared in some of the autonomous communities, which propose competing nationalist claims. Another text along these lines and with the same formal structure, "Con los brazos abiertos" (With Open Arms), is a hymn or anthem composed by Gabriel González. The refrain of the song reads thus: "Eres canto de una Euskadi / en paz, común y diversa. / Que al ritmo de todos baile / y que a todos obedezca" (You are the song of an Euskadi / in peace, common and diverse. / May it dance to everyone's rhythm / and obey everyone) (DP-2927). Not only in these lines, but throughout the song, peace is to be found in multicultural coexistence in the Basque land (Euskadi), rather than in the singular Basque identity that ETA fought for.

This sentiment is ironic in the context of the hymns dating back to the Falange (the Spanish fascist party, founded by José Antonio Primo de Rivera in 1933, whose ideology dominated the first period of the dictatorship). "Cara al sol" (Facing the Sun), for example, the official hymn of the Falange, exalts a single Spanish identity in its famous chorus:

¡España una!
¡España grande!
¡España libre!
¡Arriba España!

(One Spain! / Great Spain! / Free Spain! / Onward Spain!)

The political agenda associated with these verses was not tolerant of diversity. Rather, this unitary sense of the "Spanish people" emblematizes Agamben's argument that the concept of a people represents "the pure source of identity and yet it has to redefine and purify itself continuously according to exclusion, language, blood, and territory" (32). The statement also applies to the Spanish national anthem, which had no lyrics until these were commissioned by the Franco regime and penned by the official national/Falangist poet José María Pemán. Those lines likewise associate peace, liberty, the nation, and patriotism with the total victory of the Catholic Right:

Gloria a la Patria
que supo seguir
sobre el azul del mar

el caminar del sol.
¡Triunfa, España!
Los yunques y las ruedas
canten al compás
del himno de la fé.
Juntos con ellos
cantemos en pie
la vida nueva y fuerte
del trabajo y paz.

(Glory to the Homeland / that knew how to follow / over the blue of the sea / the path of the sun. / Triumph, Spain! / The anvils and the wheels / sing to the beat / of the hymn of faith. / Together with them / we will stand and sing / to the new and strong life / of work and of peace.)

The idea that the "Homeland" had triumphed in the Spanish Civil War implies that the vanquished represented something that was not patriotic, not really Spanish. As is typical for fascist discourse, the work described here is manual labour performed to the beat of this nationalistic hymn. What is more, we know from historical documents, including the regime's own NO-DO (Noticiarios y Documentales) films, that the people performing these tasks in the postwar period were generally prisoners of war, originally from the working class. The sticky signs related to nation, unity, religion, and peace in these lyrics, then, point to the brutal repression of that population in the postwar period and also to their banishment to prison, exile, and slums, and their exclusion from the body politic.[4] Given the fascist tone of these lyrics, it is not surprising that they were discontinued under democracy, but the ideal of a unitary state persists, as evidenced by the Spanish flags at the Atocha memorials, which did not appear as prominently in the memorials at El Pozo or Santa Eugenia, where the flag of the Spanish Republic was favoured.

Prayer cards left at the Atocha shrine also contributed to a right-wing rhetoric associated with Francoism, even as they confirmed Rosi Braidotti's assertion that "the axiom that Western secularism is predicated on the rational distinction between faith and reason ... need not lead to the conclusion that ... many Westerners are secular by default" (Braidotti, *Posthuman* 193).[5] What predominated there were images of saints associated with a particular rhetoric of the victors in the Spanish Civil War, which held that Catholics were martyred at the hands of the godless Reds, revolutionaries of the left. The prayer card of Spanish saint Maravillas de Jesús, for example, explains that she protected the monument of the Sagrado Corazón from profanation during the Second Republic, the government of which was overthrown in the right-wing military coup that initiated the Civil War in 1936 (DP-3830). St Pedro Poveda's card says that he "murió mártir a causa de la fe en 1936" (died as a martyr for the faith in 1936) (DP-390).

Other figures are linked to the dictatorship and *nacionalcatolicismo* (national Catholicism), which represented a fusion between the state and the Catholic Church about which the Spanish populace remains divided. This would be the case for the prayer card devoted to the Italian saint Gemma Galgani (DP-3816, among others), who was canonized in 1940 by Pius XII, the same pope who blessed Francoism. National Catholicism prescribed the norms of private and public morality after the Civil War, controlling the social order through regulations on education, family (marriage, baptism, death rites), public spaces, performances, meetings, festivals, the media, fashion, and even prison life. In the hands of the state, religion was often a tool of violent repression, applied with particular force to the leftists who had lost the war and were labelled as heretics by the victors. The vanquished were then employed as forced labour by the state, in the form of the Patronato Nacional de Redención de Penas por el Trabajo (National Board for Moral Redemption through Work, PNRPT), to rebuild the infrastructure and construct monuments to the victors. The PNRPT thus used moral pretexts to justify what amounted to slavery.[6]

Throughout the dictatorship, conceptualizations of modernization and modernity were complicated by the tensions between the rhetoric of Catholic orthodoxy, the economic benefits of capitalism, and the fascist, pseudo-feudalistic concept of economic order known as *nacionalsindicalismo* (national syndicalism), which proposed to eliminate class struggle by providing a form of "protection" against rapacious capitalism.[7] Even the government technocrats who eventually engineered rapid industrialization through the "economic stabilization plan" beginning in the late 1950s were members of the ultra-conservative Catholic organization Opus Dei, founded in Spain in 1928 by Saint Josemaría Escrivá, whose image is reproduced on many prayer cards at the sites (DP-3439). The prayer cards, in other words, may appear, and even intend, to simply offer religious solace, but their rhetoric upholds the right's justification of the Spanish Civil War as a religious crusade that sought to defend the Catholic Church from violent anticlerical attacks.[8]

The political, ideological, and economic valence of this particular expression of Catholicism did not end with the establishment of democracy after Franco's death. The separation of church and state was still a hotly debated topic in Spain at the time of the 11-M attacks and afterwards, yet religion is still taught in public schools, and the official ceremony for the victims of the terrorist attack was a Catholic mass held in the Almudena Cathedral.

Many of the poems at the Atocha station also express the kind of militant religious sentiment associated with national Catholicism or Opus Dei. One text represents the victims as martyrs in a holy war, citing Psalm 45: "El Señor de los ejércitos está con nosotros" (The Lord of the armies is with us) (DP-2948). Others urge the wounded and grieving to accept the will of God or to trust in the justice of God's vengeance, with language that recalls the crusades: "y si esos asesinos / mataron en nombre de 'ALÁ' / Tendrán un divino castigo / El día del Juicio Final" (and if those assassins / killed in the name of Allah / they will receive divine punishment / on Judgment Day) (DP-2937). Yet another preaches peaceful submission to authority, using the command form: "Obedeced a los que os gobiernen y aunque por ellas sufráis crueldades y contempléis maldades que vuestras mentes jamás pudieran imaginar, no amenacéis responder con la violencia" (Obey those who govern you and although you might suffer cruelties and witness evil that your minds could never have imagined, don't threaten to respond with violence) (DP-2207).

The 11-M bombers were from North Africa, with the majority (twenty-one of twenty-five) from Spain's former protectorate, Morocco, and they had invoked the rhetoric of Al-Andalus to justify their desire to reconquer the peninsula for Islam. Yet, prior to the attacks, Spanish authorities were not sufficiently focused on the jihadist threat, despite the fact the Al Qaeda had established an important cell in Spain in 1994 (Reinares 160). This blindness may be explained by the fact that the concept of terrorism was rhetorically linked during the long Franco dictatorship to internal enemies of that regime. However, the refusal by many on the right to accept the exclusive guilt of the Moroccan bombers, despite the rhetoric that the media had been using to address the "invasion" of North African immigrants (Flesler 83), resurrects yet another phantasm in Spanish cultural memory: the participation of Moroccan troops fighting with Franco in the Spanish Civil War. Franco had seized on the concept of a holy war to justify his coup as a crusade against infidels that would restore the essence of Spanish nationhood and empire. As Richards has explained, the crusade language in Francoist Civil War myths linked "the centuries-old myth of the Moorish threat ... [with] the construction of the 'Communist menace' as a modern-day Eastern plague" (Richards 129); however, this required the symbolic Cristianization of the Moroccans who fought at his side. Still, As Daniela Flesler explains in *The Return of the Moor: Spanish Responses to Contemporary Moroccan Immigration*, the Moorish "threat" still conditions Spanish perceptions of Moroccan immigrants, "awakening a series of historical ghosts related to their invading and threatening character" which explains why they have been the objects of "both subtle and explicit violence" (3). And revenge for such treatment was the motivation of more than one jihadist combatant, as Fernando Reinares explains in detail in his book on the 11-M bombings.

In part, the myth of *convivencia* – or the centuries of supposedly peaceful coexistence among Jews, Muslims, and Christians in medieval Spain – seeks to heal this wound. This is how Virtudes Téllez describes the decision to include interviews with and texts by Muslims in the Archive of Mourning, as a representation of "la pluralidad religiosa presente en España" (the reigning religious plurality in Spain) (167). This concept also appears in the poetic exercises that children in one school were assigned as a response to the bombings, with the theme "Sí a la convivencia" (DP-4911, for example). All of the students' artistic renderings contain the same poem, which unproblematically portrays peace as nature's dream.

In the story of the 11-M attacks defended by the social and political elite on the right, then, the Catholic Church and Madrid, as symbols of the Spanish nation, have been the perpetual victims, first of rebellious, murderous, and anticlerical communists in the Civil War, then of separatist terrorists associated with those defeated Republicans in the past several decades, and, more recently, of the judiciary, which refused to prosecute the "real culprits" – that is, ETA.[9] Thus, for the PP and affiliates, the sticky associations of the signs of peace (the white hands, hymns), liberty (from ETA terrorism), solidarity (in Catholicism, *convivencia*, and Spanish nationalism), and democracy in the form of a Spanish constitutional monarchy come together into a dominant narrative in which Moroccans are innocent and ETA is the real perpetrator of the bombings.

For the heirs of Franco, we could say that the story about ETA's culpability serves as an example of what Schwab calls the perpetrators' "screen memories." These

> function as a barrier between the conscious and the unconscious, and as a site of projection for unconscious fantasies, fears, and desires, which can then be decoded ... By covering one's own violent history with the memory of another, screen memories can assume both a transgenerational and a transhistorical dimension that needs to be decoded ... Looking at histories of perpetrators can reveal yet another aspect of screen memories. It is well known that narratives of perpetrators often displace perpetration onto victimhood. (22)

In a similar vein, Justin Crumbaugh has claimed that "the conservative enshrinement of victims of ETA has always performed a disavowal (simultaneous negation and affirmation) of the atrocities committed by the dictatorship" (367). Yet texts that invoke unresolved conflicts can have unintended consequences, awakening what Anne McClintock calls, in the context of 9/11, "a phantom, the ghostly mark of transgenerational guilt as yet unatoned for" (826). She is speaking of the echoes of the US atomic bombing of Japan in the "ground zero" rhetoric of 9/11, but the texts that insist on the culpability of the left and ETA may actually remind us of the uncomfortable truths about the Civil War and its aftermath: the war's origins in Franco's military coup; the supporting role of the church during the war and the dictatorship; the bombing of Guernica and Franco's deployment of Moroccan troops; the violence of right-wing extremists during and following the transition to democracy. Another ghost would be 9/11 itself and the subsequent "War on Terror," which the PP gladly joined because it gave the government carte blanche in its own war on ETA, even if, in a twist of irony, many believed that it gave rise to the Al Qaeda attack on Madrid.

El Pozo and Santa Eugenia: Franco's Heirs Sacrifice the Working Class to Their Interests

Although they contain some of the same elements (candles, flowers, written texts), the spontaneous shrines at the working-class stations of El Pozo del Tío Raimundo and Santa Eugenia bear little resemblance to the Atocha memorials. The differences are due in part to the identity of the individuals who left objects and texts at the memorials: at these stations, they were almost all family and friends of the victims leaving personalized messages (Sánchez-Carretero, "Trains" 341; Sánchez-Carretero and Ortiz 110), survivors of the attacks, or RENFE employees, and almost all of them were from the same social class. What is more, as Sánchez-Carretero and Ortiz point out, these are "tightly-knit communities with a strong neighborhood spirit" (110) and, as I shall explain, a long history of class-based resistance to state authority. These memorials therefore lack key elements from the Atocha shrines, particularly the proliferation of Spanish flags, anti-ETA texts, and prayer cards devoted to "martyrs of the Civil War," though there are prayer cards, generally to the Virgin, and psalms from evangelical churches.

These people believed a different narrative: Al Qaeda terrorists, incensed by Spain's participation in the so-called War on Terror, carried out attacks on the nation's capital, and the ruling Partido Popular sought

1.2. Poetry and graffiti at El Pozo (Archivo Histórico Ferroviario del Museo del Ferrocarril de Madrid, Debla Carbonell).

to deceive the Spanish public, placing the blame on ETA, in a bid to win re-election (Redondo 45). A supplement to this discourse appears in texts that were placed at the stations, circulated in the neighbourhoods, and published by residents of Santa Eugenia and El Pozo del Tío Raimundo, which emphasize that the bombs exploded on commuter trains carrying working-class people from the suburbs to their jobs in the city centre, along with their children, who were heading to school or the university. They also pointed out that the vast majority of the dead and injured represented a globalized proletariat doubly victimized by the political and social elites who created the conditions that led the bombers and many of their victims to seek work in Spain, and particularly in the capital. As noted in the introduction, these elites were responsible for the Urban Development Plans of 1985 and 1997, which brought about the neoliberal redesign of the capital, eliminating the *chabolas*, or shantytowns, in the traditionally leftist districts of Villa de Vallecas and Puente de Vallecas, where the neighbourhoods of Santa Eugenia and El Pozo del Tío Raimundo are located, and replacing them with new housing and shopping centres. While these changes might appear to improve the neighbourhoods, they produced forms of "everyday violence" (Coronil and Skurski 3) or "systemic violence" (Žižek). Ricardo Méndez explains that the 1997 Urbanization Plan gave rise to "una progresiva segmentación socioespacial en la que los precios del suelo y la vivienda actuaron como principal – aunque no exclusivo – factor de diferenciación entre quienes residen donde quieren y quienes lo hacen donde pueden" (a progressive socio-spatial segmentation in which real estate prices acted as the main, though not the only, factor in determining who can live where they want and who has to live wherever they can) (35). The gentrification process produced a profound political and economic rift in places like Santa Eugenia and El Pozo, which "se convirtieron, en ocasiones, en germen de contestación y resistencias locales al modelo social y de urbanización impuesto" (occasionally turned into the seed of local response and resistance to the social and urban model imposed on them) (ibid.). Many residents of those neighbourhoods opposed the Iraq War, which they saw as a battle for oil with proletarian foot-soldiers, and they saw the victims of the 11-M attacks in the same light, as cannon fodder.

This narrative about victims and perpetrators was also shaped by historical memories, which drew on another of the grand narratives about the meaning of the Civil War and its aftermath – class conflict – as well as memories of persecution under, and even after, the Franco dictatorship. Indeed, for the working class and other marginalized groups, "terrorism" would be associated, under Franco, with state-sponsored and/or -tolerated terror. They might recall violent events organized in Madrid by the fascist party, La Falange, during the years of the Second Republic leading up to the Civil War and in early Francoism; the generals who were involved with the coup d'etat that began that war and were responsible for bombing civilians in Madrid, Barcelona, and Guernica during the conflict; and the practices of the police state during the dictatorship. Another key act of urban violence that might have come to their minds occurred shortly after the end of Francoism: the assassination of labour lawyers by fascists on 24 January 1977 in their Atocha St office (five were killed and four gravely injured), followed by the kind of massive popular protest that had been forbidden during the dictatorship. The violent urban actions of the fascist paramilitary group the Guerrilleros de Cristo Rey (Warriors of Christ the King) in the late 1970s also suggested that, in Madrid, right-wing extremists could continue to act with impunity.[10]

Not surprisingly, then, the poetic texts left at the spontaneous shrines at the Santa Eugenia and El Pozo train stations, as well as the anthologies published by victims and neighbours, voice a repeated rejection of the globalized and neoliberal foreign and domestic policies of the state, claiming that they always violently sacrifice the working class to defend the interests of the elite. At the same time, the texts express a feeling of transnational solidarity, given that many of the victims were immigrants who had come to the city in search of work and lived with Spanish workers in Santa Eugenia and El Pozo. They predominantly use the lyric voice to express their individual sentiments, underscoring their desire to console the survivors and find social meaning in the deaths. In this sense, they draw on a very particular tradition of anti-fascist artists, including Pablo Neruda, César Vallejo, Miguel Hernández, Antonio Machado, Rafael Alberti, and Pablo Picasso, who figure prominently at the shrines.

"Santa Eugenia, niña, no te olvides" (Santa Eugenia, Child, Don't Forget) (DP-2988), written by "Tomás, vecino de Santa Eugenia" (Thomas, a resident of Santa Eugenia), stands in contrast to the prayer cards at Atocha. The text represents the saint for whom one of the stations was named, Santa Eugenia, as a child subject to the discipline of the state:

> Castigaron a mi niña,
> Sin recreo la dejaron.
> No se supo la lección de sociales ... ?
> ... Nunca llegaron los chavales.
> No se supo la lección de geometría ... ?
> ... Todo el barrio ha perdido la alegría.
> No se supo la lección de religión ... ?
> ... Hubo gritos, humo, sangre y desesperación.

(They punished my little girl / they took away her recess. / She hadn't learned the social science lesson ... ? / ... The kids never arrived. / She hadn't learned the geography lesson ... ? / ... The whole barrio lost its joy. / She hadn't learned the religion lesson ... ? / There were cries, smoke, blood, and desperation.)

Santa Eugenia is here the victim of punishment by an authoritarian pedagogue who recalls Franco-era teachers, imposing prescribed lessons on social issues, mathematics, and religion. The ellipses after each question and before each response indicate the silence imposed by violence and death, the missing kids, the lack of answers, which unite the entire barrio.

A poem from El Pozo, "A Todos" (To All) (DP-3109), recalls the rhetoric of the noble worker that one might expect from communist poetry of the 1930s, dedicated "A vosotros, los que tenéis el yunque en las manos, corazón encendido en ascuas de esperanza. / A vosotros, los que enterráis la semilla entre espinos, y la hacéis brotar con el aliento. / A los de la palabra ahogada" (To you, who hold the anvil in your hands, a burning heart in the ashes of hope. / To you, who bury the seed among spines and make it bloom with your breath. / To those with drowned words). Another poem, "Hoy también es primavera" (Today Is Also Spring) (DP-2704), contrasts those suffering from loss, figured as birds – doves, goldfinches, and swallows – with those who "no saben pensar / en rosas o en Primaveras" (don't know how to think / of roses or Springs) but sow only missiles. The poem repeats the phrase "los pájaros siguen pasando" (the birds keep passing by), but without optimism, as new wars accompany them, so that the final exclamation, that today is also spring, does not bring the hope of rebirth, but the return of death in "Otra primavera triste" (Another sad spring).

Although such texts dominate the horizon in El Pozo and Santa Eugenia, similar poems may also be found at the Atocha station. One of them, "11-M" by Ángel V. (DP-1788), associates the terrorists with the architects of slaughter in the Civil War. The final verses of Neruda's "Explico algunas cosas" (I Explain a Few Things)[11] serve as its epigraph, and they emblematize the "precocious mode of witnessing" (J. Gray 264) that we discussed in the introduction, one that does not pretend to know the answers about a traumatic event but registers only a stutter – "Venid a ver la sangre por las calles, / venid a ver / la sangre por las calles, / venid a ver la sangre / por las calles" (Come see the blood in the streets / come and see / the blood in the streets / come and see the blood / in the streets). For the Chilean poet, the traumatic event was the bombing of Madrid in the Spanish Civil War, and the city's sudden transformation from a space of friendship, comradery, and abundant, bustling life, to a place of violence, loss, and death. We might also recall from Neruda's poem the complicity of the wealthy, the nobles, and the church in the violence, groups that he condemns as "Bandidos con aviones y con moros, / bandidos con sortijas y duquesas, / bandidos con frailes negros bendiciendo" (Bandits with planes and with Moors, / bandits with rings and duchesses, / bandits with black friars blessing). Ángel's poem attempts something similar and indeed repeats a variation of Neruda's lines at the end of the section I cite here.

Entre raíles
De trenes reventados
De hierros retorcidos
Y cuerpos atrapados
De cuerpos desmembrados
De cuerpos en muñones

De sangre derramada
De manos sueltas, perdidas,
Que no acariciarán mas
(Por manos ocultas
que se creerán limpias)
De pies que no podrán
Hacer mas el camino
De vísceras abiertas
De corazones solos
Que dejan de latir.
...
Explota ante mis ojos,
Pero a todo color,
La imagen del Guernica.
Hoy debían llover
Lágrimas desde el cielo.
Venid a ver el llanto por las calles
Venid a oír el silencio por las calles
Venid a compartir el dolor de la calle[12]

(Between the rails / of shattered trains / of twisted tracks / of trapped bodies / of dismembered bodies / of bodies like stumps / with blood spilled / with loose hands, lost, / that will never caress again / (because of hidden hands / believed to be clean) / with feet that will never / again walk the road / with exposed viscera / with hearts, alone, / that cease to beat ... / Before my eyes explodes / the image of Guernica. / Today tears / should rain from heaven. / Come hear the cries on the streets / Come hear the silence on the streets / Come share the pain of the streets.)

The repeated parallelisms and anaphoras insistently draw us, along with the lyric speaker, to see and bear witness to the destroyed and dismembered people, whose remains haunt the scene. They are cut off from their bodies and their futures, as the repeated use of negation in conjunction with the future tense makes clear. The supposedly clean hidden hands recall the dirty tactics of anti-ETA and other state terrorism, which continued even under the PSOE government, a sign of Spain's systemic political corruption. The exploding image of Guernica alludes to Pablo Picasso's famous painting, a surreal rendering of the carpet-bombing of civilians during the Civil War. In direct opposition to the right-wing take on Basque violence as the result of ETA terrorism, then, the poem brings to the fore the most egregious cases of state-sponsored terror in the Civil War: the attacks on civilians in

Madrid and Guernica by the right-wing military, even as it channels anti-fascist poetry and art about those events.

Some Spanish newspapers (*ABC, El Mundo*) called the sites of the bombings, particularly the Atocha station, the "ground zero" of the attacks, thereby implicitly justifying Spain's participation in the Iraq War by linking 11-M to 9/11 and Madrid to New York.[13] Ana Montero's "No llaméis Zona 0" (Don't Call It Ground Zero) (DP-1340), however, rejects this parallelism:

No le llameis Zona 0
a la Avenida de las Flores,
porque aquí robaron la vida
a humildes trabajadores.
Ojala que desde el cielo
nos guarden llenos de amores,
y nos libren de vosotros, traidores.

(Don't call the Avenue of Flowers / Ground Zero, / because there they stole the lives / of humble workers. / I hope that from heaven / filled with love, they protect us, / and free us from you, traitors.)

The poem eschews the ground zero logic in favour of one that presents the working class as victims of the ruling elite, the plural "you" (*vosotros*) who joined the War on Terror in the first place. The separation between these classes is evident in the grammatical representation of the dead workers, first as victims – objects of the verb "robaron" (stole), which implies that support for Spain's participation in the war was economically motivated – and then as powerful guardian angels, the subjects of the verbs "guarden" (protect) and "libren" (free). The speaker becomes part of a collective, a "we" (*nos*) that is aided by the dead in the struggle against a dangerous plural "you" (*vosotros*) that has betrayed the nation. This argument is reinforced by the rhyme scheme: consonant rhyme in lines 2, 4, and 6, which joins the proletariat victims and the speaker together by location (the Avenida de las Fl**ores**, in Alcorcón, a working-class municipality); mourning, as symbolized by funereal flowers in the avenue's very name (*fl**ores***); the collective identity of the victims themselves (*trabajad**ores***); and love (*am**ores***). The poem then breaks the pattern of consonant rhyme in the even verses by repeating it in the odd line 7, dedicated to the members of the ruling class who are not patriots, but traitors (*traid**ores***) responsible for the attacks. The poem thus represents both the pain of loss and a call for solidarity.

"Madrid 11-M" has a similar message, presented in a series of negations, followed by a series of affirmations:

> No a la guerra
> No a la injusticia
> No al terrorismo
> No al asesinato
> No al poder
> No a la ira
> No a la venganza
> No a la mentira
> No a la opresión de los pueblos
> No al miedo
> No a perder las esperanzas
>
> Digamos un SI rotundo:
>
> Sí a la comprensión
> Sí a la unificación
> Sí a la justicia
> Sí a la esperanza por un mundo mejor
> Sí a la igualdad
> Sí al cambio
> Sí al respeto
> Sí a la libertad
> Sí a la verdad
> Sí al amor
> Sí a la paz
>
> Pero sobre todo, digamos: SI a la vida (DP-1207)

(No to war / No to injustice / No to terrorism / No to murder / No to power / No to anger / No to vengeance / No to lies / No to the oppression of the people / No to fear / No to losing hope // Let's give a round YES: // Yes to comprehension / Yes to unification / Yes to justice / Yes to the hope for a better world / Yes to equality / Yes to change / Yes to respect / Yes to freedom / Yes to truth / Yes to love / Yes to peace // But above all, let us say: YES to life.)

The repeated negations in the first half of the poem reject outright the logic from the right. These are mirrored in the second half, which proposes affirmative concepts of community solidarity in place of a politics of vengeance.

These texts use many of the same words and images we saw in the narrative from the right: terrorism, peace, war, justice, democracy, solidarity, and freedom, words with sticky associations dating from the Second Republic and the Franco dictatorship that have an entirely different valence here.

Monuments

The two irreconcilable narratives I have discussed here suggest the continuation of an unresolved battle in post-dictatorship Spain to define historical memory, create a single mourning body, and identify the perpetrators of the terrorist attack. To return to Alexander's proposition, which I cited at the beginning of this chapter, the unique characteristic of this particular trauma story is that the continued struggle to define Spanish democracy in the context of contested Civil War memories has prevented an agreement on the "nature of the victim" and "the attribution of responsibility."

The battle is re-enacted each year at the monuments that were erected at the bombing sites along the fated commuter train path, from Alcalá de Henares to the Atocha station, and in Madrid's most famous park, Retiro.[14] The construction of the monuments was itself a political struggle. The most well-known 11-M monument was inaugurated at the Atocha station after an international competition and selection by a jury with representation from only one victims' group, the Asociación Víctimas del Terrorismo (Association of Terrorism Victims, AVT), which focuses on victims of ETA.[15] As a result, the other victims' organizations, and particularly the group associated with the working-class neighbourhoods (the Asociación 11-M Afectados del Terrorismo [11-M Association of Those Affected by Terrorism]), have never recognized it as the official monument to the victims. Nonetheless the annual commemorations are held there, albeit in silence, in accordance with the demands of the Asociación 11-M (Flesher Fominaya, "The Madrid 2004 Bombing" 418). The AVT, accompanied by the conservative PP, holds a ceremony at the Bosque del Recuerdo (Memorial Forest) in Retiro Park, at which it recognizes all terrorism victims and often speaks predominantly about ETA. The PP-controlled government of Madrid did not initially approve funds for any kind of memorial at the train stations of El Pozo and Santa Eugenia; these were finally constructed thanks to the continued efforts of the Asociación 11-M, along with workers' unions and neighbourhood associations from El Pozo and Santa Eugenia. The ceremonies held there emphasize the sacrifices of the working class. In the next sections, I will discuss the monuments, the memorials, and the controversies surrounding them.

Atocha

The Atocha monument can be seen on the street (critics say it can *barely* be seen), a shimmering transparent tower of clear glass blocks jutting out of the station, visually recalling the explosions. Inside the layer of glass blocks is a clear membrane on which texts from the original memorials in the station are inscribed in a continuous, spiral text. The architects describe the rhetoric of this linguistic presentation in terms of transparency, light, absence, and structure, but also in relation to a membrane or a skin, a metaphorical representation of the tissues that connect and contain the body's separate organs:

> Esta membrana está sujeta por succión. Unos ventiladores crearán un vacío entre las dos pieles que permitirá que el monumento se mantenga en pie sin ningún elemento opaco que oscurezca la idea del proyecto. Los mensajes serán vistos a través de la piel de vidrio durante el día y aparecerán de distinta manera durante la noche ... La membrana transparente nace en el interior de la sala para hacer llegar los mensajes a la ciudad de Madrid. ("Monumento homenaje")
>
> (This membrane will be held in place by suction. Fans will be put in place to create a gap between the two skins that will keep the monument in place without a single opaque element that might shade the project's idea. The messages will be able to be seen through the glass skin during the day, but they will appear differently at night ... The transparent membrane, born inside the Atocha meditation room, will bring the messages out to the city of Madrid.)

The words here are inscribed on the "skin," which symbolically allows for continued communication between the living and the dead; the "membrane" suggests that they remain bound with connective tissue.

The monument also seeks to link the everyday activities outside of the building with the memory and grief that still haunt its inner recesses. The structure explodes out into the sky, but its glass walls allow the sunlight to penetrate down into a room with blue walls, separated from the rest of the station by a soundproof glass wall, creating "un espacio vacío, en silencio, con la luz como protagonista" (an empty space, silent, with light as the protagonist) ("Monumento Homenaje"). The "Vacío Azul" (Blue Vacuum) is a non-denominational yet sacred space for silent reflection. When mourners look up into the glass structure from the depths of that room, they see the spiral of words on the membrane illuminated by natural light. While the silence and the vacuum invoke, in a sense, the ghosts of the disappeared bodies, the trace of their identity is preserved on the wall of the meditation room in a list of the victims' names, a typical gesture in monuments to the dead. Carole Blair notes in particular that, in contemporary memorials, the inscriptions "name individuals whose lives and/or deaths have been rendered outside the cultural mainstream" (282). She is thinking of the AIDS Memorial Quilt, the monument in Alabama to civil rights activists, and the Vietnam War memorial in Washington. The names on the 11-M memorial are largely of the economically and legally marginalized: working-class citizens and undocumented foreign workers, living on the outskirts of the capital.[16]

Despite the lofty aesthetic ideals of its creators, the Atocha monument has often not functioned as planned, in large part because the PP government of Madrid has not adequately funded its maintenance. The first problems surfaced just two years after its installation, and they have continued off and on since that date, with blame affixed to the party in power by the newspapers ideologically aligned with its rivals.[17] The image in the 8 March 2016 edition of *ABC* by José Ramón Ladra portrays the complete collapse of the membrane, dramatizing how partisan battles have effectively undermined the memorial intent of the monument, converting the victims into political capital. Although the site has since been repaired, its frequent inaccessibility over the years due to its various states of disrepair and to the poor signage designating its location, seems to symbolize the neglect and forgetfulness surrounding 11-M and its victims, which stand in stark contrast to the attention afforded victims of the Spanish Civil War and of ETA terrorists.

El Bosque del Recuerdo

The same kinds of conflict and neglect have characterized El Bosque del Recuerdo, located in Retiro Park. Originally created by Isabel la Católica, queen of Castile, as part of a monastery, Retiro became a palatial garden during the reign of Felipe II in the sixteenth century. More recently, the park has figured into neoliberal plans to convert Madrid into a global city and tourist destination. Benjamin Fraser describes in detail the processes whereby the redesignation of the park from a recreational site to a tourist attraction and site for capital accumulation required that "class conflict ... be erased from the landscape and minority-groups removed or policed ..., written out of that place's history" (683). Fraser also documents the increased policing of the park beginning in the mid-1990s, aimed particularly at racialized immigrant populations (689). It should not be surprising, then, that the site for the *bosque*, in a previously neglected isolated corner of the park called la Chopera, was not chosen randomly: it was a social space utilized primarily by Ecuadorians, who, as immigrants, were portrayed in ads distributed at bus stops by the "ultra right-wing group *Democracia Nacional*" as "dangerous, unnatural, and a threat to the park and its users" (Masterson-Algar 85, 86). Araceli Masterson-Algar argues that the repurposing of this area for an 11-M memorial was intended to eliminate the Ecuadorians' weekly get-togethers and effectively erase their collective memory in favour of a one designed to honour one particular concept of the Spanish nation (102).[18]

Even though the site is dedicated to the victims of 11-M, as evidenced by its 192 trees (one for each of the dead) surrounded by a moat, it effectively invisibilizes them. A large plaque dedicates the site "a todas las víctimas del terrorismo / cuya memoria permanence viva en nuestra convivencia / y la enriquece constantemente" (to all victims of terrorism / whose memory stays alive in our *convivencia* / and enriches it constantly). In other words, it is a tribute not to the 11-M victims, but to all victims, inscribed into a plurality defined as *convivencia*, which, as I have discussed earlier, is a concept linked to a Francoist notion of *Hispanidad*. The AVT's annual memorial ceremonies reflect this insistence on subsuming the 11-M incidents into a narrative about terrorism in general, with an emphasis on ETA. Like the Atocha memorial, the Bosque del Recuerdo has fallen into disrepair, to the extent that the dying trees had to be painted green for the 2017 commemoration, according to a report by *El Mundo*. The newspaper had taken quite a critical stance toward Podemos, which emerged from the "Indignant" or 15-M movement that began on 15 May 2011, organized by the authors of the *pásalo*, among others, as a response to the 2008 economic crisis. It is not surprising, then, that the article blames the degraded condition of the site on budget cutbacks by the Podemos party mayor Manuela Carmena, which resulted in insufficient watering and plant care. The article also points out the role of the neoliberal penchant for privatization, as maintenance of the site had been contracted to a private firm, Acciona, through 2021. In fact, Acciona was awarded the ten-year, ninety-five million euro, contract for eight historic parks in Madrid by the PP government of Madrid, not the Podemos party or Mayor Carmena, in 2013.

March 11th Plaza in Alcalá de Henares

Other official monuments are located in Alcalá de Henares, a historical site associated with Spain's imperial past, designated as a UNESCO world heritage site in 1998. The birthplace of Miguel de Cervantes, a bishopric before becoming part of the diocese of Madrid, and the original location of the Complutense University, Alcalá is now the home of the University of Alcalá, an important branch of the National Library, and the Cervantes Institute, which promotes Hispanic culture. None of the bombs went off in Alcalá, but the commuter line along which the trains exploded has its origin there, and twenty-seven residents lost their lives. The small square outside the station, renamed the Plaza 11 de Marzo in 2014, is dominated by an enormous abstract monolith, accompanied by a column listing the residents of the city who perished on the doomed commuter line. Another monument in that space, the first dedicated to 11-M (in 2005), includes a group statue of nine victims, who, both in their physiological features and their dress, appear to be Spaniards, though the victims included immigrants, and the station itself is located in an immigrant neighbourhood.

El Pozo del Tío Raimundo and Santa Eugenia

Distant and distinct from the sites associated with cultural heritage, the train stations and neighbourhoods of El Pozo and Santa Eugenia have remained largely invisible in the official acts recognizing those affected by the bombings. This neglect extends to the benefits accorded to the victims, including the construction of monuments, which have been erected and funded only thanks to the determination and concerted effort of people living in the neighbourhoods.

The abstract concrete monument to the 11-M victims in El Pozo, designed by the architect José María Pérez González (also known as Peridis), towers above visitors to the site. Looking through the structure from one end of it, you feel the power of an enormous train, but from the side you see that it is broken into pieces, like the trains themselves on that fateful day. This static monolithic structure is bathed at night in soft light and surrounded by the flowing waters of a fountain, suggesting the continuity of life, with death looming in its midst. Peridis explains that the monument contains the four elements – "la piedra, metáfora de eternidad; el aire, de aliento; el agua, de vida, y las flores, de afecto" (stone, metaphor of eternity; air, or breath; water, of life; and flowers, of affection) – and that the falling streams of water represent tears ("La inauguración"). In the background are thirty-one lithographs by the painter Juan Genovés (1930) and the graphic artists El Roto (Andrés Rábago García, 1947) and Forges (Antonio Fraguas de Pablo, 1942), embedded behind panes of glass in a great wall.[19]

The El Pozo monument hosts the annual commemorative acts of the Asociación 11-M, Comisiones Obreras (Workers' Commissions, CCOO), the Unión General de Trabajadores (General Workers' Union, UGT), and the Actors' Union of Atocha, along with the neighbourhood associations of El Pozo and Santa Eugenia. The inauguration itself demonstrated the conflict we have been discussing: the aforementioned groups had organized a ceremony for the afternoon of 11 March 2014 and invited the PP mayor of Madrid, but he did not respond and instead arranged for a separate act without consulting the victims or the neighbourhood organizations (Efe). Another emblematic incident occurred on 14 November 2015, the day after the terrorist attack in Paris, when the site suffered damage to the glass panes due to vandalism. Ángeles Domínguez, the president of the conservative Fundación Víctimas del Terrorismo (Victims of Terrorism Foundation [FVT], created in 2001 as a result of the Antiterrorist Pact signed by the PP and the PSOE), ascribed the vandalism to irresponsible citizens of El Pozo who wanted to draw attention to themselves. The AVT president, Ángeles Pedraza, pointed out that monuments to ETA victims have also suffered from destructive acts by left-wing groups and claimed that the El Pozo vandalism was a way for those elements to respond to the Paris attacks and "escenificar su posición a favor del terrorismo" (stage their pro-terrorist position). Finally, Pilar Manjón believed that the acts were an attack on the Asociación 11-M and its anti-war, pro-peace agenda (Macías). In sum, even violent and destructive acts that disrespect the victims are cause for acrimony rather than unity.

In Santa Eugenia, the neighbourhood association La Colmena (The Beehive), frustrated by the lack of material support from the Popular Party government of the Community of Madrid and angered that the victims of the poorer communities had not been consulted in the design of the other sites, also raised money to create its own memorial ("Monumento a las víctimas"). A statue, completed in 2007, seems not to be a wholly effective remembrance: the small figure is not prominently displayed on the grounds of the station, but across the street, in an isolated, weedy patch. Nonetheless, the residents host annual commemorative events at the site, including a ceremony with local schoolchildren, who leave flowers and sing a well-known pop song, "No dudaría" (I Wouldn't Hesitate) by Antonio Flores (*El blog del Guernica*), whose theme is anti-violence. Flores, born in Madrid in 1961, was the son of singer Lola Flores, who played the Franco-era prototype of the Andalusian gypsy in numerous films, and Roma guitarist Antonio González.[9] Although Flores might have easily lived isolated by his parents' wealth, he instead immersed himself in life on Madrid's streets during the famous *movida madrileña*, as I will discuss further in the following chapter, and he was a popular figure with residents. His popular cover of Joaquín Sabina's song "Pongamos que hablo de Madrid" (Let's Say I'm Speaking of Madrid) made him a kind of symbolic ambassador for the city. What is more, the choice of a song by an artist with strong Andalusian roots visiblizes the fact that immigrants fleeing extreme poverty in Andalusia had flocked to the neighbourhoods surrounding the El Pozo and Santa Eugenia stations during the dictatorship.

The sticky associations behind the rhetoric of the grassroots memorials and the polarizing images of public mourning in the yearly commemorations of 11-M and the narratives that accompany them – including newspaper articles, television programs, blogs, memorials, videos, books, and scholarly articles – place the remembrance of this event alongside the Pacto del Olvido, as an open wound in the national psyche. Along with debates about the monuments' initial funding and continued maintenance, the official sites and ceremonies are emblematic of the continued struggles over the meaning of the events and the culture of "forgetting" in Spain, enshrined in the Pacto del Olvido at the heart of the transition to democracy. Still, the performance at Santa Eugenia suggests an alternative form of memorialization that draws on cultural phenomena unrelated to the Civil War. This kind of bodily enactment of culture will be the focus of chapter 2.

Chapter Two

Circulation and Performance in Memorial and Media Sites

Although symbolic markers referencing Civil War memories may have dominated the media's response to the 11-M attacks, in the preponderance of materials at the grassroots memorials, and at the annual commemorative events at the monuments, the dynamic and temporal dimensions of mourning and memory destabilize those dominant narratives. Indeed, the memorials themselves, as well as the texts and other objects placed there, persist "not as a stable entity but as fundamentally a mnemonic *process*" (Erll 27). The memorials and the poetry in them, then, reflect "the 'dynamic turn' in memory studies (which] is itself part of a larger shift within culture studies away from such a focus on individual products to a focus on the processes in which those products are caught up and in which they play a role" (Rigney 348).

Even the writing at the grassroots memorials was not static, as the photos might suggest; rather, it evolved over time. The earliest writing was inscribed on the walls and columns, and this graffiti conveyed the "immediate reactions and the most violent expressions of hate, as well as of love and solidarity, leading to a combination of insults aimed at politicians and terrorists and messages of peace and the possibility of creating a better world" (Sánchez-Carretero, "Madrid Train Bombings" 253). Especially as the government's story continued to unravel, visitors added other kinds of texts, which papered over the graffiti, forming a palimpsest of messages, in which sentiments against politicians and terrorists, and in solidarity with the victims, dominated (ibid. 249). These acts, along with the processes of public reading and writing, singing, and prayer, functioned as what Diana Taylor calls the "repertoire" that "enacts embodied memory-performances, gestures, orality, movement, dance, singing – in short, all those acts usually thought of as ephemeral, non-reproducible knowledge." Repertoire, she argues, "allows for individual agency," and it "requires presence – people participate in the production and reproduction of knowledge by 'being there,' being a part of the transmission" (20).

The memorial spaces, as loci of reflection and mourning, hosted a wide variety of religious, spiritual, musical, and communitarian activities that sometimes reinforced, but often disrupted, the rhetoric of the dominant social narratives I have described in the preceding chapter. The 11-M memorials, for example, and particularly the shrine in the Atocha station, were literally the sites of prayer, as the prayer cards I mentioned earlier imply. However, not all of the services or devotional objects drew from the traditions of national Catholicism and Opus Dei. There was room as well for the liberation theology, Buddhism, Islam, Protestantism, Gnosticism, and Judaism, as the documents collected from the sites and photos of activities taken at them attest. Such responses reflect the real religious diversity of the Iberian Peninsula today.

The circulation of poems in the grassroots memorials also reflected the dynamic processes of cultural remembrance and its connections to collective memory. Some remembered poems were posted in public places to be read, reread, and commented upon by others. Others denote a very personal kind of contact among people at the shrines and beyond, requesting that readers copy the poem and pass it on, functioning in this sense like the *pásalo* text message on 13 March. The circulation of previously hidden or suppressed texts, as well as those from different generations and musical traditions, also comes to form a kind of connective tissue between the present and the past in living memory, as well as performing the recuperation, as it were, of a body of literature. Songs may play a role in these processes, but they may also help to shape the memory of the event and, in performance, inscribe the body into the text as breath, movement, and voice.

In this chapter, I will suggest that these forms of lyrical expression, remembering, and sharing represent complex processes of embodiment, mourning, and performance that reveal the dynamic processes of cultural memory.

Collective Memory in the Grassroots Memorials

Most of the poems posted in the memorials were written by, or allude to, Spanish and Latin American authors associated with the losing side of the Spanish Civil War and anti-Franco sentiment (for example, Miguel Hernández, Pablo Neruda, Rafael Alberti, César Vallejo, Antonio Machado, Blas de Otero, Federico García Lorca, Gabriel Celaya), a population whose voices were largely silenced during the dictatorship through exile and/or censorship, forms of what Aleida Assmann calls

2.1. Buddhist prayer in the Atocha station (Archivo Histórico Ferroviario del Museo del Ferrocarril de Madrid, Francisco M. Gil García).

the active form of forgetting, which "is implied in intentional acts such as trashing and destroying" (A. Assmann, "Canon" 97–8). The genocidal drive of Franco's government aimed at extinguishing not only the people associated with the so-called *vencidos* (vanquished), but also their memory. The Partido Popular (PP) government continues to resist the investigation of secret graves, with an insistence that the survival of democracy depends on forgetting the past; but in the memorials, the poems of artists who fought against the regime become part of the performance of remembrance. In this sense, they may stand in for the unrecovered bodies of those who died in the war or were assassinated and often buried in unmarked graves during the dictatorship.

Such enforced silence could have eradicated the collective memory of the ideals of the Second Republic; indeed, it was intended to do so. As Jan Assmann writes, collective memory is in danger of disappearing altogether within three generations when "it is not supported by any institutions of learning, transmission, and interpretation; it is not cultivated by specialists and is not summoned or celebrated on special occasions; [and] it is not formalized and stabilized by any forms of material symbolization" (111). Aleida Assmann adds that "[a]cts of forgetting are ... violently destructive when directed at an alien culture or a persecuted minority. Censorship has been a forceful if not always successful instrument for destroying material and mental cultural products" ("Canon" 98).

The reappearance of these poets in the memorials and in the texts of other poets writing about 11-M, however, suggests the continuation of the cultural memory begun by the passing or singing of forbidden texts during the Franco dictatorship. Díaz-Mas explains that the works of these poets could be mobilized by common citizens due to the popularization of poems by the most-cited poets – Hernández, Machado, Alberti – in the songs of *cantautores* like Joan Manuel Serrat and Luis Eduardo Aute, the singer-songwriters of late Francoism and the post-dictatorship who set many poems by forbidden authors to music in the 1960s and 1970s (107). This transmediation of poems into songs renewed, but also transformed, their significance, making the texts newly relevant, including for the younger generations who had no direct knowledge of the Spanish Civil War and had learned about it only in schools and other state cultural institutions and only from a Francoist perspective. It allowed the memory of the vanquished left to persist. In this sense, the language of that entire persecuted community, and their poems, constitute traces of resistance – or "una entrada imprescindible para permanecer en la memoria colectiva" (an indispensable gateway for remaining in collective memory) (Macciuci 18) – which prove that "the absent past is also part of reality" (Reyes Mate 22). The songs put the struggles of the working poor against the dictatorship into a broader historical perspective, so that such people perceived their present as a continuation of the past. The poetry was thus uniquely able to sustain an oppressed population that was obliged to suffer in resigned silence, as Michael Richards has explained (140).[1] Indeed, Richards sees their very silence as a form a resistance, rather than surrender or passivity, as it ensured their survival and that of future generations. "This," he writes, "was social and cultural reproduction in the aftermath of and in the face of the worst defeat imaginable" (ibid.).

At the same time that the *cantautores* set these poems to music and thus resuscitated a particular collective memory, other mechanisms were in motion to return this corpus to canonical status in the nation's cultural memory. To wit, foreign and/or exiled writers, singers, and academics preserved, shared, and curated the forbidden poems in universities and cultural institutions abroad, and poets and intellectuals in Spain (most famously, Vicente Aleixandre) maintained private libraries and circulated texts clandestinely in bookstores and literary groups. The poems thus came to form part of the literary canon, a mechanism of enduring cultural memory, which "supports a collective identity" (A. Assmann, "Canon" 100).[2] From this secure location as "great works," the censored poetry garnered a cultural legitimacy within Spain that endures to this day: such poems are taught in schools, and their memory is preserved through performance and other forms of cultural remembrance, including, particularly in the case of Miguel Hernández in Madrid, the naming of institutions and even neighbourhoods. Indeed, Hernández is the single most-cited poet (sixteen texts) in the archival materials I consulted.

The poems by Machado, Hernández, and Alberti that had been popularized by the *cantautores* of the Franco years were not the only Spanish-language songs in the shrines. There were also several lyrics written or sung by the counterculture stars of the *movida madrileña*, who had celebrated a gritty, grungy Madrid bursting with creative energy in the first decade and a half after Franco's demise.[3] One mourner posted the lyrics of Joaquín Sabina's "Yo me bajo en Atocha" (I Get Off at Atocha, 1998), with a critical difference, changing the line "su dieciocho de julio, su catorce de abril" (its 18th of July, its 14th of April) to "su dieciocho de julio, *mi* catorce de abril" (its 18th of July, *my* 14th of April; emphasis in the original) (OB-1). The dates mark the beginning of the Spanish Civil War, on 18 July 1936, after a coup d'etat by General Franco and others against the Second Republic, which had been proclaimed on 14 April 1931. This mourner clearly identifies with the leftist sentiments of the Second Republic, which sought to give voice and power to the working class and other marginalized groups. Another Sabina text in the shrines, "Pongamos que hablo de Madrid" (Let's Say I'm Talking About Madrid) (DP-4575), was popularized by Antonio Flores when he covered it in a rock version on his 1981 album *Al caer el sol* (At Sunset).[4]

In 1994, Flores also performed "Sólo le pido a Dios" (I Only Ask of God) in concert in Gijón with Ana Belén (stage name of María del Pilar Cuesta Acosta), who popularized the song by Argentine composer León Gieco in Spain, after recording a cover of it on her 1984 album *Géminis*. Díaz-Más explains that the song "aparece en varias ofrendas dedicadas por personas argentinas, a veces junto a un dibujo de la bandera de su país" (appears on many objects dedicated by Argentinians, sometimes accompanied by a drawing of their flag) (110). Mexican music also shows up in the form of the ranchera "Pa' todo el año" (For the Whole Year).

Visitors to the grassroots memorials did not limit their repertoire to Spanish-language texts: they also papered the sites with anti-war lyrics in English, sometimes accompanied by Spanish translations. These texts include John Lennon's "Imagine," U2's "Sunday Bloody Sunday," Bruce Springsteen's "Empty Sky" (bilingual), and Sting's "Fragile."[5] Another text contains the lyrics of a song, "Sorrow," by the punk rock group Bad Religion, from their album *The Process of Belief*: "Let me take you to the hurting ground / Where all good men are trampled down." In part, these song lyrics offer evidence of music's global language and reach and of the variety of musical cultures that spoke to different populations affected by the attacks. They also point to a particular form of dissent in the post-9/11 environment, one that would be likely to appeal to a society that had protested massively against Spain's participation in the Iraq War.

Pop Music and the Cultural Industry

In March 2005, a group of both well-known and unknown musical artists put out an album of thirty-one songs dedicated to the victims of 11-M, *No os olvidamos* (We Won't Forget You), produced by BMG/ARIOLA. A handful of these songs were composed specifically in response to the attacks, but most had come out before the bombings. The proceeds from the album sales were donated to the Fundación Víctimas del Terrorismo (FVT). The title of the album is also the title of a blog dedicated exclusively to victims of ETA, but here it refers to a line from Elena Bugedo's 11-M song "De Madrid al cielo" (From Madrid to Heaven).

This musical collaboration in the name of solidarity with the victims clearly recalls prior global efforts like the Live Aid concert (1985) and the "We Are the World" recording (1985), as well as more recent massive musical events in the United States, which were also broadcast internationally, in the years following the attacks on the Twin Towers. The songs on *No os olvidamos* cover a broad range of music styles, but they contain few overt political messages beyond a desire for peace and intercultural understanding. They include ballads by a variety of singer-songwriters and pop groups (Elena Bugedo, the Catalan singer Marina Rossell, Luis Eduardo Aute, Ismael Serrano, La Oreja de Van Gogh, Ana Torroja, Carlos Choouen, and the Palestinian-Spaniard Marwan); flamenco-infused songs from performers like Andy & Lucas (who contributed a song against domestic violence), Arcángel, Clara Montes, Aurora Guirado, and Antonio Orozco; covers of songs like "Imagine" and "A Dios le pido"; a musical version of Neruda's poem "Para mi corazón" (For My Heart) in Juan Valderrama's "C/ Neftaly n°12" (12 Neftaly Street); and a Hebrew/Arabic collaboration between the Israeli singer David Broza and the Palestinian musician and composer Said Murad on "Belibí" (In My Heart).[6] Together, these songs reflect the cultural paradigm that Guillem Martínez and others call CT, or the Culture of the Transition – that is, the de-activation of culture's critical function in favour of its potential for generating stability and cohesion (see the discussion in the introduction).

The insert for the album contains several texts that explain how the artists came together in the interests of inclusiveness, togetherness, healing, and peace, and in the belief that solidarity matters more than celebrity.[7] In the insert, Javier Gurruchaga writes, for example, that the purpose of the album is to "rendir homenaje a todas las víctimas del 11-M y, en general, a todas las víctimas de todas las guerras del mundo por los siglos de los siglos" (to give homage to all of the victims of 11-M and, in general, to all of the victims of all of the wars in the world from time immemorial).[8] The Portuguese Nobel laureate José Saramago contributed a paragraph, under the heading "El rostro de un pueblo herido" (The Face of a Wounded People), that emphasizes solidarity (variations of the word appear five times), particularly the way in which "el recuerdo de la solidaridad pasada refuerza la solidaridad que el presente necesita, y ambas, juntas, preparan el camino para que la solidaridad, en el futuro, vuelva a manifestarse en toda su grandeza" (the memory of past solidarity reinforces the solidarity that the present requires, and together they prepare the way so that solidarity, in the future, can again reveal itself in all its glory). Only Pilar del Río's paragraph broaches the topic of lies, social injustice, and an unjustifiable war, hinting at the culpability of the PP.

The insert also contains two lyrical texts. One is Manuel Francisco Reina's poem "Poemas en los andenes" (Poems on the Platforms), which may also be found on the website of the Asociación 11-M Afectados del Terrorismo.[9] In this text, the speaker/poet is likened to the mourners who left poems and flowers at the shrines – "Abandono versos en los andenes. / Deshojo flores manuscritas" (I abandon verses on the platforms. / I pull the petals from manuscript flowers) – and he expresses lyrically the ways those personified texts stood in for sympathetic citizens, offering "anónimos abrazos" (anonymous embraces) and a "caricia del consuelo / como un paño de voz para el llanto del silencio" (a caress of consolation / like a voice cloth for the silent weeping). Poetry, this text argues, may play a vital human role in tragic circumstances, embracing the mourners, holding their tears, guiding them, and providing a space for remembrance in a place defined by dismay. The text links this process to the sacred and to cultural memory, in the form of the manuscript, the folio, and the rosary; and later to song, in the trill of the bird. The melancholic but steady cadence of the poem also offers a soothing retreat from the chaos of sudden death and traumatic loss. There are no violent enjambements or syntactical ruptures, but rather a series of parallelisms – the repetition of long phrases preceded by verbs conjugated in the first person, denoting the soothing activities performed by the speaker, for example, or the opening and closing that refer to the transformation of the train platforms, covered with poems in lieu of broken bodies and blood, taking the place of absence and silence.

The second text in verse in the insert contains the lyrics of Elena Bugedo's song "De Madrid al cielo." The title is taken from a common saying in praise of Madrid, the disputed origins of which date back to the seventeenth century, and which had become part of a tourist campaign for the city. It appears frequently in the grassroots memorials. The song repeats common images from 11-M and 12-M – including the crowds, smoke, flowers, candles, and white hands – and advocates that everyone simply to go forward together with hope. The refrain is stark and straightforward:

> Llenaremos las calles por ti
> Prenderemos velas a nuestro paso
> Con las manos blancas y así
> De Madrid al cielo, que no os olvidamos

(We will fill the streets for you / We will light candles along our way / With white hands and thus / From Madrid to heaven, we will not forget you.)

The song lacks the lyrical and structural complexity of "Poemas en los andenes," but its simplicity, sentimentality, and plaintive melody struck a chord in Madrid, where it became a kind of anthem for many mourners.[10] Indeed, when *No os olvidamos* was ready for the market, an article about the album in *El Mundo* led with a paragraph about Elena Bugedo, who had been entirely unknown at the time of the attacks, and merely listed the names of the other famous artists who collaborated on the project (Aparicio).[11] The song was so successful, I suspect, because it sought to heal the continued rift in Spanish society by erasing all of the political and ideological controversy from the events, folding everyone, unproblematically (but also uncritically) into a common "we."

The same could be said for the other most popular 11-M song, "Jueves" (Thursday), which came out in 2008 on the album *A las cinco en el Astoria* (At Five O'Clock in the Astoria) by La Oreja de Van Gogh, a group that had contributed a different song, "Geografía" (Geography), to the *No os olvidamos* album. "Jueves," which topped the charts in Spain, tells an unrequited love story that takes place on the train, apparently based on a true story taken from the diary belonging to one of the victims, which was found in the rubble. The speaker is a young woman who takes the same train each morning and has fallen in love with someone that she doesn't dare to talk to. In the penultimate stanza of the song, that person approaches her and tells her that s/he takes the same train as well just to see her. The flash of love, however, coincides with the explosion of the train: the first kiss is the last, and she leaves the gift of her last heartbeat.

The sentimental melodrama of the story appears as a different kind of remembrance on the 2009 video released by Sony Music Entertainment España. Rather than simply representing the plot of the story and repeating the traumatic images of the explosions, the video begins with close-ups of people of various ages, races, and genders, including children and a baby, who stand in for the dead, before cutting to the lead singer, Leire Martínez, in live concert, and then back and forth between her and the others, who fade out toward the end. This is the same gesture we saw in the monuments that list the victims' names, or the newspaper stories that relate their individual lives. The singer and the viewers can easily see themselves as one with, or potentially one of, the victims of senseless violence because Martínez's voice comes from their mouths as they seem to sing the words of the song.[12] Although the gesture is meant to rehumanize the victims and represent their differences, the video visually presents an image of a diverse population singing with one voice (Martínez's) and telling one story about the event.

Hip Hop

The YouTube video of Arma Blanca's hip-hop song "El último tren" (The Last Train), from its 2007 album, *Autodidactas*, has received nearly half a million visitors since it was uploaded in August 2007. This figure does not approach the popularity of "Jueves," which had been viewed more than forty-one million times by October 2018,[13] but it is nonetheless significant, especially considering that hip hop began to spread in Spain only in the 1980s after young Afro-Spaniards discovered it through African-American soldiers at the US Army base in Torrejón (Elola). Much of the early hip-hop scene took place in a discotheque in Torrejón called Stone's, which closed in 2002 (Marcos). It entered Spanish culture first through the phenomenon of break dancing before passing to graffiti, with famous figures like Muelle (Juan Carlos Argüello), and then to musical composition. The first major collaborative album, *Madrid Hip Hop*, was produced by Troya in 1989, the same year that the first big hit single, "Hey, Pijo" (Hey, Preppy) by MC Randy, came out (*Dos platos*). Significantly, hip hop incorporated Spaniards of African and Latin American descent, people such as El Chojín from the group Base Aérea Torrejón (Torrejón Airfield Base), whose father was from Ecuatorial Guinea, or the Congolese Frank T (Franklin Tshimini Nsombolay) from El Club de los Poetas Violentos (The Violent Poets' Club), a demographic that is barely represented at all on the Spanish pop scene (Elola).

Initially, Spanish hip hop addressed class issues in the districts of Campamento and Vallecas, where the movement took off (*Dos platos*), drawing on "the creative capacities conditioned by the often harsh realities of people's everyday surroundings" (Bradley, n.p.). These districts were among the neighbourhoods served by the commuter line that carried the bombs on 11-M: Santa Eugenia is located in the district of Villa de Vallecas, and El Pozo is in Puente de Vallecas.[14] Commuters on that train line can see clear evidence of hip-hop culture in the graffiti on all of the available surfaces along the tracks, particularly in the stretch between Entrevías and Torrejón. These images and tags, I would argue, are much like the texts at the grassroots memorials at El Pozo and Santa Eugenia, covering under-used urban spaces with words and images that testify to the presence of a marginalized population that contests the dominant narratives of urban development. Other hip-hop activities, including skateboarding and break-dancing, also belong to public urban spaces, occasionally resignifying them, as with the case of the Plaza de Colón, which was designed to celebrate Spain's imperial past and not as a playground for post-colonial youths (Marcos). The ideological orientation of hip-hop artists in Spain varies greatly, running the gamut from the far left to the far right, the former becoming increasingly anti-capitalist and the latter with pronounced xenophobic tendencies that became violently Islamophobic after 11-M (Rodríguez Jiménez 120).[15]

Scholars have made the case for hip hop as a poetic form in the English language and in Latin America. Adam Bradley, for example, writes that, "not all rap is great poetry, but collectively it has revolutionized the way our culture relates to the spoken word. Rappers at their best make the familiar unfamiliar through rhythm, rhyme, and wordplay. They refresh the language by fashioning patterned and heightened variations of everyday speech" (n.p). As Bradley explains, rap simultaneously imposes and undermines order, with rhythm imposed by the beat and disrupted by syncopation and stress, known as "the MC's flow, or cadence."[16] In Spanish, African-infused oral rhythms had already made important contributions in verse early in the twentieth century in, for example, Nicolás Guillén's *Motivos del son* (Motifs of Son Music, 1930), and Federico García Lorca likewise adapted the cadences of flamenco song in his *Poema del cante jondo* (Poem of the Deep Song, 1921) and of jazz in *Poeta en Nueva York* (Poet in New York, written in 1929–30),[17] but hip hop has introduced new metrical forms and rhyming patterns, particularly during the advent of groups like El Club de los Poetas Violentos and Zona Bruta in the 1990s (*Dos platos*). It does so even while it challenges traditional Spanish metrics, which are determined by the number of syllables per line, by subordinating the syllable to the beat. In Spanish, as in English, "[o]ne line, in other words, is what an MC can deliver in a single musical measure – one poetic line equals one musical bar" (Bradley, n.p.). The beat, moreover, is determined solely by the MC, not by the traditional stress of any given word. The rhyme scheme can also be quite complex, incorporating external and internal rhyme, often consonant (most oral poetry in Spanish uses assonant rhyme), which further complicates the listener's ability to separate and structure the lines. The mix, meanwhile, may be reminiscent of John Cage's radical poetics, incorporating ambient sounds, non-musical sounds that might reproduce the effect of onomatopoeia, and/or recordings of different kinds.

We find all of these elements in Arma Blanca's "El último tren." The verses seem impossibly long in print; however, the oral version uses stress to effectively reduce them to four beats. The sound of the breath within the lines produces a hiatus, and the absence of a breath at the end of a line creates enjambement. Here are the first lines and the chorus, with slashes marking the breaths and bold print indicating the stress (though some stresses, particularly on the rhyming words, are stronger than others). Consonant (at times approximate) rhyme is underlined.

Salgo de **ca**sa escojo la aglomeraci**ón** en un vag**ón** a los at**as**cos,/
debajo de la ca**pu**cha a**so**ma el **ca**ble de los **c**ascos,/
suena **R**asco and Cal**i** **A**gents[18] / a la**s** **on**ce tengo e**xa**men
mental**m**ente lo re**p**aso a cada **p**aso escribo **H**endes,[19] /
vidas converg**en**tes, / en el andén de un tr**en** todos pre**s**entes,/
pero au**s**entes de un modo incons**ci**ente/ rumbos dife**r**entes,/ rutinas
dependientes miradas indife**ren**tes nos da i**gual** quien **ha**ya enf**r**ente,/
pen**di**entes de ser siempre puntu**a**les, / se**gui**mos los ritu**a**les
y **e**so es lo que a**quí** nos con**vier**te en igu**a**les/
...
[Estribillo]
En el **último** **tr**en, / cada **vi**da se **fue**,

en **me**dio de ese and**<u>én</u>**, /aca**bó** su ca**m**<u>ino</u>,/
pregúnta**te** cuando es tu **fin** y **tu** dest<u>ino</u>
y nadie **sa**be si a su **la**do puede ha**ber** un ase**s**<u>ino</u>. ("Letra")

(I leave my house I choose the crush of a trainwagon at the hub / under my hoodie you can see the cord of my headphones / Rasco and Cali Agents are on / at eleven I have a test / mentally I review at each step I write Hendes / convergent lives / on a train platform with everyone present / but absent in an unconscious way / different routes / interdependent routings / indifferent looks it's the same to us whoever's in front of us / always worried about being on time / we followed the same rites / and that is what makes us equals here.

REFRAIN: On the very last train / every life went off / in the middle of the platform / it reached the end of the line, / ask yourself what are your ends and your destiny / and you don't know if beside you there sits an assassin.)

The song tells intertwined stories of the passengers on the train from the perspective of a young male Spanish speaker, until the third stanza, in which the speaker is one of the bombers recounting his horrific childhood in the context of an implacable god and constant war, before coming to Spain and suffering class oppression and exploitation. These tales of angry young men are subordinated to the rhythm of the song, the implacable rhythm of the trains, and the cadence of death, which becomes regular in the refrain. Meanwhile, the breath and the vocal stress inscribe the human body into the very structure of the text, combating in this way the dehumanizing processes of economic misery, hopelessness, and violent death.

The mix contributes strongly to the song's effectiveness. It begins with the noise of the train moving along the tracks, and the stanza divisions are punctuated with the particular dinging sound used on the commuter train when it is about to enter a station.[20] The video ends with a recording taken from one of the video cameras in the Atocha station, which shows passengers ascending an escalator, fleeing the first explosion, when another bomb goes off, and they disappear. The mix includes the recorded voice of a woman calling someone named Montse to tell her that they have been evacuated from the train. The phone call is interrupted by two explosions, and we hear the sound of the woman screaming before she is abruptly cut off. The song ends with a dial tone, recalling the phones that would never be answered ringing on the tracks.

The impact of the song can be measured in part by the number of hits and the comments on the YouTube site, which functions in much the same way as the grassroots memorial, as a space for reading and writing. There, visitors have inscribed their own personal stories about 11-M, their readings of the lyrics, comments about the song's merits, and, as always happens on such sites, a series of extreme remarks, as well as polemical and vitriolic exchanges regarding the events themselves and the song's take on them.

This chapter has explored how the sharing of lyrical texts allows them to circulate in the public sphere, where they constitute part of the complex fabric of collective and cultural memory. This process has preserved and disseminated a multiplicity of interpretations, voices, and expressions of emotion across decades – from the poets of the Second Republic to the Franco-era *cantautores,* and *movida* artists to hip-hop MCs – which allow us to complicate the Manichean narratives put forth by the two major political parties about 11-M, as well as the homogenizing mechanisms of a culture industry that has abandoned its critical role. Chapter 3 will continue to explore the mechanisms that resist the petrification of memory – paradoxically, it would seem – in archives and anthologies.

Chapter Three

Archives and Grassroots Anthologies: Preservation, Social Action, and Affect

Once the materials from spontaneous shrines have been removed from the original site to an archive, the collection, cleaning, and cataloguing of the artefacts by professionals (academics, anthologists, and museum experts) contribute to a process of "hertitagization" and institutionalization of the structures (Margry and Sánchez-Carretero 17). Every archive, Jacques Derrida reminds us, "is at once institutive and conservative. Revolutionary and traditional ... [I]t keeps, it saves, but in an unnatural fashion, that is to say in making the law (nomos) or in making people respect the law" (Derrida 12). It has also been argued that the archiving process desacralizes the memorial, in much the same fashion as the display of religious artefacts in museums and libraries re-appropriates them for history by separating them from the context in which they are or were sacred, meaning that "the archive is the opposite of the memorial space of the church: It is the unhallowed bureaucratic space of a clean and neatly organized repository" (A. Assmann, "Canon" 102). It has also been claimed that the archive does a poor job of preserving affect because the trauma – as registered, in the case of 11-M, in the emotions and shattered bodies – escapes the classificatory drive of the archiving endeavour. What is more, Ann Cvetkovich reminds us that archives of trauma do not house "the forms of violence that are forgotten or covered over by the amnesiac powers of national culture, which is adept at using one trauma story to suppress another" (16). For these reasons, theorists, including Cvetkovich, Derrida, and Diana Taylor, among others, have suggested alternatives to the traditional concept of the archive, including anti-archives, digital archives, repertoire, and counter-archives, which might resist the incorporation of the artefacts of radical and grassroots political movements into the institutionalizing, historicizing, conservative, and/or neoliberal thrust of the traditional archive.

These forms of resistance characterize the archives and the processes of archiving in relation to 11-M, which maintain the affective force of the traces of the event. The Archive of Mourning, for example, was created in part as a way for anthropologists to process their own feelings, and in a sense their work embodies that affective relationship to the people and places they studied and preserved. Paul Ricoeur also points out that an archive "is not just a physical or spatial place, it is also a social one" (167). Objects in the archive may also retain traces of affect, or the "persistence of the original impression" (416). With these theorists in mind, I will argue here that the dynamic and affective processes I described in the previous chapter have continued even after the sites have been dismantled and the objects stored in archives, meaning that archives do not necessarily represent the kind of petrification of living memory that Nora's concept of *lieux de mémoire* brings to mind.

Archives, Libraries, and Affect

The archive removes objects from circulation, storing them in a place hidden from public view. The Archive of Mourning, for example, is housed in the small library maintained by RENFE, the Spanish railway company, far to the back of the Train Museum, which is located in the working-class Delicias neighbourhood, not far from the Atocha train station. As with most libraries in Spain, investigators must obtain prior permission to access archival materials, which the staff of the library bring out to the tables. The library itself is open to the public, and it is often visited by parents and/or grandparents with small children in tow, who come to look at the materials available on the shelves. These individuals sometimes encounter a scholar like myself leafing through archival materials and may thus chance upon the documents and objects that have been stored away, of whose existence they had been previously unaware.

This does not necessarily imply, however, that the archive's founders are entirely removed from the original traumatic event or that they view their endeavour from a cold, distant remove. On the contrary, Cristina Sánchez-Carretero's introductory essay to her edited volume of anthropological studies related to 11-M combines an objective, scientific approach with a description of their affective roots and intended social effects:

> De alguna manera, el ir a las estaciones para documentar lo que estaba ocurriendo era también la forma de responder, desde nuestra profesión, a una necesidad de acción ante una situación traumática. La necesidad de «hacer algo» desde aportaciones más individuales que institucionales, es

> una de las claves precisamente de este tipo de memoriales y, en el fondo, es lo que también guió el inicio de este proyecto. (*El Archivo* 19)
>
> (In some sense, going to the stations to document what was happening was also a way of responding, from our profession, to our need for action when faced with this traumatic situation. The need to "do something" as a more individual than institutional contribution was precisely one of the key features of these types of memorial, and it was also what inspired this project [i.e., the anthropological study of 11-M by the Agencia Estatal Consejo Superior de Investigaciones Científicas (the Spanish National Research Council, CSIC)].)

What we see here, and what I felt in my own research in the archive, was the "detour [that] takes us away from abstract questions of method into what lies outside the metadiscursive talk about method, which is, well, us, our involvement" (Gordon 40). And the objects themselves retain their emotional impact: a summer of immersion in this particular archive taught me that lesson very well. What is more, ten years after the bombings, my examination of some of the artefacts in the Archive of Mourning elicited stories and comments from the RENFE employees working in the train museum; professionals, scholars, and regular citizens consulting RENFE's archives;[1] and individuals who happened to enter the museum's library, which suggests that the objects still hold what Pierre Nora calls the gestures and habits of true memory (13).

Ramón Mayrata's 11-M poem about the library, "Entre escombros, fragmentos de aquellos días" (Amidst the Rubble, Fragments of Those Days), also illustrates how the archive may be an affective site, and a social one.[2] The work appears in the volume *Homenaje a las víctimas 11-M* (Homage to the 11-M Victims), put together by the Comisiones Obreras Unión Sindical de Madrid-Región (Workers' Union Commission of the Madrid District), which places the lithographs I mentioned in the previous chapter, some of which were incorporated into the El Pozo monument, alongside narrative and poetic texts. The contribution of Ramón Mayrata to this volume is set in the context of the Alcalá de Henares branch of the Spanish National Library, where he conducts research and the doomed commuter train line begins, and the Atocha train station in Madrid, which is five hundred metres from his home. As he puts it, "Durante años he vivido, aún vivo, entre una y otra ciudad, llevando conmigo un equipaje de sensaciones coincidentes o encontradas" (For years I lived, I still live, between one city and the other, carrying with me the baggage of coincidental or accidental sensations) (Comisiones Obreras 63). The text begins by prosaically setting the scene of a typical research day: "Mañana en la Biblioteca Nacional. Abro un libro. Silencio. En estas circunstancias leer es una especie de sordera. Más tarde, un minuto de público silencio. Congregados – personal y lectores – en el jardín" (Morning in the National Library. I open a book. Silence. It these circumstances, reading is a form of deafness. Later, a minute of public silence. Gathered – staff and scholars – in the garden.) The bombings make it clear for the speaker that the archive is an affective site defined by human relationships: "El muchachito de la sección de publicaciones periódicas. Tan amable. No ha acudido hoy a trabajar. La familia llama una y otra vez angustiada" (The kid from the periodicals section. So pleasant. He hasn't made it to work today. His family calls over and over again in anguish). The speaker describes his mundane activities from the day before, but, when he arrives at Atocha, the prosaic language becomes suddenly metaphoric, personifying the station and distancing the violence of the scene, while at the same time signalling how the sight has impressed itself into the speaker: the inside of the station is "un párpado en que centellean, incandescentes, las luces rojas de bomberos y ambulancias" (an eyelid on which the red lights of firetrucks and ambulances twinkle, incandescent). The text then immediatedly switches to verse, and the poetic structure, along with the metaphors, both provide distance and communicate something more than a mere description of events, as the lights become the radiant point of contact between heaven and earth, darkness and oblivion:

Donde la tierra es obsuridad
y el aire lo olvidado, lo visible
reúne el cielo y la tierra
en un punto luminoso.

(Where the earth is obscurity / and the air is the forgotten, the visible / brings the heavens and the earth together / in a luminous point)

The stanza begins with dark earth and ends in a luminous point, so that obscurity and light embrace and bring together the lines and images between them: the forgotten and the visible in line 2, heaven and earth in line 3. The structure of this stanza thus creates and reflects what Rowland describes as "the epiphanic moment, truncated traumatic recollections, silences beyond the black print, and the emotive space that need not be repressed behind the supposed objectivity of testimonial facts" (4). The effect of the entire text is to convert the library from a mere repository of archival documents into an affective site, characterized by the interactions among the people working there in various capacities, bound together by strands of verse and threads of metaphor.

Cybersites

A Space for Words

The original shrines at the train stations were dismantled by petition of the RENFE station workers in June 2004 and replaced with computerized *espacios de palabras* (spaces for words) (Sánchez-Carretero, "Madrid Train Bombings" 246, 252). These electronic sites remained in place until 2007, providing a mechanism for travellers (tourists, students, workers) passing through the stations to write messages. The technology of the sites dramatically altered the collective act of writing at the grassroots memorials because, rather than reading other peoples' discourse and then adding to a palimpsest of texts, visitors interacted with a computer screen and keyboard individually or with small groups of family members, classmates, or friends.[3] The technology also required a certain degree of computer literacy – and, minimally, the ability to type – whereas even an illiterate person could leave an object at the original sites. Yet even those with the capability of writing on the computer lose the kind of physicality that handwriting involves, and the particular textures and connotations of writing materials, which at the shrines included whatever paper people had on hand (textbook and notebook pages, medical prescriptions, and so on). Thus, in some senses, the revamped sites changed the relationship between visitors and the original objects placed there by mourners, even if some of those objects may have been reproduced electronically and visible at the location. But the technology did allow for continued physical contact with the sites, as visitors first touched the screen with their hands, adding their own imprint to what had become an iconic symbol of solidarity with the victims, before contributing their own words. At the same time, that symbol, which, as I have explained, initially appeared in response to ETA violence, as well as the other images on and surrounding the screen (taken from some of the original texts at the memorial), may have conditioned their interpretation of the events and their own writing.[4] The act of touching evokes a kind of physical contact with other mourners and with the dead, even if what the writers touch is a cold screen rather than the textures of paper, clothing, cardboard, and so forth – objects that provided the writing materials in the original shrine, and that had been in intimate contact with those affected by the bombings.

The texts written on this electronic site are likewise conditioned by its technological characteristics. Of the approximately sixty thousand texts archived by the Agencia Estatal Consejo Superior de Investigaciones Científicas, most take the form of brief messages, but there are nonetheless several poetic entries, including lyrical texts, quotes from poems and songs, and even full-length poems. Also recorded on the site are the geographical origins of the authors – Valencia, Bilbao, Granada, Barcelona, Pamplona, Asturias, Tenerife, the Netherlands, Mexico, Peru, Uruguay, Argentina, Chile, Bolivia, Venezuela, and so forth – so that the messages come to represent a coming together of far-flung bodies in a commemorative act, particularly at the Atocha site. The messages appeared on a website, which was later discontinued, and they were finally stored in the Archive of Mourning.

The poetic texts at the sites, like those in the original memorials, were quite varied. There are selections from César Vallejo, Antonio Machado, Martin Luther King Jr, Miguel Hernández, John Donne, St Augustine, and Gandhi. Lola Díaz from Jerez de la Frontera quotes verses recalling the ideal of *convivencia*, but from an Islamic source, Al-Zubaidi, the preceptor of the second Caliph of Córdoba, Al Hakam II (915–76): "Todas las tierras en su diversidad, son una, / Y los hombres todos, / Son vecinos y hermanos" (All the lands, in their diversity, are one, / and all men / are neighbours and brothers) (ME-4 3715). Rather than folding Islamic culture into an ideal of *Hispanidad*, Díaz highlights the peaceful nature of enlightened Islamic leaders. Of the original poems at the site, some are simply prosaic texts written in verse form, occasionally with rhyme; others are brief but more suggestive, contrasting strongly with the rather cold image of the site's mechanical output. A poem from "lorenaaa" conjugates the verb "to cry," with a final difference that marks the indifference of the assassins or oppressors: "yo lloro / tu lloras / el llora / nosotros lloramos / vosotros llorais / pero ellos nunca lloran" (I cry / you cry / he cries / we cry / you all cry / but they never cry) (ME-4 9878). The text replicates the style of Gloria Fuertes's poems, which use the "found forms" of grammar and institutional forms to make social critiques. A survivor of the attacks writes, "Últimamente llueve más de la cuenta en Madrid, son los ángeles que están llorando" (Lately it has been raining more than usual in Madrid, it is the angels who are crying) (ME-4 6452) (this image will become the central motif of an entire novel *El mapa de la vida* (The Map of Life, 2009) by Adolfo García Ortega).[5] Mario from Madrid asks his dead friend, "Que hay amigo / al otro lado del silencio?" (What is there, my friend, / on the other side of silence?) (ME-4 13330). His evocative question, addressed to his absent friend, cannot be answered, leaving a haunting silence of its own.

The preceding texts came from the Atocha site (ME-4 in the archive). In El Pozo (ME-2) and Santa Eugenia (ME-3), where the losses were most direct and personal, the authors are primarily RENFE workers, parents, *afectados*, and friends. Their messages are characterized by the use of rhetorical questions, apostrophes addressed to the deceased, and metaphors to represent grief, anguish, and the haunting absence of the dead. In these texts, nature is not beautiful or soothing, but oppressive. In the place of crying angels, thunderclouds threaten and torment: "nubes de tormenta en n pecho angustiado. la vida sigue" (storm clouds in an anguished breast. life goes on) (ME-3 90). In a similar vein, a RENFE ticket-seller in Santa Eugenia writes that, "cuando vosotros os fuisteis mis lagrimas calleron como caen las hojas de los arboles en otoño" (when you went away my tears fell like leaves that fall from trees in autumn) (ME-3 710). Another text evokes the absent victims, whose yawns still haunt the early morning trains: "vagones vacios dnde los primeros bostezos aun se escuchan" (empty train cars where the first yawns can still be heard) (ME-3 1018). Yet another suggests iconic rendering of the dove of peace, undermined by a rhetorical question about reality: "una paloma de la paz forman nuestras manos. de que han servido?" (our hands form a dove of peace. what good have they done?) (ME-2 659). Peace slips through our fingers; we cannot grasp it.

Traces and Stitches

The website of one of the victims' associations, the Asociación 11-M Afectados del Terrorismo, maintains an online exposition, "Trazos y puntadas para el recuerdo" (Traces and Stitches for Remembrance). The name of the site was taken from an art exposition organized in 2005 by the association, with lithographs by artists from the collectives Artistas Plásticos Sin Fronteras (Artists without Borders) and the Movimiento por la Paz, el Desarme, y la Libertad (Peace, Disarmament, and Freedom Movement, MPDL). These works were later integrated into a mural behind the sculptural monument erected at the El Pozo train station and were incorporated along with poetic texts into a book titled *Homenaje a las víctimas 11-M* (Homage to the 11-M Victims). On the tenth anniversary of the attacks, they reappeared at the Cervantes Institute, in an exposition titled "Trazos y puntadas para el recuerdo. Una ventana de paz en Madrid, 10 años después" (Traces and Stitches for Remembrance. A Window on Peace in Madrid, Ten Years Later), which also included works from a group of artists that had been on display in Santa Eugenia.[6] Another exposition was organized in 2017 at the Carlos III University.

The poetry section of the website includes both original compositions and texts from the shrines at the stations, and it functions like the grassroots memorials in that it includes texts by recognized and unknown writers, which the association did not solicit but which "como abrazo de ternura de una sociedad solidaria, hemos recibido y el cual lo hemos convertido en un instrumento de cultura didáctica, con el cual poder trabajar valores como la paz, la libertad, la justicia, la solidaridad, la ternura, la interculturalidad, el recuerdo, la cooperación, la no violencia" (we have received like a tender embrace from a community in solidarity, and which we have made into a didactic cultural tool with which to promote values like peace, freedom, justice, solidarity, tenderness, interculturality, remembrance, cooperation, and non-violence) ("Trazos y puntadas," n.p). Here we might point out the sticky associations that bring the didactic practices of the famed *ateneos populares* (working-class athenaeums) instituted under the Second Republic (which offered free instruction on diverse cultural themes for the working class), together with concepts of freedom, justice, solidarity, peace, memory, cooperation, and intimate interpersonal affective ties within a class-based family defined by its leftist values. The site remains open to new texts, thereby maintaining its dynamic quality.

Grassroots Anthologies as Archives

11-M: Palabras para el recuerdo – *Testimonio and Social Action*

Perhaps more than any other neighbourhood in Madrid, El Pozo del Tío Raimundo embodied resistance, resiliency, and class consciousness in the face of Francoist oppression. Indeed, the introduction to the anthology *11-M: Palabras para el recuerdo* (11-M: Words for Remembering), a collection of texts compiled by the Asociación de Vecinos y Amigos del Pozo del Tío Raimundo (Association of Neighbours and Friends of El Pozo del Tío Raimundo) articulates precisely this kind of collective spirit, which draws on one the grand narratives about the Civil War that Richards describes: class conflict. After a brief presentation by Iñaki Gabilondo, to which I will return later, the book begins with a narrative text authored by the Neighbourhood Association, which offers a genealogy beginning with the founding of El Pozo when Tío (Uncle) Raimundo arrived from Asturias in the late twenties. After the Civil War were "[a]ños de vencedores y humillación de vencidos; de cárceles repletas de los derrotados; de mujeres de media España con la cabeza rapada a modo de escarnio y escarmiento, ante el recocijo de los caciques y las bendiciones del clero" (years marked by the victors and the humiliation of the vanquished; of jails overflowing with the defeated; of women from half of Spain with their heads shaved as a form of mockery and punishment, to the great pleasure of the caciques and with the blessing of the clergy) (Asociación de Vecinos 10). During this time, El Pozo continued to grow as a marginalized community of poor, hardworking immigrants who together built and maintained a space where they could "levantar la cabeza y proclamar la dignidad de pueblo trabajador" (raise their heads and proclaim the dignity of the working class) (13). In this reading, the *chabolas* (slum dwellings) were "puntas de lanza" (lance tips) (14) in a class war, refuges for a persecuted class of people under Francoism, and one of the heroes was, to their surprise, a priest: Father Llanos, who arrived in 1955 (13). It was in that community, the narrative continues, that a true democratic spirit was formed: "Pozo democrático" (democratic Pozo) (15), "punto de referencia y emblema de la lucha por las libertades democráticas" (a reference point and emblem of the battle for democratic freedoms) (17). Far from the image of filth and delinquency that justified the dismantling of the *chabolas*,[7] the last of which fell in 1986, this text highlights the intellectual and political nature of the residents through the 1960s, "enfebrecidos con debates revolucionarios" (feverish with revolutionary debates) in those times of "clandestinidades, de miedos y de carreras, de octavillas lanzadas por las noches" (clandestineness, fear, and running, of pamphlets thrown at night) (17).

As the introduction to the anthology explains, poetry (particularly social poetry) played an important role in this process. Not surprisingly, then, many of the texts (not all are poems) in the collection are testimonial in nature, and they express concepts of democracy, solidarity, and class consciousness, blaming President Aznar for the attacks and thanking the emergency personnel and medical workers. Some are collectively written by groups of schoolchildren from El Pozo, Entrevías, and Alcalá de Henares, many of whom were directly impacted by the events. Most seem to be rhymed exercises designed by teachers to help students manage grief, of little literary interest, perhaps, but moving testimonials from witnesses who suffered direct losses. One of the best of the student poems is "El atentado" (The Attack). Here is a fragment:

> El buen quehacer de unas gentes
> quedó marcada en tragedia:
> en la frialdad de la noche
> con desmesurada violencia,
> desgarrasen las entrañas
> a tanta flor indefensa,
> que sólo mal cometieron,
> el de ser de clase obrera.
> Un funesto Once de Marzo,
> teñida quedó la niebla,
> por la sangre derramada,
> de una silenciosa guerra. (64)

(The good work of some people / was marked by tragedy: / in the cold of the night / with immeasurable violence / they ripped open the insides

/ of so many defenceless flowers / whose only sin was / being from the working class. // On a fateful Eleventh of March, / the fog was stained, / with the spilled blood, / of a silent war)

This poem seems again to echo Neruda's "Explico algunas cosas," which I discussed in chapter 1, although the blood shed this time is the result of a silent war on the working class. The author, Cruz Moreno Aranda, composed it on 26 March 2004, when he was a student in Padre Mariana Public School, located in the neighbourhood of Entrevías, another stop on that ill-fated commuter train line. It is written in the ballad form (eight-syllable lines with assonant rhyme in the even verses) – symbolically placing its young author in the traditional role of the minstrel, declaiming his verse in the public square to a popular audience. In using this form to recount the violence that the working class suffers, he recalls the tradition of Federico García Lorca's *Romancero gitano* (Gypsy Ballads, 1928). The allusion to Lorca, who was assassinated by right-wing Nationalists in 1936, at the beginning of the Spanish Civil War, also appears in this poem's final lines, "Si somos hojas caducas / cuando el viento nos cimbrea " (For we are withered leaves / swayed by the wind) – which bring to mind the ending of the Andalusian poet's *Llanto por Ignacio Sánchez Mejías* (Lament for Ignacio Sánchez Mejías, 1935).[8]

Palabras ends with a poem by a well-known social poet, Enrique Falcón, an advocate for *poesía en resistencia* (resistance poetry). Although Falcón is not a resident of El Pozo, or even of Madrid, he lives in a similar neighbourhood in Valencia, called the Barrio del Cristo (Christ's Quarter). His poem, titled "Vientres de Madrid y de Baghdad" (Wombs of Madrid and Baghdad), opens with an epigraph from Eugen Drewermann's *Contra la injusticia* (Against Injustice), which speaks of how war turns all civilian victims into brothers, united by an "inesperado cordón umbilical" (unexpected umbilical cord). Falcón's poem elaborates on this image in its critique of war, particularly the ways in which it converts the working class into animals sent to slaughter. It is, in fact, in those dehumanizing acts that the speaker is able to perceive the hand of the masters and their dogs of war:

Sólo entonces
os he visto.

En la nuca partida del suelo iraquí.
En la sangre bramando por la grava de Atocha. (160)

(Only then / did I see you. // In the shattered nape of Iraqi soil. / In the blood bellowing on Atocha's gravel.)

The visionary speaker, who also witnesses in El Pozo "los ombligos de los hombres / abiertos y a cuchilla por los perros del Amo" (the navels of men / open and put to the blade by the Master's dogs) (160), becomes both one with the oppressed and their avenger. In lines that echo the name of El Pozo and the image of the interior of the Atocha station, the speaker joins "el pueblo sin puñal" (the daggerless people) (160) and embodies their anger: "soy el hombre que cuelga de un ombligo, / la cólera enterrada en los pozos del mundo" (I am the man who hangs from a navel, / the fury buried in the wells of the world) (161). The poem concludes with a stanza that begins with the same lines as the first but ends with an image that refigures the dehumanization and the navel of the intervening stanzas:

> Sólo entonces
> os he visto,
> a los unos y a los otros, sangre terca unida ahora:
> desde entonces sea el hombre
> yo bramo en vuestro propio
> cordón umbilical. (161)

(Only then / did I see you, / both of you, obstinate blood united now: / since then may the man / myself bellow in your own / umbilical cord.)

The stanza performs several transformations and reversals. The blood of the civilian victims of adversarial nations is united, linguistically in the speaker's pronouncement that he sees them together, and structurally by their inclusion in the same verse. And, finally, the navel split open by the master's dogs, the navel from which the speaker hangs like an umbilical cord representing suppressed anger, brings them all together as one man, the speaker, who voices their common anger in their own umbilical cord. This poem exemplifies one of the emblematic responses of poets to the bombings, an embodied form of poetic realism and social engagement.[9]

At the same time, the poem illustrates a serious issue: the erasure of women in discussions of socio-political and geopolitical conflict. This erasure is especially surprising in a poem in a volume compiled by the Neighbourhood Association of El Pozo, given that it has been a woman, Pilar Manjón, who has most strongly represented and fought for the 11-M victims in that district. Yet Falcón's poem folds "el pueblo" (the people) into the category of "hombres" (men); in fact, the singular and plural forms of the word appear four times. Women appear twice, and only in the synecdoche of their wombs: in the title and in the line, "Yo cuido de los vientres de las novias perdidas" (I take care of the wombs of the lost brides). This protective, gentlemanly gesture might seem insufficient in the face of the virulent misogyny of jihadism, which also permeates Western society, a topic to which I shall return in the conclusion.

11-M: Palabras para Daniel y cartas al director – *Archive and Mourning*

This chapter ends with a discussion of another anthology, *11-M: Palabras para Daniel y cartas al director* (11-M: Words for Daniel and Letters to the Editor, 2006), published with his own funds by Eulogio Paz Fernández, the father of one of the victims – Daniel Paz Manjón, who died in El Pozo. Daniel was also the son of the long-time president of the Asociación 11-M Afectados del Terrorismo, Pilar Manjón, an activist who has suffered brutal personal attacks on Twitter and the media for her assertion that both political parties were using the victims for political advantage in the year following the bombing. In a similar gesture, the dedication of the father's book is directed to his son, but also to those he holds responsible for his death, who listen to their "gods of war and terror" (17). This and the other initial texts by Paz, along with a prologue by novelist Juan José Millás titled "Cierre la puerta con cuidado" (Close the Door with Caution), are followed by the first part of the book, which is divided into three sections: "En la Estación de El Pozo, lugar del crimen" (In the El Pozo Station, Scene of the Crime); "En el Instituto Nacional de Educación Física (INEF)" (In the National Institute of Physical Education); and "En el Acto de Homenaje a Daniel" (In the Memorial Ceremony for Daniel). The second part consists of the father's letters to the editor of *El País*, insisting on the obscenity of the politicization of 11-M, especially by the PP; these were never published, and some were never even sent, and they therefore hint at a kind of silencing in which the press is complicit. The book concludes with an essay written by Daniel and a classmate, Miguel Rivera, "Sociología del deporte: Violencia y deporte" (Sociology of Sports: Violence and Sports).

Paz's book combines many elements of the memorial, the archive, and the monument. The initial texts of the first part, "Words for Daniel," are much like the ones that were posted at the grassroots memorials, as we see in this poem written by Paz in April 2004, titled "Ausencia" (Absence):

> Dolor de ausencia,
> de no poder verte más tú
> vivo, feliz, sonriente.
>
> Dolor de ausencia,
> de no poder verte más yo
> cordial, profundo, alegre.

Dolor de ausencia,
dolor total,
dolor de muerte. (19)

(Pain from absence / from you not being able to see you any more / alive, happy, smiling. // Pain from absence, / from me not being able to see you any more / affectionate, profound, joyful. // Pain from absence, / total pain, / death pain.)

Divided in three tercets, with an insistent parallelism that emphasizes the conjunction of pain, absence, and former joy, the text seems to exemplify how poetry can give structure to grief in the immediate aftermath of tragic death, allowing the distraught mourner to articulate the terrible loss. It is followed by a narrative, in which Paz explains how he returned to the El Pozo station in April 2004, and began transcribing into a notebook all of the messages to his son that people had written at the grassroots memorial. Then, suddenly, as in Ramón Mayrata's text, the narrative turns into a poetic lament, as the grief becomes too great for the father to continue in prose (23–4). After the poem come several pages with the short messages and poems that others had directed to his son, making the notebook itself a kind of partial archive of the El Pozo memorial site, with a very personal criterion of selection. The first part of the book ends with another poem titled "Ausencia," written a little over a year later, in August 2005:

El sonido del agua
jugando
en la orilla.

El rumor de las hojas
movidas
por el viento.

El canto de las aves
que buscan
su alimento.

Cielo azul,
pardas sierras;
campos amarillos,
verdes arboledas.

Tristeza infinita.
Mortal ausencia.

(The sound of water / playing / on the shore. // The murmur of the leaves / moved / by the wind. // The singing of the birds / seeking / nourishment. // Blue heavens, / brown mountains; / yellow fields, / green groves. // Infinite sadness. / Mortal absence).

The poem's structure is similar to the first one – three tercets – but it adds a quatrain and an ending couplet. The tercets are organized around sounds of joyful life in natural settings; the quatrain adds a colour palette; and the couplet marks separation from the natural world occasioned by infinite sadness and death. Although it is no less of a lament than the first poem, this one is more complex in terms of its structure, rhythm, and imagery, portraying the beauty of nature and of life before marking the speaker's absolute alienation from it in his infinite sadness. The absence of the child has dealt him a death blow.

This anthology is a kind of archive, but its intent is to rescue the texts, and perhaps even the lost child, by creating a more permanent monument to keep his memory alive through the circulation of texts beyond the graveyard of the archive. This gesture later expanded to a blog, a site that is analogous to that of the Asociación 11-M Afectados del Terrorismo because it likewise announces events relevant to those affected by the tragedy, and it contains sections on books and videos, although they are not as thoroughly developed and interactive as the other site.[10] The book and this site are poignant testaments to one individual's effort to keep alive the memory of his dead son by drawing on, and contributing to, the collective memory of the event.

As with the spontaneous shrines, the gathering of poems into websites, archives, and grassroots anthologies was meant as a memorial to the victims, inspired first by the individual rather than the institutional or professional impulse to react to crisis. Like the queer archives described by Ann Cvetkovich in *An Archive of Feelings*, these sites, simultaneously personal and political, contain materials ignored or undervalued by institutions of public culture (243) but particularly meaningful to the archivists, whose work, inspired by grief, allowed them to restore some kind of order after this traumatic event. They therefore serve as "repositories of feeling" (244), and, as such, they resist the totalizing interpretations of 11-M's significance, subtly undermining the narratives carefully constructed by political elites in Spain and beyond.

PART TWO

Poets, Cultural Politics, and Crisis

As we saw in the first part of this book, the vast majority of those who sought refuge and solace in poetry after the bombings, and who used the genre to voice political protest, turned to poems written by politically engaged artists who had suffered personal loss or oppression at the hands of Franco's forces during and after the Spanish Civil War and who had wrestled with how to bring together their simultaneous commitment to aesthetic innovation and democratic, sometimes revolutionary, principles. But, what is the role of poets today in times of crisis? To witness? To heal? To promote social change? To reflect critically? Can poetry still live up to those expectations? Should it? Can it speak of crisis without commodifying it? These have been burning questions for Spanish poets in the post-Franco period, and for their critics, but also for other writers and observers. This becomes apparent in *Leaving the Atocha Station* (2011), the first novel by an American poet, Ben Lerner. It is, ironically, the best-known response by a poet to 11-M,[1] and it raises many issues that the second part of this book will seek to address.

Lerner's novel chronicles a year in the life of a young American poet named Adam Gordon, who is in Spain on fellowship when the attacks occur, supposedly working on "a long, research-driven poem exploring the [Spanish Civil] war's legacy" (23), although he admittedly knows little about the war. Throughout the novel, Adam somewhat listlessly (in the style of the Beats) but insistently wrestles with the problems of engagement, or of not wanting to really engage but at the same time to look like he is, and of profound aesthetic and personal experiences: the desire for them and the pretension of having had them.[2] He casually puts forth his views on the vulturine nature of the culture class in response to tragedy and senseless death.[3] And he wonders about memory in relationship to the virtual and the real. Adam is speaking of himself much of the time but also of the Spanish intellectuals and artists of his age with whom he interacts on his year abroad, before and after 11-M. Indeed, the tensions highlighted throughout *Leaving the Atocha Station* – between a leftist politics based on an abstraction of the proletariat and the comforts made possible by inherited wealth, cultural legitimacy, and globalized capitalism; between a poetics of engagement and the economics of grief; between a simultaneously aesthetic and affective experience of poetry and "the echo of poetic possibility" (9) – have been at the centre of discussion and debate among Spanish poets and their critics since the Transition.

These issues are manifest in the initial responses by Spanish poets to 11-M, collected into two anthologies published in 2004: *Madrid, once de marzo: Poemas para el recuerdo* (Madrid, March 11th: Poems for Remembering), edited by Eduardo Jordá and José Mateos, and *11-M: Poemas contra el olvido* (11-M: Poems against Forgetting). Each volume opens with a preface describing the genesis of the project and its organizing logic in terms that recall the dynamic spontaneity of the grassroots memorials, the affective professionalism of the anthropologists of the Agencia Estatal Consejo Superior de Investigaciones Científicas (the Spanish National Research Council, CSIC) who organized the Archive of Mourning, and the socio-political intent of the grassroots anthologies. The editors of *Poemas para el recuerdo*, for example, describe the window of the Rafael Alberti bookstore as a spontaneous shrine displaying poems and testimonies, metaphorically represented as cries, laments, sighs, prayers, and farewells (11); and the poets' computers, they say, replicated that gesture in bringing the poems together in an anthology (12). The editors of *Poemas contra el olvido* liken the circulation of printed poems to the black ribbons and clothing that appeared at memorials throughout Madrid after the attacks, and they describe their work as anthologists as an act of solidarity (7).

Despite these similarities, the anthologies differ from one another in their conceptualization of the collective response. *Contra el olvido* contains exclusively Spanish-language poetry by Latin American and Spanish authors, capped with an epilogue by a Moroccan exile living in France but writing in Spanish.[4] The editors call this collection, "un canto a la vida, a la libertad y al mestizaje. A la convivencia de culturas, tradiciones, convicciones políticas y religiosas, a la integración, a la tolerancia. El siglo XXI o es el siglo del mestizaje o no será" (a song to life, to liberty, and to miscegenation. To the co-mingling of cultures, traditions, political and religious convictions, to integration, to tolerance. The twenty-first century will be about cultural and racial integration, or it will not be) (7). The word *convivencia*, as we discussed in the first part of this book, recalls Franco-era myths of a medieval paradise, transposed here onto the multiculturalism of neoliberal societies. The word *mestizaje*, for its part, is a code word for assimilation, represented in this anthology by monolinguism. The community that sings of life, liberty, and tolerance is one forged through a common language, spoken by assimilated people living within the borders of continental Spain. For its part, *Para el recuerdo* brings together poems in the major languages of Spain (Castilian, Basque, Galician, and Catalan). As in *Contra el olvido*, this is a linguistic creation of an imagined nation, one that in this case favours a multi-national representation of the Spanish territory but that in the process might invisibilize immigrants and other people who have occupied or currently occupy the same territory, including Moroccans, but also Eastern Europeans, Romani, or sub-Saharan Africans. In lieu of *convivencia*, this anthology advocates for "la unidad y la concordia" (unity and concordance), or for the peaceful co-existence of autonomous nationalities within a single country, symbolized by their representation together in this volume.

The anthologies also suggest different interpretations of the event itself and the identity of its victims, which surface in the beneficiaries of their sales. Proceeds from monolingual *Contra el olvido* went to the Asociación Víctimas del Terrorismo (AVT), which, as we have discussed, is linked to the right-wing Partido Popular (PP) and focuses primarily on victims of violence by ETA (Euskadi Ta Askatasuna [Basque Country and Freedom]) and would not favour the linguistic politics of *Para el recuerdo*. The latter volume supported the Fundación Víctimas del Terrorismo (FVT), which, as I mentioned in chapter 2, represented an uneasy truce between the PP and the Partido Socialista Obrero Español (PSOE) regarding the victims of terrorism.

Despite these political notions of nation and victim, the prefatory remarks to the volumes do not offer a clear theorization of poetic responses to crisis or trauma beyond rather vague notions of "giving voice to the dead/afflicted," "affirming life," "expressing emotions," or "coming together." In part, this incoherence is a result of the anthologists' professed goal of being broadly inclusive, inviting poets "de todas las generaciones y tendencias" (of all generations and tendencies), in the case of *Para el recuerdo* (11), and "de todas las promociones y generaciones de nuestro país y a otros poetas amigos de países lejanos" (from every group and generation of our country and other poet friends from distant countries) in *Contra el olvido* (7).[5] These appear to be grassroots efforts of organization among the population of recognized poets, mobilizing them in the same way the archive project did with anthropologists. Still, given the rigid and conservative institutional concepts of Spanish literary groups and generations, and the limitation of non-Spanish contributors to the personal friends or acquaintances of the anthologists, we can hardly expect a broadly representative sampling of contemporary poetry or an expansive understanding of the event. Other types of identity – including sexual, religious, national, and racial identities – are also invisibilized, subsumed under the Spanish or Iberian categories of language, nation, class, and family that constitute the imagined "we" who were all on those trains.[6]

As collective sites, these anthologies move in a very different direction from other responses – the erection of the grassroots memorials at the train sites, at which anyone could participate; the preservation and analysis of those original texts by CSIC anthropologists; and the political organization of the 13-M protests, summoned via text message. Instead, the books maintain the habitus of a certain Spanish-language literary field (Bourdieu 214), which imbues the editors with the power to determine who is a legitimate writer, worthy of inclusion in the volume (224). And here the coincidences are telling: twelve poets appear in both volumes, and, in seven cases, with the exact same poem. Most of these poets, moreover, are well known and/or heavily anthologized and therefore confer literary value on the enterprises: Dionisio Cañas, Antonio Colinas, Eduardo García, Pablo García Casado, Luis García Montero, Martín López-Vega, José Antonio Muñoz Rojas, Benjamín Prado, and Manuel Rivas. Two were emerging voices: Elena Medel had won the Premio Andalucía Joven (Andalusian Youth Prize) in 2001 for her first book, *Mi primer bikini* (My First Bikini), and Josep M. Rodríguez had two books to his name, one published by a small local press in Lleida and the other by the prestigious Pre-Textos. Both writers had new books come out in 2004. Jesús Munárriz, the remaining poet whose texts appear in both volumes, is the editor at Hiperión, one of the most important publishers of poetry in Spain.

Rather than assuming the counterhegemonic socio-political function that informed the El Pozo anthology that we discussed in chapter 3, these anthologies contribute to the processes of canonization and consolidation of current and future market share, supporting what Guillem Martínez and his collaborators call the CT (Cultura de la Transición [Culture of the Transition]), which is apolitical and vertical by design. The cultural products produced under this regime are inward facing but not critical enough to threaten the CT, and they are marketable only to the Spanish audiences for whom they are designed as a political tool to maintain an unproblematized stability, even in the face of increasingly polarizing economic policies (Martínez, "El concepto"). It is not surprising in this context that, as Jonathan Mayhew asserts, the hegemonic poetic group that emerged in the 1990s does not care if the authorizing "'forms of power' belong to left, right or center: what these poets share is a desire to achieve institutional status" (*Twilight* 51). Raquel Medina goes further, noting the coincidence between all the institutions of symbolic value, a veritable poetry mafia, in promoting a canon that translates into sales of a national product for a global market (523–4), including libraries and classrooms in Spain and abroad. These would seem to be apt descriptions of the cultural politics articulated in the prefaces of these two 11-M anthologies, which could indeed be characterized as politically neutral, inward-looking, and self-promoting, despite the conflicting poetic and aesthetic positions of the poets united in their pages.

What is more, the fact that both volumes mention their potential sales highlights not only the generally limited market for poetry, but also the potential capitalization of/on grief by people not directly affected by the violence. Lerner represents this issue in two critical scenes of *Leaving the Atocha Station*, which take place following the 11-M attacks. One of Adam's friends, Arturo, had planned an exposition at his upscale gallery in the posh Serrano district for March 12th, and he decides, on Adam's suggestion, not to cancel: "I heard myself saying that he should cover one of the larger paintings with a black cloth as a memorial, a visual moment of silence. He thought this was a great idea ... ; soon the decision was made that all the paintings would be covered for a couple of days, if they could get the painters to agree" (121). Adam wonders, however, about how they will handle the commercial angle: "Would they also cover the little placard bearing painters' names and prices?" (121–2). After the 12-M demonstration, he writes that, when he arrived at the gallery, "it was packed ... The paintings were covered in what looked like black felt ... The placards were uncovered ... People were looking at the covered paintings as if they weren't covered, looking long and thoughtfully at the black felt and then reading the placard. I wondered if any of them would sell" (124). The scenes lay bare the exploitation of grief for fame and fortune, as well as the literally blank canvas that art provides the grieving, much like the poems Adam describes earlier as "screens on which readers could project their own desperate belief in the possibility of poetic experience" (38).

We should also note that the poems in these anthologies were never actually posted at the grassroots memorials but, rather, appeared in bookstore windows, in the culture section of newspapers like *El País*, or on poetry blogs. These locations, removed from the sites of the bombings, imply a lack of direct engagement with the public before, during, and after the events. In other words, these poems did not participate in the dynamic reading and writing process we described in chapter 2, but remained at a remove. As archives, however, the anthologies provide diverse, if admittedly limited, snapshots of poetic practice in Spain at that historic moment, as well as a record of the first responses of a considerable number of poets to 11-M. In this sense, they are valuable resources.

Many of these first poems, like those written immediately after 9/11, qualify as "symptom not diagnosis. All that is registered, really, is the confusion, and the desperate resort to the familiar – the clichéd, the stereotypical – that is often the result of shock" (R. Gray 171). For example, some – like the poems by José Manuel Caballero Bonald, Enrique Baltanás, José Cereijo, or Benjamín Prado – express anger and a desire for vengeance that dehumanize the terrorist, either in Judeo-Christian terms (e.g., with reference to Cain and Abel) or in the condemnation of all religious extremists. Others reduce women to stereotypes of victimhood or culpability: we see a noble mother originally from the provinces who dies on the train (José Vidal Valicourt), bad mothers who raised terrorist sons, in contrast to saintly Spanish ones (Álvaro Salvador), or Madrid as the mother of working-class children (Antonio de Padua Díaz). Still other poems reflect the rhetoric of the photos we discussed in part 1: "los trenes heridos" (the wounded trains); "una pierna sola en un andén" (a leg alone on the landing); "una plaza compartida" (a shared square); "Íbamos todos / en los trenes" (We were all on those trains); "en todos los paraguas del dolor repicaba / la piedad de la lluvia" (on all the umbrellas of pain pealed / the pity of the rain).[7] Yet others remit to the rhetoric of the Civil War or social poetry from the Franco era to explain the events: "no pasarán" (they shall not pass), the cry of the Republican defenders of Madrid in the war in Francisco Díaz de Castro's "Atocha" (Jordá and Mateos 47), or an echo of Gabriel Celaya's poem "La poesía es un arma cargada de futuro" (Poetry Is a Weapon Loaded with the Future) in Inmaculada Moreno's "Volcán de sangre y hierro" (Volcano of Blood and Iron), where she writes that "el dolor es un arma – ésta sí – / cargada de poderes" (pain is a weapon – this one, yes – / loaded with powers) (ibid. 118).

The anthologies also provide a sense of the competing poetic trends in Spain at the time of the bombings.[8] They reveal the limitations of some aesthetic tendencies, including the poetry of experience and some forms of social poetry, which attempt to address 11-M through abstractions. Other tendencies appear renewed or emerge more powerfully in response to the events. Some poems echo the poetics of the grassroots memorials or of hip hop, inscribing affect and traces of the body and the flesh into the text. Others decline transcendence in search of an affective, transformative engagement, in a condition of radical vulnerability.

Still others foreground the media technologies that simultaneously promise liberation (for example, the *pásalo*, the Internet, digital imaging) and make possible ever more subtle forms of control, including enhanced surveillance, targeted policing or military operations, and a political economy based on marketing algorithms. Together, the less traditional poems move beyond an exclusive focus on Civil War and Francoist issues, Spanish poetic form, and secular humanism to broader social and aesthetic considerations. The ensuing chapters will explore how these trends became more visible in response to 11-M, not only in the anthologies, but also in some key texts not included there: Ana Rossetti's "Ciudad profanada," Tina Escaja's *Codigo de barras*, and Pedro Provencio's *Onda expansiva*.

Chapter Four

Body, Affect, Flesh

One of the most unsettling elements of the *El País* photo we discussed in part 1 is the way in which it foregrounds the chaos of the body turned into flesh – the messiness of it, the confusion, the anguish – in the form of the bloody limb on the tracks and the man sitting, desolate, in the foreground.[1] In the background are people dressed in their everyday clothes, tending to the injured and traumatized, and covering the dead. The image also portrays, then, an affective, embodied response to the dehumanizing disruption of order, including the order of the body itself, which is the objective of war and terror. The countless acts of spontaneous generosity in the following days, including donations of blood, clothing, transport, and logistical assistance, and the posting of poems and other texts at the grassroots memorials, represented further acts of solidarity that demonstrated that "the body is less an entity than a relation" (Butler, "Rethinking" 19), dependent on infrastructural support. And, indeed, 11-M exposed the ways in which a broad sector of Spanish society had become increasingly vulnerable, not just to terrorism or war, but also to the policies of the political elite that had degraded their "infrastructural support," leaving them "radically unsupported under conditions of precarity" (ibid.), even before the crisis of 2008.

Mayra Rivera argues that these questions of vulnerability and relationality can also be figured in connection to the flesh. Like Butler, Rivera critiques the concept of the self-contained body, which "[a]s a theoretical category ... fosters an illusion of completeness and wholeness easily naturalized, normalized, and deployed as part of cultural systems of representation" (7). In contrast, "flesh is conceived as formless and impermanent, crossing the boundaries between the individual body and the world" (2). These related but contrasting concepts seem particularly apt for addressing an event in which people witnessed the instantaneous transformation of bodies into flesh, and/or the laborious and emotional tasks of scraping, collecting, bagging, identifying, and burying that flesh that was of, but was not, the bodies of the dead.[2] Rivera traces a genealogy of the term *flesh* in Christian theology (in the Gospel of John, Letters of Paul, Tertullian, liberation theology) and philosophy (in Merleau-Ponty, Foucault, Nancy, Irigaray, Butler) that allows her to elaborate an understanding grounded in the materiality of the body but not limited to its boundaries. Rather, she theorizes broad socio-political implications tied to both profound *vulnerability* to the other, as well as *relationality* in the form of the host, where the flesh "is shared, becoming part of many bodies, transformed into the very flesh of those bodies that partake from it" (23). A poetics of the flesh, she theorizes, is one that is "attentive to loss and opacity, interruption and silence" (3), an aesthetic that is "indispensable for addressing histories marked by disruption, displacement, and irrecoverable loss" (2–3).

For both Butler and Rivera, the acknowledgment of our common vulnerability is profoundly feminist in the sense that it "exposes the disavowed dependency at the heart of the masculinist idea of the body" as self-contained and independent (Butler, "Rethinking" 21). At the same time, the concept of the flesh as relational, plural, and indeterminable resists the inscription of gendered or other cultural representations upon it. To be perfectly clear, then, though feminist, Rivera's poetics of the flesh and Butler's concept of vulnerability are not "just about women." Rather, by addressing the "material conditions and effects of human practices" (Rivera 9), they propose forms of agency based on relationality that might avoid the political dead end of Foucauldian concepts of discipline and discourse, on the one hand, and disembodied abstractions of engagement, on the other.

Other lines of affect theory consider relationality and encounter beyond the limits of conscious knowing, the individual body, or even the human.[3] In this context, we discussed in chapter 1 the affective relationship to objects in the grassroots memorials, and how their "sticky associations" came to cohere into narratives tied to socio-political identities and shared emotions. Poetry, certainly, can participate in that process, simply upholding the value and "truth" of commonly held ideas, identities, and beliefs, but it can also disrupt discourses about identity, contest them, and reveal their fictitiousness – alienate them – by either highlighting the mechanisms of their construction or creating dissonance, attaching to objects, bodies, and flesh an affective valence outside of, or in conflict with, the norm. It can also do so by portraying the movement from one physical state to another, as in exile or gesture.

This chapter begins with a discussion of what I see as a disembodied poetics based on sentimentality, in the case of the poetry of experience, or political abstraction, in the case of some social poetry. In both cases, I argue, the lyrical subjects speak from a position of "knowing" and seek to provide order and meaning to their readers. In contrast, other poems register and reproduce semantically and/or structurally the disordering effects of the traumatic events, foregrounding the speaker's own unknowing body and/or psyche. Finally, we will examine a series of poems that elaborate an affective poetics of the flesh grounded in movement, relationality, and vulnerability.[4]

Disembodied Poetics

The poets of experience and the "voces del extremo" (extremist voices) of poetic realism (Iravedra 51) have radically different ideas about the function of poetry, the poet's ideal interlocutor, and the nature of reality. Nonetheless, they share a belief in their ability to understand reality and communicate it plainly and directly in the poetic text, and, in this sense, they fit squarely within the paradigm of secular universalist humanism.[5] This section will argue that both tendencies respond to 11-M with a disembodied poetics based in abstraction.

The poems by the "poets of experience" that are reproduced in the anthologies *11-M: Poemas contra el olvido* and *Madrid, once de marzo: Poemas para el recuerdo* suggest that their adherence to the dominant paradigm of socio-political order and relationality made it nearly impossible for them to respond critically or affectively to the events, their underlying causes, and the aftermath. These limitations are evident in "Soneto herido" (Wounded Sonnet), the 11-M poem by Luis García Montero, the best-known representative of this tendency. García Montero's career as poet, university professor, literary critic, member of literary prize juries, and regular contributor to *Babelia*, the weekly literary supplement of *El País*, exemplifies the group's consolidation of cultural capital in the post-Franco era, in which political stability and economic prosperity were the guiding values (see, among others, Cantelli 17; Martínez; Mayhew, *Twilight* 60; Medina 520; Villena 24). As we might expect, then, "Soneto herido" appeared in both of these anthologies and, on 15 May 2004, in *Babelia*.

The speaker in the poetry of experience generally presents himself (he is usually male) as a "normal" – read "bourgeois" – citizen who uses plain language and a facile tone to talk about "universal" themes, while at the same time situating himself as a public intellectual and adherent to traditional literary forms. "Soneto herido" epitomizes this aesthetic. The poem obliquely references the *El País* photo, replacing the chaotic horror of dismemberment and death with an orderly list of emotions and meanings that the poet attributes to the events, which reflects the rhetoric of cohesion in the 12-M demonstration and the photos of umbrellas united under the rain.

La lluvia en el cristal de la ventana
el aire de una plaza compartida
el pañuelo de sombras de la vida
la noche de Madrid y su mañana,

el amor, la ilusión del porvenir,
el dolor, la verdad de lo perdido,
la constancia de un sueño decidido,
la humana libertad de decidir,

la prisa, la política, el mercado,
las noticias, la voz, el indiscreto
deseo de saber lo silenciado,

el rumor, las mentiras y el secreto,
todo lo que la muerte os ha quitado
quisiera devolverlo en un soneto.

(The rain on the windowpane / The air of a shared square / life's shaded handkerchief / Madrid's night and its morning, // love, the dream of the future, / pain, the truth of what's lost, / the constancy of a decisive dream, / the human freedom of choice, // haste, politics, the market, / the news, the voice, the indiscreet / desire to know what has been silenced, // rumours, lies, and the secret, / all that death has taken from you, / I would like to give back in a sonnet.)

In the first stanza, the objects and the flesh strewn on the tracks, as well as the crowds of protestors, have been converted into a sentimental but impersonal representation of Madrid, in which there are no people and no conjugated verbs. The tears shed by mourners appear metaphorically at first, as rain on the windows, and then metonymically, through the handkerchief; solidarity is evoked by the shared air in the plaza; the continuation of life is conveyed as the city moves from night to day. The second quatrain knowingly lists what was lost – the future and the past, love, dreams, free will – and the pain that endures. In the alternation between veracity and illusion (the chimera of a future, the truth of what was lost, the constancy of a dream, the freedom of choice), it foreshadows the brief uncertainty that appears in the next four lines – in the rumours, lies, and secrets about the perpetrators – along with the desire that drives the accelerated rhythm in those verses: that is, in contrast to the first two stanzas, in which a full line and considerable adjectivization are dedicated to each image or emotion, here we find two to three unadorned nouns per line (haste, politics, market; news, voice; rumour, lies and secret). Only one – the indiscrete desire to know what's been silenced – extends further, but the enjambement nonetheless reflects haste and curiosity, propelling the reader speedily from line 10 to line 11 and then to line 12, which gives the answer: rumours, lies, and the secret. The poem thus reflects the movement and instability of those days, but it does not pause to consider their profound implications. The ending couplet finally features a person: the lyric speaker, identified with the poet and seemingly located at a safe reserve, addressing an unidentified plural "you," and expressing the desire to offer us/them all that death took away, neatly wrapped up and resolved in the sonnet form itself, and previously outlined in the orderly lists.[6] Rather than forging a collective or a shared experience or engaging ethically with those affected by violence, the speaker/poet of "Soneto herido" retains his distance and authority as he seeks to convey to readers an orderly, sanitized meaning of the events, erase the anguish and anger of those affected, and symbolically project onto them the comfort of his neatly refined inner sanctum.[7] Despite its technical competence, the sonnet represents an apolitical, sentimental abstraction suggesting a simple return to the established order, presented in a dispassionate, measured tone, and with facile rhythm.

The text by another poet of experience, Felipe Benítez Reyes, is no less problematic in this regard. Titled "Una mañana" (One Morning) and written in prose, it presents what the speaker calls, at the end, a "cúmulo de ilusiones pequeñas convertido en humo" (a collection of small dreams turned to smoke) (27), in the form of the personal stories of those whom the poet considers to be representative victims. Each of these narratives, however, is reduced to the person's job and/or the beginnings of a heterosexual love relationship that will never be consummated. This practice of identification, like the vignettes published with the photos in the newspapers, is intended to humanize the dead, but it does not convincingly portray their individuality. What is more, the stories and the language in which they are recounted can only be described as formulaic and sentimental. "Enrique iba al trabajo por primera vez ... y estaba ilusionado: ese sueldo indigno le permitiría vivir de un modo un poco menos indigno, y podría comprarse de vez en cuando algún disco y alguna camiseta" (Enrique was going to work for the first time ... and he was thrilled: that disgraceful salary would allow him to live in slightly less disgraceful manner, and he could buy himself every now and then a record album or a shirt) (26). "Abdil había conseguido regularizar su situación hace apenas un mes; se acordaba de su tierra y de su gente, por supuesto, ... pero le consolaba el espejismo de haberse instalado en su futuro" (Abdil had gotten his papers just a month earlier; he missed his land and his people, of course, ... but he was consoled by the mirage of having settled into his future) (ibid.). "Elena se había levantado con el propósito de decirle a su compañero de oficina que estaba enamorada de él desde la primera vez que lo vio" (Elena had awoken with the intention of telling her co-worker that she had been in love with him since the first time she saw him) (ibid.). Each vignette represents a stereotyped identity, but they have common traits – modesty, timidity, integrity, hope – and a common aspiration toward a comfortable normality in Spain with a decent job and family. Again, sentimentality leads to only the abstraction of engagement.

This failure to engage affectively may also manifest in social poetry that is highly critical of the social order and in which the lyric speakers explicitly align themselves ideologically with those affected by the bombings. Like "Soneto herido," many of these poems are technically competent and effectively communicate a message. The problem is that the lyric speakers "are completely stabled; they *know*" (J. Gray 267), and the poets employ "a language of immediacy, of presence, a language in which nothing will be figurative" (ibid. 262). This is one of their goals – to make literature accessible, but to the working class rather than the middle-brow reader whom the poets of experience address. Another is to make poetry a political tool, in the most direct sense possible, by stating a position and inspiring listeners to provoke a change.

Antonio Orihuela's "11-M" is exemplary of this direct style of expressing indignation and condemnation:

> Yo me manifesté contra la guerra.
> Hice todo lo que un ciudadano puede hacer contra la guerra.
>
> Pegué carteles,
> di recitales,
> fui a la huelga general contra la guerra
> que mi pequeño sindicato convocó contra la guerra.
>
> Hablé, donde pude, contra la guerra.
>
> Ahora, el gobierno de mi país en guerra
> me pide que me manifieste
> porque el enemigo
> ha empezado a tirarnos bombas.
>
> Querían
> ir a la guerra
> y sólo disparar ellos.

(I demonstrated against the war. / I did everything a citizen can do against the war. // I put up posters, / I gave recitals, / I went to the general strike against the war / that my little union organized against the war. // I spoke, where I could, against the war. // Now, the government of my country at war / asks me to demonstrate / because the enemy / has begun to drop bombs on us. // They wanted / to go to war / and be the only ones to shoot.)

The speaker in the poem declares his physical and ideological position repeatedly: unlike the speaker of "Soneto herido," he is in public spaces, performing repeated acts "against the war" (a phrase that appears five times), not alone, but in collaboration with a collective that defends the rights of workers. The government, which is "at war" and "wanted to go to war," is set up in opposition to these citizens. Of course, the Partido Popular government did not see 11-M as an act of war – it denies that terrorism is a form of warfare, and it denied that 11-M had any relation to the Iraq War – but the voice of the speaker overwhelms any possible counterargument with its anaphoric insistence on "war," which appears seven times in the poem. The final stanza represents the "wisdom of the people," who see through the rhetorical manipulations of the political class and call a spade a spade. They, and the speaker, know what the problem is, and thus use "faithful language addressing a stable traumatic event" (J. Gray 264). The poem has the impact of an angry political protest, like many of the texts posted at the grassroots memorials, but it rather simply upholds a classical leftist rhetoric that pits the noble worker against the exploitative ruling class, and it is therefore unlikely to linger in the mind or move anyone who doesn't already agree with the speaker's explanation of events. What is more, as in the poem by Enrique Falcón that we discussed in chapter 3, the poet seems unaware of the gender implications of his rhetoric: the nouns that he has chosen to discuss war and the protests against it grammatically represent all of the actors as masculine: the citizen (*un ciudadano*), the government (*el gobierno*), the enemy (*el enemigo*), and the plural representatives of the government (*ellos*).

These knowing aesthetics also characterize David González's "En el cielo como en la tierra" (In Heaven As It Is on Earth), which ends with these lines:

y los paraguas de sus mayores,
de luto riguroso
guardan cinco minutos de silencio
en memoria de las manos, limpias,
que los sostienen.

(and the umbrellas of their elders, / in full mourning / observe five minutes of silence / in memory of the hands, the clean hands / that are holding them)

The poem references the famous 12-M umbrellas, which it links to death, as they are clothed in black, and it mentions the obligatory moments of silence after such tragedies. Apparently, the elders holding the umbrellas are respecting the working-class people who died, as these are often represented synedochically as hands ("en memoria de las manos" (in memory of the hands)). The final twist is clever, revealing that the only hands they actually respect are their own, supposedly clean ones, which have actually been sullied by clandestine state violence, as I mentioned in my analysis of the poem "11-M" by Ángel V. in chapter 1. The hypocrisy of the self-interested mourners, pointed out ironically by the speaker, is not hard to capture, and, once we are in on the joke, we easily identify with, or else reject, his knowing, critical position.

In these examples of poetry of experience and social poetry, the poet speaks from a place of knowing, which "suggests that the danger lies not in writing about disaster but in the pretense of understanding it" (J. Gray 262). Like American philosopher Martha Nussbaum, all of these poets find that "abstract universalism is the only stance that is capable of providing solid foundations for moral values such as compassion and respect for others" (Braidotti, *Posthuman* 39) and political critique. Indeed, García Montero sees common civic values, experiences, and language as essential for combatting the nefarious form of individuation propagated by neoliberalism (Iravedra 49), a topic we shall discuss in the following chapter. Nonetheless, these universal values can only be consolidated by overlooking differences (in gender, race, ethnicity, religion, and so forth) upon which hierarchies and inequalities have been unquestioningly structured.

Emotion, Flesh, Gesture

In contrast to these *knowing* texts, others portray the kind of *not knowing* that Michael Rothberg associates with the prophetic mode of witnessing after 9/11 ("There Is No Poetry" 149). Some poems offer an embodied form of emotional response, cognitive dissonance, and connection, whereas others represent the attacks as acts of violence perpetrated on vulnerable bodies. Still others develop an affective approach more akin to the poetics of the flesh or even of the gesture, that most ephemeral trace of the body.

Angelina Gatell's sonnet "11 de marzo de 2004" conveys a renunciation of authority, as the speaker repeats the ways in which pain has stripped her of language; in its place are the bodily manifestations of grief – laments, cries, tears.[8] From the first stanza, the attempt to fix feeling in language is attenuated, literally interrupted by the phrase, "no sé, quizá" (I don't know, perhaps), set off, not simply by commas, but by hard dashes.

> Sólo el dolor acude cuando intento
> buscar esa palabra que podría
> – no sé, quizá – tocar la luz del día,
> dejar en ella impresa mi lamento.
>
> Sólo el dolor. No tengo otro argumento.
> Voy y vengo por él. Sólo él me guía.
> Consumo el pan que brinda a la agonía.
> Subo a su torre. Grito a contraviento.
>
> Oigo a lo lejos, otra vez, la vida.
> Se yergue de la muerte, decidida
> pero no hay tiempo ya para el olvido,
>
> ni voluntad, ni espacio. Roto el canto
> sólo mi voz, desordenada en llanto,
> es cuanto queda de lo que he perdido.

(Only pain shows up when I try / to find the word that might be able to / – I don't know, maybe – touch the light of day, / leave impressed on it my lament. // Only pain. I don't have any other argument. / I come and go because of it. Only it guides me. / I consume the bread that it offers to agony. / I climb its tower. I shout against the wind. // I hear far off, again, life. / It rises up from death, determined / but there is no more time for forgetting, // or will, or space. The song broken / only my voice, disordered in tears, / is what remains from what I have lost.)

The rhythm of the poem performs the speaker's sobbing uncertainty, with frequent pauses interrupting the flow of the verses, and enjambements disordering the sonnet's structure. The text is punctuated with negations, and with the insistent repetition of insufficiency – in a word, "sólo" – that also invokes the loneliness of grief.[9] The poem begins and ends with pain, the speaker's pain, and with what she – not someone else – has lost, and cannot be adequately described with words. Thus, although the sonnet form intends to bring "the ordering power of the imagination" to bear on "the disordering force of the loss" (Orr 219), Gatell's poem offers a kind of embodied witnessing based on emotion, rather than facts, images, or memories.

Antonio Méndez Rubio represents the dissolution of a coherent sense of the individual and collective body through the confusion of the senses, time, space, and form in "La música que oiremos" (The Music We Will Hear), until the speaker is finally possessed by undecidability at the end of the poem.[10] That speaker, who appears in the first person only in the final stanza – "Escucho: el sí y el no / me han poseído" (I listen: the yes and the no / have possessed me) – is never gendered, and the subject of the verbs is uncertain: it is plural, or else an object (light, sun), or even simply the unspecified "lo que" (that which). The verbs themselves often appear without person, as infinitives or gerunds, or in the passive voice, even when describing cries of anguish: "desconociendo / otra vez el lugar allí / donde se grita" (unknowing / again the place there / where one screams). Rhetorical questions, the conditional tense, negations, paradoxes, and qualifiers reinforce this sense of not knowing and not being able to say, but the single conjugated verb – "Escucho" (I listen) – marks the receptivity that defines the relationship of the speaker to others in their shared condition of radical vulnerability: "Estar perdidos / siendo otros en los otros: dando en nada" (To be lost / being others in the others: coming up with nothing).

Rather than registering perplexity and dissonance, Clara Janés's 11-M poem "Todo es muerte en el aire" (All Is Death in the Air) draws on a Buddhist understanding of time, reality, and human existence to weave a series of connections – between all and each, transience and firmness, the lost face and the face that shows itself, blood and water, blood and tears – that suggest our common vulnerability to death.[11] Although the poem begins with images of blood and wounds that cannot be washed away, it does not heighten the vengeful reaction to violence, although it does allude to it. Instead it proceeds with discrete affirmations in each sentence, which, combined with a series of repetitions, allow us to reconsider the images that came before, creating calm through its mantra-like rhythm and structure that lead us to a contemplative state, allowing for a meditation on the repetition of violence in world. This process is apparent in the opening lines:

> La lluvia no puede borrar la sangre. El rojo que emana de la herida es más firme que la insistencia del agua. La lluvia se mezcla con las lágrimas. Y son ríos de lágrimas los que corren desde el cielo hasta la tierra y despliegan el negro de los paraguas como banda de luto sobre la muerte. Todo es muerte en el aire. Todos miran la muerte y pierden el rostro. Sólo el rostro de la aflicción se muestra.
>
> (The rain cannot erase the blood. The red that emanates from the wound is firmer than the water's insistence. The rain mixes with tears. And they

> are rivers of tears that run from heaven to earth and open the black of the umbrellas like a band of mourning over death. All is death in the air. All look at death and lose their face. Only the face of affliction shows itself.)

In the poem, repeated first-person plural commands ("Let us") re-create the act of invocation, of prayer, as does the symbolic lighting of candles in love, not hate. The poem paints a still image that is concrete and present, yet it also traces the movement of rivers and processions, which, along with the tropes of repetition, inscribe both a past and a future into the present moment. The palate is limited to red, black, and white, which the transparency of rain, tears, and a river attempt to wash clean. The individual is erased, as we are in death and fear – "Todos miran la muerte y pierden el rostro" (All look at death and lose their face), "el estallido que sembró en todos los corazones el pánico" (the explosion that sowed panic in all the hearts) – and the response becomes collective, expressed in the first-person plural. The pain of death for the individual is acknowledged, and it is personified here: "Solo el rostro de la aflicción se muestra" (Only the face of affliction shows itself). But the lack of possessive pronouns and site-specific descriptions along with the insistence on plurality inscribe this particular instance and these particular individuals into a history of violent death that comes to embrace all such painful losses and the rituals that accompany them: "Muerte que se expande como las ondas sonoras del estruendo y abarca todas las muertes distantes hasta los confines más lejanos en el tiempo y el espacio" (Death that expands out like the sonic waves of the boom and reaches all the distant deaths in the farthest confines of time and space). Instead of attempting to synthesize information and reach a conclusion, the poem offers a contemplation on the pain of violent death that does not efface it, offer a solution, or call for vengeance, but rather represents all of the dead as grievable. In contrast to the Catholic response discussed in chapter 1, Janés's text reproduces the Buddhist mechanisms of meditation, prayer, and contemplation, while also invoking a sense of community, or communality, beyond the borders of family, state, or language, thereby creating a unique space for responding to terrorist acts from a collective vulnerability.

Other poets approach the question of vulnerability by portraying the flesh affectively, as does Isabel Pérez Montalbán in "Identificación de cadáveres" (Identifying Cadavers). The cadavers of the title are not whole, but only the flesh and the objects that loved ones carried. The speaker is a witness – "He visto" (I have seen) – obliging readers to see as well the manifestation of grief in the parents' refusal to identify flesh, to acknowledge death: they "no reconocen" (don't recognize), "rechazan" (reject), "retrasan" (delay), "reniegan" (renege), "precisan la genética y la duda" (require genetics and doubt), and "dilatan la esperanza" (stretch out hope). The speaker registers their anguished denial, their rejection of the dehumanization wrought by violent death that turned their beloveds' flesh into an alienated object, something that no longer belongs to them: "la carne de su carne, / ... lo inerte que fue suyo" (the flesh of their flesh / ... that inert thing that was theirs) (135). Their postponement of the inevitable shows how they hold onto the hope of life, registered in the affective simile that brings back their gum-chewing kids: "dilatan la esperanza como un chicle / mil veces masticado" (they stretch out hope like a piece of gum / chewed a thousand times). The gum is what Sara Ahmed calls a "happy object." "If objects provide a means for making us happy," she writes, "then in directing ourselves toward this or that object we are aiming somewhere else: toward a happiness that is presumed to follow" (34). What will follow in this case, however, is not happiness but despair, and what was once a happy object is now a source of alienation. The same is true of the flesh in the second stanza: "hay dedos de un cadáver ya sin brazos, / y una pierna infantil sin ningún nombre" (there are fingers from a cadaver without arms / and a child's leg without a name) (Pérez Montalbán 135).

After enumerating these and other remains with tenderness in the first two stanzas, the speaker envisions an embodiment that is "both performative and relational" (Butler, "Rethinking" 21), elaborated in terms of everyday routines (abandoning the warm bedsheets, eating an early-morning breakfast, turning off the lights, running to catch the train, answering a cellphone) that, over time, have come constitute a "shared horizon in which objects circulate, accumulating positive affective value" (Ahmed, "Happy" 38). Interspersing with these routines a series of actions that evoke death (autopsying, turning cold, embalming, moving away, interrupting, taking away, not answering), the speaker shows how the absence of the dead will haunt the familial space, and asks again and again who decided to interrupt these routines forever.

In the final stanza, the speaker again becomes witness, this time to the vision of the flesh of the dead – the flesh of the flesh of the parents – and the objects they carried, which, personified, go off in search of the lost people to whom they belonged and their own "futuro / mutilado sin jueves, su después imposible" (future / mutilated with no Thursday, their impossible afterwards) (Pérez Montalbán 136). The speaker obliges us to see and feel the formerly inert objects, including the flesh, as living beings that persist after they have been brutally ripped from their everyday context (body, family, routine), to experience them as affective, as "[s]harded elements [that] remix to shared effect" (Massumi 75). They affect us, and we recognize ourselves in their vulnerability. Naming them as "Hijos todos de la mañana niña" (All of them children of the morning child), the poem asserts that they are of the same flesh, members of a single family, the flesh of all of our flesh. Thus, although we don't know to whom the last object, "el corazón sin brújula" (the heart without a compass), belongs, it seems to implicate all of us – the dead, the grieving parents, the speaker, and the reader. Its bewildered vulnerability suggests the composite reflex of a collective body to the destructive disorder wrought by trauma.

The flesh may also have sacred connotations, even as it alludes to gender norms, as Rivera points out, recalling Judith Butler's "styles of the flesh" (*Gender Trouble* 139). One of the Spanish poets who has most effectively brought together such sacred and material implications of the flesh in the post-Franco era is Ana Rossetti (Ana Bueno de la Peña).[12] The erotic in her poetry often marks the violent encounter of a vulnerable body, generally coded as feminine (though not necessarily female), and the destructive, dehumanizing desire associated with masculine power. In her poems, it is not the biological sex of the victim and victimizer that matters, but rather the ways in which the latter inscribes a gendered identity on his or her prey. The texts thus theorize our perception and construction of erotics by codifying the rhetoric of the erotic gaze and revealing the gendering of violence, or the violence implicit in gendered power relations. Another repeated motif in Rossetti's work is the representation of the body in architectural terms: an early poem, "Inconfesiones de Gilles de Rais" (Unconfessions of Gilles de Rais) from *Los devaneos de Erato* (The Frenzies of Erato, 1980), for example, refers to what the murderous pedophile calls the "columna tersa" (terse column) of his victim; likewise, the feminized body in *Virgo potens* (1994) is a citadel, and the book is replete with images of holy war waged on that battleground.

Rossetti's rendering of what could be called our contemporary religious wars, "Ciudad profanada," originally composed as a protest against the Iraq War,[13] also draws on a gendered rhetoric of violence and victimization to represent the calculated planning and execution of an attack on a city by falcons ("city" is feminine in Spanish; "falcon" is masculine). That image might recall St John of the Cross's "Tras un amoroso lance" (Upon a Quest of Love), in which the soul's quest for union with God is figured as a falcon's hunt for prey. Yet the reference for Rossetti's text is from the Book of Ezekiel, in which, as punishment for idolatry and heresy, Jehovah destroys and humiliates Jerusalem, figured as an unfaithful wife and a prostitute. Thus, in Rossetti's poem, the city and its architecture appear as a violated body, and the justification of the violation is framed in religious terms. But the poet highlights the quivering vulnerability of that body in the second half of the text:

> Como a un cuerpo sin más bastiones, almenas o parapetos que diez dedos atemorizados y dos brazos insuficientes, saquean sus entrañas exhibidas,

horadan las membranas tensadas de sus vidrieras y esparcen sus vísceras temblorosas: cables, plomo, arena, hierros retorcidos. Convertida en burdel y en festín, se escupe sobre la ciudad la descarga lasciva del desprecio, arrancan las simientes del útero estremecido, cauteriza todo el tiempo anterior y la somete a la pesadilla de un presente continuo. Igual que en el cuerpo mutilado se cercena la memoria del tacto, el contacto, la caricia – ese cuerpo que alguna vez fue amado, consolado, defendido y que ahora es violado y estigmatizado con fuego – , así se clausuran los paisajes: se arrebata el hogar, la escuela, la tumba, los rincones queridos, los lugares de las historias de las gentes, como si se arrancara la piel de los huesos; y la materia trabajada por la edad y la experiencia es demolida, despojada de su eternidad.

(As with a body with no greater bulwarks, turrets, or parapets than her ten terrified fingers and two inadequate arms, they sack her exposed entrails, pierce the stretched membranes of her windows and scatter her trembling viscera: cables, lead, sand, twisted iron. The city is turned into a brothel and a feast, the lascivious discharge is spit upon her, the sperm is ripped from her shuddering uterus, all previous time is frozen, and the city is subjected to the nightmare of an eternal present. Just as with a mutilated body, the memory of touch, contact, caress is cut off – the body that once was loved, consoled, defended, and is now violated and stigmatized by fire – , there the landscapes are closed off; the school, the tomb, the beloved nooks and crannies, the places of people's stories, as when the skin is ripped from the bones; and the material wrought from age and experience is demolished, stripped of its eternity.)

The poem graphically represents the ways in which acts of war, precipitated by religious fanaticism and blind hatred but strategized coolly, destroy the fabric of society, exposing the vulnerability of the body. Especially vulnerable are the bodies of women, which often count among the spoils of war. Women readers in particular will recoil at such graphic images of raped and mutilated women, spit upon and stigmatized by their murderous violators, but these kinds of images have often stirred men's passions, serving as erotic stimulation (as Rossetti has repeatedly shown) and/or as a justification for future wars, figured as acts of vengeance by other men. This poem instead insists on how they have become "radically unsupported" (Butler, "Rethinking" 19), bereft of history, touch, protection, love. By evoking the support that has been withdrawn and concluding with the assertion that "ninguna captura es sagrada" (no seizure is sacred), the poem seeks to perform a disenchantment of violent death and contest the logic of every war waged cunningly in the name of the sacred on feminized bodies.

Jorge Riechmann's "Un día después del once de marzo" (One Day After the 11th of March) also foregrounds human vulnerability and the blood that flowed after the bombings. Like Rossetti's poem, it figures the city as a body; however, it suggests that the cycle of blood letting can be remedied through the sharing of blood, beginning with blood donation as a literal and concrete form of relationality and support. The poem begins by reciting the vengeful logic of an eye for an eye, a tooth for a tooth, "la regla arcaica" (the archaic rule) (149), which it rejects: "una sangre / no lava la otra" (one blood / does not wash the other away) (ibid.). The exception to this rule comes in the flowing of donated blood, figured as a form of communication: "Sangre de vena a vena difundiendo / las palabras preciosas: no estás solo" (Blood from vein to vein spreading / the precious words: you are not alone) (ibid.). In the next stanza, the litres of donated blood multiply until, in the next, they become an overwhelming force of solidarity that can literally combat the tribal hatred of the poem's opening stanzas: "Espesa sangre amiga que rebasa / las medidas, las bolsas, incontables los litros que bombean / limpias arterias en Madrid" (thick blood of friendship that overbrims / any measure, the bags, countless litres that bomb / clean arteries in Madrid) (149). In the final image, this generous, loving blood flows to hundreds of millions of hearts on Earth, now "corazones lúcidos" (lucid hearts) (150). The poem, like the donated blood, has resignified the meaning of the archaic rule: one blood does wash away the other. Grounded in the word made flesh and the flesh made word, it aptly illustrates Jacques Rancière's assertion that "[p]olitical statements and literary locutions produce effects in reality" (35).

Possession and sacrifice underlie the violence of nationalism and Abrahamic religions in Julia Piera's "Atlas de muerte" (Atlas of Death).[14] The text is an invitation to exile, to a liberating dispossession. It opens with an epigraph by the film-maker Chantal Akerman – "The land one possesses is always a sign of barbarism and blood, while the land one traverses without taking it reminds us of a book" – that parallels the ending of Rossetti's poem. The reference to Akerman also brings to mind questions of exile, the Holocaust, the deep bond between mother and daughter, and the everyday oppression of women, as well as an aesthetic that defies conventional notions of time, place, memory, the body, and identity, obliging the viewer to perceive these otherwise.

All of these inform Piera's approach to 11-M in "Atlas de muerte," a poem that dissolves the gendered hierarchies of Abrahamic religions and nations. Thus, the speaker and the female-gendered addressee are construed as equals – "tú / igual que yo" (you / the same as I). And, although the addressee is described as "avergonzada" (ashamed) and "arrepentida" (repentant), the issue at hand is not original sin: she is ashamed of *borders* and repentant of *nationalisms*, and the speaker invites her to leave them behind.

> Ve tú
> igual que yo.
>
> Compra el último billete
> con sangre de cabras y de toros
> para extraer de tu biografía un milagro.
>
> Empaqueta tu confusión,
> paga el exilio
> y que un atardecer,
> en los extremos del mapa
> abierto de miel y jengibre
> a tientas, y avergonzada de las fronteras
> acaricies blancas mariposas naciones.
>
> Jugarás
> al frontón con la muerte
> pero ve tú
> igual que yo.
>
> Esperaré. Abiertos
> así los brazos, de par en par
> hemisferios, a que la muerte
> acoja su revancha
> venid!, y arrepentida de las naciones
> trace testamento en atlas sin tierra. (133)

(Go forth, you, / the same as I. // Buy the last ticket / with the blood of goats and bulls / to extract from your biography a miracle. // Pack up your confusion, / pay your exile, / and may you, some day at dusk, / at the far reaches of the map / open and made of honey and ginger / feeling your way and ashamed of borders / caress white butterfly nations. // You will play / pelota with death / but go forth, you, / the same as I. // I will wait. With arms / wide open, like this / hemispheres on which death / takes its revenge / come!, and repentant of nations / trace your testament in an atlas without land.)

The poem brings together a number of signs associated with national and religious identities, only to blur their borders, substituting for them the exilic imagination. The first line clearly echoes Genesis 12:1, when

God tells Abraham, "Go forth out of thy country, and from thy kindred, and out of thy father's house, and come into the land which I shall show thee." As reward for his obedience, God says that "I will make of thee a great nation" (12:2) and "I will bless them that bless thee, and curse them that curse thee" (12:3). This blessing justifies the construction and defence of the nation consecrated by God, as well as the destruction of the enemies of that nation. Abraham does not appear only in the Judeo-Christian Bible, however: he is also the father of prophets in Islam, where he is known as Ibrahim, and he is likewise willing to sacrifice his son to God, who finally accepts an animal offering, as in the second stanza of Piera's poem. The religions are brought together as well in the "mapa / abierto de miel y jengibre" (map / open and made of honey and ginger): the reference evokes a drink called zanjabeel that the righteous are given in the Quran as well as the description in the Old Testament of the Promised Land as flowing with milk and honey. Animal sacrifice also appears in the form of bull fighting, which has disputed origins (Basque? Christian? Roman? Celtic?) but is now identified largely with Spain. Indeed, under the Franco dictatorship, bull fighting was consecrated as an intrinsic part of national identity, and the debates about outlawing it in Catalonia in recent years have been tied to the push for Catalan independence from the Spanish state. The *frontón*, meanwhile, refers to the arena for the Basque game of pelota (known in the United States as jai alai); which is one element of cultural identity in Basque nationalist discourse. Indeed, Julio Medem's 2003 documentary about the Basque question was titled *La pelota vasca: La piel contra la piedra* (Basque Ball: Skin against Stone).

The poem, then, alludes to but also silences the identities of the possible 11-M perpetrators – Islamists, ETA, or the Judeo-Christian invaders of Iraq. In place of those masculinized national and religious signs, the speaker offers her female interlocutor ephemera – a magical map, a miracle, white butterflies, an embrace with hemisphere arms, and an imaginary atlas, one without nations – and, like Akerman, only "the traces, the hints and the inferences of the past" (Lebow 46). Finally, in its silences and omissions, in the imprecise location and identity of the speaker and the addressee, Piera's "Atlas de muerte" performs what Rivera describes as a "poetics of the flesh," one that "displays light and obscurity, visibility and invisibility, connections and gaps" (158).

This is also an apt description of Lola Velasco's 11-M poem, "El aliento del cazador" (The Hunter's Breath). Rather than creating a stable system of signifiers or imagined biographies, Velasco traces almost unbearably delicate and ephemeral gestures, which transpire in an indeterminate space of transition reminiscent again of Akerman's interior and exterior geographies, simultaneously marked and unmarked by evanescent signs of identity.

Se gira contra la pared
y su antiguo torso
de nadadora
flota
en la luz
del mediodía,
con la dignidad
del ciervo herido
que sabe
que cruza el río
por última vez.

Los bosques
ahora son abrazos
que asfixian
y miro al cielo
con la veneración
de quien ya no cree en nada.
Lo que existió,
tiene aire.

Se gira contra la pared
y de esta manera
se despide del mundo.
La tierra corrige huellas,
teje un visillo invisible
de pisadas,
los hilos que miden
la estatura de nuestra soledad.

Yo también caminaré descalza
hasta volverme pálida
como mi madre. (175–6)

(She turns to face the wall / and her ancient torso / of a swimmer / floats / in the light / of noon / with the dignity / of a wounded deer / that knows / it is crossing the river / for the last time. // The woods / are now embraces / that smother / and I look at the heavens / with the veneration / of one who no longer believes in anything. / What existed, / has air. // She turns to face the wall / and in that way / she bids farewell to the world. / The earth corrects footprints, / it weaves an invisible curtain / of footsteps, / the threads that measure / the stature of our solitude. // I will also walk barefoot / until I grow pale / like my mother.)

There are no concrete details of the bombings, no media images, no victim biography in this poem, which only hints at the violence of this woman's death: in the hunter of the title (though his presence is limited to his breath); in the deer's wound; in the smothering embraces of the woods. Instead, the poem creates a minimalist, performative portrait of subtle, dignified gestures of farewell, grief, transience, and continuity.

The first stanza portrays a woman on the border between life and death, on the verge of farewell, turning to the wall. Her body is also in a liminal state, simultaneously weighty – her "ancient torso" is reminiscent of a classical sculpture – and as buoyant as a swimmer, as she floats on the midday light. Those lines highlight the ambiguity of the boundary between life and death, as a single word – "flota" (floats) – alone on line 4, serves to transition the woman from the previous vigorous activity of a swimmer to the stasis of floating, and from the earth to the ethereal light. At the same time, "flota" joins the two realms, not only in a literal, structural, and grammatical sense, but also as an embodied gesture. As if to emphasize further the ephemerality of the moment and the image, the poem transitions to another, as the woman's dignity is represented as a wounded deer that knows it is crossing the river, Lethe, into oblivion. Knowing that deer go to the woods to die, we might imagine the gesture of the animal turning toward the woods, mirroring the woman's turn to the wall, so we are not surprised that the words "Los bosques" (the woods) open the following stanza. These associations are not explicit, but rather suggested by what Brian Massumi calls "the shimmers of reflection and language" (75). What is more, the continuous movement from one image to the next, from one state/place to another, from one stanza to the next, highlights the tension inherent in the *gesture*, which is simultaneously static (paused, so to speak, as it is observed and/or recorded) and dynamic, on the verge of becoming something else (Agamben 55).[15]

The dying woman is altogether absent from the second stanza, and, along with her, the graceful, light images of dignified transition. They are replaced here by nothingness: airlessness, doubt, solitude. Even an embrace brings death. The lyric speaker appears for the first time halfway through the stanza, looking up at the heavens, surrounded on one side (the first three lines) by the smothering embrace of the woods/death, and on the other (the last four lines), by doubt, the finality of death ("existió" [*existed*, in the preterit tense]), and air. The reader might also equivocate because the signs of nature in this stanza – forests, heavens, air – defy their traditional symbolic significations and thus do not offer solace or meaning. The third stanza begins by repeating the first line of the poem – "Se gira contra la pared" (she turns to face the wall) – and thus seems to emphasize finality, as do the images of the lost traces and the invisible barrier of footsteps that again leave the speaker in solitude. They seem to lead to what Ricoeur calls "profound forgetting, forgetting through the effacement of traces" (415).

It is perhaps in the recognition that the path to oblivion is one that we all must eventually walk that the speaker finds solace in the final stanza, projecting a future when she will literally and figuratively follow in those footsteps, "unforgetting" them, so to speak, or testifying to the "persistence of the original impression" (Ricoeur 416). The adjective "descalza" (barefoot) grounds that image of inevitable vulnerability before death in the contact of her flesh with the very earth that erased the traces of the dead woman, figured in the last line as her mother. The trace of the mother also remains in her gestures of farewell, the fleeting images that shimmer in the memory, and the gestures of the speaker herself taking her mother's place, walking in her footsteps. Despite the poem's deceptive simplicity, the embodied subtlety of these gestures, of the transformations of the body into flesh, the flesh into its trace, and the trace into a path, resists an easy resolution, inviting, or even requiring, attentive rereading and contemplation.[16]

The diverse approaches to a poetics of the flesh in these texts offer a vital alternative to the certainties of both sentimental and social poetry, which rely on abstracted, secular notions of the human.[17] The affective representation of the flesh and its impermanence seems particularly apt for engaging with the shattering impact of the 11-M attacks on seemingly stable concepts of individual and social bodies without reconstituting their borders. Beyond the normalizing frames of knowledge, they make possible what Butler defines as "apprehension," which "is less precise, since it can imply marking, registering, acknowledging without full cognition. If it is a form of knowing, it is bound up with sensing and perceiving, but in ways that are not always – or not yet – conceptual forms of knowledge" (*Frames* 5). This formulation of knowing as apprehension, along with Rivera's poetics of the flesh, signals a postsecular turn, particularly in feminist thought, which does not necessarily lead us back to the kinds of "politicized religion" (Braidotti, *Posthuman* 36) that underpin terrorism or pre-emptive war. Rather, they suggest a form of the sacred that allows mutable, alternative collectives to emerge from the evanescent traces and shards of a common vulnerability, figured as flesh. Piera's and Velasco's poems also point toward intermediality and the virtual, respectively, and they thus provide a starting point for considering the technological and economic mechanisms that shape what has come to be known as the posthuman, which will be the focus of the following chapter.

Chapter Five

Pixel, Bar Code, Algorithm

In contrast with cultural objects that referenced or sought to reproduce the effects of the photos we discussed in part 1, some 11-M poetry seeks to foreground the complex implications of digital images themselves, along with other new media objects and marketing strategies structured by the mathematical logic of the computer. In a sense, the principles of knowledge and identity that emerge from new media and globalized capital would seem to run counter to the postsecular understanding of the body and the flesh that we discussed in the previous chapter, since they imply not simply a post*humanist* posture, but the advent of the post*human*, in which the data-driven, algorithmic logic of computers and the needs of the market work together to influence perception, subject the body, and configure consciousness. Nonetheless, several theorists have argued that these new media are also "potentializing" (Massumi 43). On the one hand, technological advances in the form of prostheses enhance human capabilities, converting us into what Donna Haraway deems as cyborgs. But we must also address the ways in which our interactions with computers structure our understanding of reality and relationality, a topic we touched on briefly in our discussion of the *Espacio de palabras* in chapter 3.

In his classic book, *The Language of New Media*, Lev Manovich succinctly outlines the characteristics of new media objects and some of their social implications. Unlike old media objects made up of continuous data, he explains, new media objects are composed of a sampling of discrete data points, numerical representations, that are "usually not units of meanings in the way morphemes are" (29), and are "subject to algorithmic manipulation" (27). Thus, although computer images, representations of space, or word documents appear to conform to our expectations, their actual underlying structure "follows the established conventions of the computer's organization of data" (45). This logic also defines post-industrial economics, which uses algorithms to market aggressively to individual preferences. Manovich notes that this new organization of labour and production impacts both individual and social identities: it replaces mass production, which required a conformity of taste and habits that shaped the individual liberal subject, with post-industrial production, which markets seemingly infinite options for customization, emphasizing individuation over tradition and social cohesion (41). In a similar fashion, N. Katherine Hayles writes that "the posthuman view privileges informational pattern over material instantiation" (2) and, performing an "erasure of embodiment" (4), configures the "human being so that it can be seamlessly articulated with intelligent machines" (4). We have already discussed the impact that this political economics had on the urban organization of Madrid in the post-Franco era. Still, Hayles and other theorists of the posthuman and the virtual also find affective traces and the potential for social change in this form of disembodiment; indeed, in the case of 11-M, the *pásalo* serves as an example of the circulation of affect that could "enable triggerings of change" (Massumi 43). Considerations of the implications of these concepts in literature had also appeared before 2004, not only in Hayles's book, but also, for example, in Espen Clarseth's *Cybertext: Perspectives on Ergodic Literature* (1997) and Loss Pequeño Glazier's *Digital Poetics: The Making of E-Poetries* (2002). In Spain, they were theorized by the artists of the Nocilla Generation, or Afterpop, in the early 2000s as well, and Agustín Fernández Mallo exemplified them in his first novel, *Nocilla Dream*, published in 2006, the first instalment of his Nocilla Experience trilogy.[1] For Fernández Mallo, the potentiality of the affective trace is represented poetically in what he calls "postpoesía" (postpoetry), which explores, "la nueva forma de representación de los fenómenos por ordenador que según los filósofos de la ciencia ni es experiencia ... ni es teoría ... sino otra cosa más poderosa que ambas y entre las cuales flota simulada" (the new form of phenomenal representation by computer, which, according to the philosophy of science, is neither experience nor theory but something more powerful than either that floats between them as a simulation) (*Postpoesía* 31). This explanation is similar to Massumi's formulation of the "event-dimension of potential" as "in-between" that "is in no sense a hybrid or mixture" (76). "In itself, it is composed not of parts or terms in relation, but of modulations, local modifications of potential that globally reconfigure (affects)" (ibid.).

Despite the ubiquity, at the time of the 11-M events, of new media objects (cellphones, computers, video games) and technologies in Spanish culture, particularly the culture of the young, there are few examples of poetry in the two 11-M anthologies *Madrid, once de marzo: Poemas para el recuerdo* and *11-M: Poemas contra el olvido* that engage the underlying organizational principles and aesthetic implications of these media and technologies.[2] Fernández Mallo's untitled 11-M poem is one of them, a text that exemplifies the fragmentation of reality, knowledge, and experience in the information age. It is divided into two sections, each with its own subsection, yet none of the divisions presents a coherent image or idea, and, despite their sequential numbering (1, 1.1, 2, 2.1), they do not offer a linear development in thought or time, beyond the assertion that the whole is more than the sum of its parts, citing Ilya Prigogine, known as the poet of thermodynamics: "$f_1(x) + f_2(x) + f_3(x) + \dots f_n(x) < F(x)$" (Fernández Mallo 62).[3] The formula also applies to the relationship between pixels as discrete data points, the realities they record in real time, and the emotional impact of the images that they come together to form: "Amanece en el televisor / gente corriendo malherida" (Dawning on television / people running gravely wounded) (62). The lines effectively represent the blurring of reality on the screen, the locus of the dawning, not of the day itself, but of the severely injured and their movements in real time, in distinct contrast to the viewer, who must be immobilized to witness it (Manovich 104). The television screen is the bearer of bad news in these lines, and it serves to exacerbate the distance between the viewer and the injured. The modularity inherent in the "fractal structure of new media" (ibid. 30) also appears ominous, as a reference to the still-unknown identity of the attackers appears, not as a person, but as a computer virus, or malware, suggesting the reproducibility of the destruction: "un software desconocido arrasa / una ciudad a trozos pixelada" (an unknown software razes / a city pixilated into pieces) (Fernández Mallo 62).

This sense of isolation typical of the discrete samples of new media (pixels, characters, scripts) also appears in the first section of the poem, where "soledad" (solitude or loneliness) is repeated three times over the course of eleven lines. It shows up in the first line: "La soledad no tiene dimensiones" (Solitude has no dimensions) (61). The subsequent lines offer a metaphorical elaboration of that idea that literally moves us to the "seeping edge ... where potential, actually, is found" (Massumi 43), in the point of contact between the virtual and the real: "La soledad es un extrarradio moteado / de irreconciliables objetos, / (aguarda la materia / la patada que le devuelva fe en su silueta)" (solitude is a mottled periphery / of irreconciliable objects, [it holds the matter / the kick that might restore its faith in its silhouette]) (61). In the final instance, solitude, already constituted metaphorically as an edge made up of irreconciliable objects like pixels, is represented as a digital image that can be enlarged or shrunken, like Alice in Wonderland: "la soledad se hace doble; / por fractal aritmética / se reduce a ½ al mismo tiempo" (solitude becomes double; / by a mathematical fractal / it shrinks to ½ at the same time) (61). Despite the mathematical logic behind the computational image and the solitude of the person facing the screen, there is something here that eludes rationality, materialized in the interface and transformed by the imagination.

Searching for meaning(s), the lyric speaker turns to other discrete points of data, quotations from literary texts, personified as their authors (Thomas Mann, Ernesto Sábato, René Thom, Emil Cioran), some of whom appear to materialize and literally accompany him, mimicking the function of human memory or the "zapping" potentialized by hypertexts.[4] The fragmentary nature of those excerpts also exemplifies the computational process of sampling, which "turns continuous data into discrete data, that is, data occurring in *discrete* units: people, the pages of a book, pixels" (Manovich 28), which can then be organized into a new media object. Although this process is generally automated, and thus both invisible in the final product and beyond the control of the person who perceives the object, Manovich explains that "[n]ew media is interactive. In contrast to old media where the order of presentation is fixed, the user can now interact with a media object. In the process of interaction the user can choose which elements to display or which paths to follow, thus generating a unique work. In this way the user becomes the co-author of the work" (49).

Despite its repeated allusions to mathematical structures, the poem ends with an implicit critique of rationality, as the speaker and his interlocutors depart, "racionales" (rational), without leaving a mark. And, in line with an earlier critique of the certainties of metaphor – "*se muere por exceso de metáfora*" (*you die from too much metaphor*) (62, emphasis in the original), the poem ends with a simile, an approximation, of their parting: "como se escinden las líneas / de un haiku destrozado / aunque excesivamente exacto" (like the splintering of lines / in a haiku destroyed / but exceedingly exact). We may apprehend a connection between the fractured haiku and the razed city, between the lines of one and the pixels of the other, each of them an illusory image of exact and enduring order that can be brought down by splintering or by the replication of malicious code. At the same time, the replication of affective ties, as with the sharing of even shards of literary texts, may create something akin to resistence. What lingers, as in some of the poems that we studied in the previous chapter, is this imprecise and ephemeral sense of both loss and connection.

In both of his 11-M poems, Josep M. Rodríguez also evokes the space in between the real and the virtual where perception and apprehension take place, figured as the computer or television screen. In "Las semillas del viento" (Seeds of the Wind), his literal and figurative awakening involves a subtle shift in perspective on the "edge of the virtual, where it leaks into actual" (Massumi 43). The first image that confronts the speaker is fleeting and imprecise, as is the simile that follows:

> Blando y escurridizo sol
> de un día
> escurridizo y blando
> como una medusa. (Contra el olvido 153)

(Soft and slippery sun / of a day / slippery and soft / as a jellyfish.)

The structure of the first three lines implies an attempt to grasp the image, through the *retruécano* – the repetition and reversal of the initial adjectives (*blando* and *escurridizo*) in the first and third lines – and the spacing that puts "de un día" apart on a separate line that visually continues and links those same lines. The fact that the day modifies the sun, and both are modified by the same slippery adjectives, however, makes the image even more elusive. These lines are followed in line 4 by a simile, which, as a literary figure, suggests diffuseness; this effect is multiplied in this stanza by the elusiveness of both the initial image and the jellyfish. All of this suggests a blurriness that we might expect to dissipate as the eyes open further and focus, an idea that materializes as "certainty," but is repeatedly denied in the following lines. What has broken and blurred that certainty is the television image ("Enciendo la televisión, / veo" [I turn on the TV, / I see]), representing a reality that, the speaker asserts, will not take shape without his witnessing it: "el horror necesita de mis ojos" (the horror requires my eyes). The screen in many senses would seem to serve as a barrier separating viewers from reality, leaving them untouched and giving them the control to filter out what they don't want to see. At the same time, however, it is the interface between the virtual and the human, and, in this poem, reality bleeds through, literally colouring the initial image with blood in the final lines, transforming the slippery simile into a concrete metaphor: "Blando y escurridizo sol / de un día en el que sangran las medusas" (Soft and slippery sun / of a day when jellyfish bleed) (153). Rodríguez's second 11-M poem, "Frente al televisor" (In Front of the TV), continues this meditation on the screen, showing how the images and silence are captured by it, but, even when we turn them off, they penetrate our consciousness and our space.

In Javier Rodríguez Marcos's poem "Solo en casa" (Home Alone), consciousness and space are breached by marketing. The text never describes the attacks, but it links them implicitly to globalized capital in the form of advertising for Visa and Citroën (not capitalized in the poem) on the television set:

> El anuncio de visa
> (y en ella Dublín, supongo)
> Se mezcla en tu cabeza
> con frases, desperdicios
> de la cena, papeles
> ¿te gusta conducir? No sabes
> lo que citröen puede hacer por ti.

> (The visa ad / (and in it Dublin, I suppose) / Becomes mixed in your head / with phrases, leftovers / from dinner, papers / do you like to drive? You don't know / what citröen can do for you.)

The juxtaposition of these objects, places, and phrases appears random, even meaningless, perhaps, but it represents structurally the ways in which contemporary networked subjects are never actually alone but rather surrounded and interpellated by new media objects with voices that get into their heads, shaping perception and creating desires that seem to be uniquely their own. In this informational environment, traditional concepts of time, space, and relationality are unrecognizable; and the structure of the poem, the syntax, the sequence of events, and the punctuation likewise disrupt legibility. The attacks themselves appear in the form of "Los muertos por los suelos / de esta casa vacía, / su sangre, tu costumbre" (the dead on the floor / of this empty house / their blood, your habit). They are associated only by implication with the forces of global capital: Citroën cars and Repsol gas may remind us of the motives for the Iraq War, and their television ads become confused with "anuncios de paz, discursos, guerra" (peace posters, speeches, war). Although the speaker moves to turn off his conscience by turning to the television, the repeated Repsol ad reminds us again of the latent violence disguised as entertainment and desire in the post-industrial network society, and the ways in which propaganda, like terrorism, targets us.

In Tina Escaja's *Código de barras*, the concepts of perception and control in the age of mass media and cyber cultures are linked more explicitly to the free market and the Bush doctrine (some of the texts first appeared in a 2006 exposition titled, "The Only Bush I Trust Is My Own"). In this book, perception is conditioned by the logic of the barcode. In one image, for example, the American flag is composed of a series of codes that include the slogan not of the United States but of the Spanish fascist party, La Falange – "Una, Grande, Libre" (One, Great, Free) – which casts the alliance between Spain and the United States in the light of authoritarianism. The poems, meanwhile, interrogate the truth behind the American Pledge of Allegiance, as modified in 1954: "one nation, under God, indivisible, with liberty and justice for all." Indeed, an underlying theme of the book concerns the ways in which the steps taken to preserve a certain concept of freedom following war violence often result in the sacrifice of freedom itself. In the exposition, the bar codes were literally "read" by a scanner, and the scanned text (sometimes in English) was often in tension with the written Spanish words. Some texts are now online, and you can use your mouse as the scanner to reproduce the effect.[5] What is particularly interesting is the contrast between the impersonality of the code itself and the mechanized voice it produces in English, Escaja's recorded voice in Spanish, and the subversive message of empowerment hidden in the barcode, as in the poem "Quiet Zone: Lugar de Silencio," which ends with three barcodes, with text that reads: "Silence," "bleeds," "indifference," a near translation of the last line of the poem, "El lugar del silencio es la indiferencia" (the quiet zone is indifference). The barcodes themselves are silent until we activate them, and on the website, the voice says, "I speak," thereby demonstrating the latent potentiality of the virtual.

Escaja's 11-M poems can be found in *Código de barras*, grouped after the barcode signifying "Códigos de identificación" (Identification Codes). In this section of the book, the bars suggest imprisonment or entrapment in an impossible situation brought on by the pressures of globalization: they are prison bars, prostitute bars, guns held high by child soldiers that look like bars, the glass cage of the officer in the Department of Homeland Security who will separate a mother from her family, and so forth. The poems themselves are rather straightforward condemnations of globalized capitalism, nationalism, and state violence. "Esmeralda" suggests an association between shopping and violent death through the image of a dead woman, fresh from the morning's shopping, covered pitilessly with a plastic bag: "ahora espatarrada y rota se muestra / con la piedad y el abrazo de una bolsa de plástico" (now legs sprawling and broken she appears / with the compassion and the embrace of a plastic bag) (40). Similarly, in the poem "Pentagramas marinos (Masacre en Madrid)" (Marine Staves (Massacre in Madrid)), the poor dead are in the streets like "basura rota, descalabro y residuo de un asfalto manchado" (broken garbage, ruin and residue of a sullied asphalt), and their trace may be found again in the black garbage bags used to collect their remains, "notas negras" (black notes) (42) on the bars of the musical staves from the title. The poem concludes with an explicit expression of disenchantment of religion that recalls the ending of Rossetti's poem: "Dios no es grande" (God is not great).

The most sustained critique of the codes and algorithms that regulate identity in post-industrial Western society comes long after the initial anthologies appeared, in a book published in 2012, Pedro Provencio's *Onda expansiva* (Shock Wave), in which they are explicitly linked to patriarchy, nationalism, and the dehumanizing mechanisms of capitalism, evils that the book seeks to reveal and affectively counter. Each of the poems is dedicated to one of the dead from the 11-M bombings, whose name, birthplace, and years of life constitute the title, as if each text were a gravestone. In this sense, the text replicates the 11-M monuments that name the dead and often offer a biography of each individual, or the poem "Una mañana," by Felipe Benítez Reyes. Provencio, however, rejects this logic, this attempt to forge recognizable, grievable identities on the bodies of the dead, which might become some kind of "identidad cuantificadora" (quantifying identity) (14), "identidad cuantitativa" (quantitative identity) (25, 194), "identidad rentable" (profitable identity) (28), "identidad insuperable" (unbeatable identity) (41), "cálculo identificador" (identificatory calculus) (45, 66, 188, 198), "hipóstasis identitaria" (identitarian hypostasis) (53, 69, 144), "identidad legitimadora" (legitimizing identity) (64, 123), "identidad cuantificable" (quantifiable identity) (72), "identidad ejecutiva" (executive identity) (99), "identidad en masa" (mass identity) (132), "identidad justiciera" (righteous identity) (180), "identidad no enajenable" (inalienable identity) (189), "identidad distributiva" (distributive identity) (197), "identidentidad" (identidentity) (210), "identidad referencial" (referential identity) (75, 218), or "referencias idénticas" (identical references) (224). These identitarian terms come from the mouths of the elite in the central section of each text, as I will explain below, and they become mixed with the discourse and algorithmic logic of the stock market, commodification, insider trading, identity politics, and the three monotheistic religions to determine the value of human life, not coincidentally confirming that some lives matter more than others and some deaths are perfectly justifiable. Among these disposable people are the poor, "apostates," and women.

Identity, then, is represented as part of the problem that gave rise to the attacks. Thus, the texts under each name are not linked to the person, not even to that person's or the poet's gender, nor are they entirely separate from the other texts; rather, they refer directly to those texts in their repetition of motifs and names. Each body is "less an entity than a relation, and it cannot be fully dissociated from the infrastructural and environmental conditions of its living" (Butler, "Rethinking" 19). These bodies circulate like flesh, "an element transformed as it is given"

(Rivera 23), and "an ambivalent term that names a rather slippery materiality ... [with a] propensity to change ..., crossing the boundaries between the individual body and the world" (Rivera 2). Nonetheless, Provencio's book insists that the recognition of individuality is key to humane treatment, as we see in this part of the poem, "Abel García Alfageme (España, 1977–2004)":

> Dos átomos de un mismo elemento – por ejemplo, dos átomos de P en el grupo fosfato de un nucleótido – nunca son iguales: difieren como consecuencia del carácter particular inducido por la posición que ocupan en la cadena de reacciones químicas donde son considerados. De ahí que los enlaces, como los intervalos musicales, contengan una actividad energética extremadamente versátil, en gran medida opaca – o transparente: el efecto es el mismo – , que hemos de analizar hasta donde nos sea possible, sin fáciles concesiones rentabilizadoras, si queremos llegar a comprender el comportamiento más íntimo de la materia. (78)

> (Two atoms of the same element – for example, two atoms of P in the phosphate group of a nucleotide – are never identical: they differ as a result of the unique character induced by the position they occupy in the chain of chemical reactions where they are being analysed. Thus, the bonds, like musical intervals, contain an extremely versatile energetic activity, that is largely opaque – or transparent, the effect is the same – , that we must analyse to the best of our ability, without facile, profitable concessions, if we want to come to understand the most intimate behaviour of matter.)

This is precisely the thrust of *Onda expansiva*, as the author explains in his prefatory remarks. Each person who dies as a result of this kind of violence, he writes, "queda para siempre con un gesto interrumpido de ir a decir algo" (remains forever with the interrupted gesture of being about to say something), and so, attentive to this "deseo de decir" (desire to speak), "se han recopilado los siguientes textos atribuidos a quienes recibieron con la muerte el carácter de autores en Madrid el 11 de marzo de 2004" (the following texts have been compiled, attributed to those who received with their deaths the quality of authors in Madrid on 11 March 2004) (9). Note the gesture here in the passive voice of erasing Provencio's protagonism and instead ceding his place to the multiple voices of others.

The structure of this powerful book imitates in many senses Bach's music,[6] intricately weaving together individual voices and choral interludes over the course of more than two hundred pages. Each of the poems has three parts. At the top, we find a first-person text (in the form of verse or narrative) from the perspective of an individual (not reduced to any identity) who comes to participate in a multi-voiced collective of the dead over the course of the book. In the middle of the page and between brackets, there is a chorus of voices representing the elite, which brings together and repeats religious, financial, class, and nationalistic discourses that self-righteously justify (and even sarcastically laugh about) the violence of exploitation, war, or abuse. Along the bottom of the page and in italics, we find the voice of the poet/musician. The separation between victims and artist is not absolute, however, as the victims often call out to the bard (alternately called "el arpista" [harpist] and "el escriba" [scribe]), appropriate his/her words, and take on her/his characteristics as author and composer. The bard likewise comes to be described in some of the same terms as the dead. Another element that changes throughout is the kind of instrument to be played: the harp, the zorna oboe, the aulos (a precedecessor of the oboe from Ur), the sitar (India), the kundama (Polynesia), the likembe or zanza (central Africa), the lythophone (Indonesia), the syrinx (Greece), the murali flute (India), and the viela sarangi (northern India and Pakistan). Many of these instruments, their sounds and their functions, as well as numerous musical forms and sacred texts are described in the book's endnotes, which are themselves moving lyrical pieces. What remains the same throughout the book is the caustic, cruel, and calculating discourse literally at the centre of the page and, symbolically, of the problem, which has to do with the relationship between religion, identity, money, and power. Here we have the same phrases repeated over and over: "el trabajo os hará libres" (Auschwitz's motto, "work will set you free," which later becomes "power will set you free"); "matadlos todos y Dios elegirá a los suyos" (kill them all, and God will find his own): "algo habrán hecho si han venido por ellos" (they must have done something if they've come to get them); "está escrito" (it is written); "nuestra forma de ser" (our way of life); "no tienen nuestra fe" (they don't share our faith); "Dios lo quiere" (it's God's will); and so on.[7]

The book is also a powerful condemnation of sexism and systemic violence against women. Provencio repeatedly confuses the gender identities of the victims and the scribe/harpist, so that they do not conform to the individuals' bodies. He also mentions misogyny explicitly, in the voices of the dead and the artist: "*Quién en mi casa se escupió a sí mismo cuando nací mujer?*" (*Who in my house spit on himself when I was born a woman?*) (55, emphasis in the original). The strongest text about this topic, however, comes in the poem "María Dolores Fuentes Fernández (España, 1975–2004):

> Cuando nací mujer,
> mi padre apaleó a mi madre,

"tú tienes la culpa, inútil,
se la echaré a los cerdos," pero Dios
en forma de vieja centenaria
lo impidió riendo: "Déjala viva;
que sufra" (73)

(When I was born a woman, / my father beat my mother, / "it's your fault, useless woman, / I'll throw her to the pigs," but God / in the form of a hundred-year old woman / forbade it, laughing: "Leave her alive; / let her suffer")

It is also important to note that Provencio does not attribute this virulent misogyny to any culture or religion in particular, but rather to patriarchal systems that use religion to subjugate entire classes of people.

Indeed, the book offers a strong critique of gods and religions, which abstract human suffering in the service of certain principles. It instead suggests an alternative in the "desdiós" (disgod or ungod) and the profoundly human understanding of the individual experience of pain and interrupted life, represented here as interrupted speech. The critique extends even to sacred music: "Qué música es ésta que requiere intérpretes / muertos recientes and recién nacidos?" (What music is this that requires singers / newly dead and newborn?) (59). The story of Job provides a concrete example of the unjustifiable sacrifice of innocent people to an implacable God, as he figures in all three monotheistic religions, offering a model of unbending faith in the face of adversity. In numerous texts in this book, he becomes linked to the innocent victims of the attacks, and he rebels, articulating a stinging critique of moral values based on human suffering: "Y Job no volvió a confiar en el Dios que se ríe de la angustia del inocente" (And Job never again trusted in the God that laughs at the anguish of the innocent) (22). Recalling the 11-M poems that mention the devastating effects of the attacks on human bodies, this book repeats the image of the eye without an eyelid, which again links Job to the bombing victims, and the missing or seared tongues, which symbolize both the elites' desire to see and their will to silence. Near the end of the book, in the poem dedicated to Marta del Río Menéndez (España, 1964–2004), we read, "Ten piedad de tu dios, recréalo para el recién nacido y no para tus antepasados" (Have pity on your god, re-create him for the newborn and not for your ancestors) (177). This echoes an earlier poem, in the voice of Rex Reynaldo Ferrer (Filipinas, 1984–España, 2004), although, there, God is still the monotheistic one, with his name capitalized: "Ten piedad de tu Dios, no lo hagas responsible / de su capitular ni de sus advocaciones financieras, / llévale infieles vivos, es lo que más le gusta" (Have pity on your God, don't hold him responsible / for his capitulation or for his financial advocations, / bring him live infidels, which is what he likes best) (69). Near the end of the book, in the poem "Neil Fernando Torres Mendoza (Ecuador, 1966–España, 2004)," "God" is again capitalized, but this time as Goddess, counteracting the numerous previous texts in which women are shown to be despised in monotheistic religions. The critique of religion as a power structure, however, is not limited to those faiths; on the contrary, the bard in "José María Carrilero Baeza (España, 1965–2004)" writes, "Yo en la voz del verdugo / sólo en el libro sagrado significa / yo en la voz de la víctima" (I in the voice of the executioner / only in the sacred text means / I in the voice of the victim) (44). And the penultimate poem, "Yaroslav Zojniuk (Ucrania, 1956–España, 2004)," asserts that

> Los ingredientes del dolor no han cambiado nada con los siglos. El Neandertal lloraba igual que el Cromañón. Quizás por eso, los métodos y los instrumentos de tortura varían muy poco de una época a otra. Apórtense ejemplos procedentes de clanes rivales, de dioses únicos, de sectas y herejías, de dioses multiples, de identidades enfrentadas, de ofertas y demandas, de verdades con poder, de pérdidas y ganancias, etc. (225)

> (The ingredients for pain haven't changed a bit over the centuries. The Neanderthal cried in the same way as the Cromagnon. Perhaps for that reason, the methods and instruments of torture vary little from one age to the next. Examples may be provided by rival clans, by sole gods, by sects and heresies, by multiple gods, by clashing identities, by supplies and demands, by truths with power, by profits and losses, etc.)

The conclusion of the book, clearly, is quite pessimistic. The last text, "Csaba Olimpiu Zsigovski (Rumania, 1978–España, 2004)," tells us that "El escriba ha encontrado la pieza / que faltaba en el arpa / pero no sabe qué hacer con ella" (The scribe has found the piece / that was missing from the harp / but doesn't know what to do with it) (226). Meanwhile, the voice of power remains unchanged: "[así está escrito / yo siempre he dicho / (risas sarcásticas) / qué le vamos a hacer]" ([so it is written / I've always said / (sarcastic laughter) / what can you do about it]) (226). And the scribe ends the book with these lines: "El aire desgastado por el dolor / ahoga a los recién nacidos" (The air worn down by pain / drowns the newborns) (226). Still, the beautiful book remains to instruct us in these terrible lessons, and to animate and give voice to the victims of such heartless and calculated violence.

When the 11-M bombings occurred, Provencio was working as a teacher in a Vallecas school, and he continued to do so afterwards, interacting intimately on a daily basis with a population directly affected by the loss of life or permanent injuries caused by the explosions.[8] It was the need to process this tremendous pain that gave rise to his book, which provided a space for reflection, developed over the course of several years. The presentation of *Onda expansiva* took place in the Muga Bookstore on Pablo Neruda Avenue on 14 March 2014, ten years to the day after the Partido Popolar lost the election because it tried to manipulate the 11-M tragedy by attributing the attacks to ETA. The event included a reading of the text in three voices, those of Provencio, his wife (the actress Aurora Herrero), and his son (the actor Julio Provencio), accompanied on the clarinet by Salvador Vidal. The bookstore owners worried about the implications of celebrating and selling a book of this nature and took every measure to avoid the appearance that they were exploiting the pain of others, respectfully asking permission: first, symbolically, of the dead and then, literally, of the survivors (Aigor). This performance of the poems, like the songs, prayers, and writing we discussed in part 1, endeavoured to maintain an embodied, affective connection between the text, the poet, and the reader in the public sphere, potentializing collective experiences and organizations.

The book and the performance offer powerful examples of the affective turn in Spanish poetry and society that was already in the air in 2004, coupled with an engaged critique of the institutional discourses that promote and justify policies that leave so many vulnerable to violence. By the time it was published, a hopeful new form of networked politics had emerged, in the form of the 15-M movement, which would endeavour to harness both new media technologies and affective relationality to effect social change. The poems we have discussed in this chapter sound a cautionary note, however, reminding us that the mass media are, as Brian Massumi explains, both potentializing and inhibiting (43), subject to control and usurpation by the "capitalist mode of power" (88).

Conclusions

This book has argued that 11-M marked a critical turning point in Spanish society and politics in which poetry played a unique and vital role. The bombings, protests, and subsequent reactions by-passed the frameworks that had been established by the Culture of the Transition for maintaining order through a common understanding of Spanish society, history, politics, and economic policy. Instead, the events and those who wrote about them revealed the emergence of a latent new sensibility, informed and shaped by both communication technologies and post-humanist thinking. It found its political expression in the *pásalo*, which enabled the rapid organization of a massive collective response to what the Internet had revealed to be the lies of the political class and the collaboration of the media in spreading and supporting those falsehoods. This same sensibility surfaced in the public sphere through the various processes of reading, writing, singing, and circulating poetic texts, which we could see as "shards of intentions and conscious memories" (Massumi 75) that did not coalesce into the coherent messages or narratives that had regulated order in the post-Franco state, but, rather, as in the poetry we discussed in chapter 4, appeared as "shimmers of reflection and language" (ibid.). They created impressions that were apprehended, rather than knowledge that was imparted, and they shared those impressions through mutable, informal, non-hierarchical, and affective networks of communication and memorialization made possible by new media technologies. For the Spanish elites who in 2004 still maintained their faith in traditional media, the "truths" of the Transition (political stability, the importance of forgetting the past, the economic miracle, and so on), a single state religion, and political parties, the power of this essentially poetic sensibility came as a surprise. In contrast, it resonated strongly with Spanish poets who had already been exploring forms of expression and ethical engagement beyond the options afforded by secular humanism and the Spanish poetic tradition.

Our awareness of these processes may allow us to recognize that the centrality of the narratives I described in the first chapter of this study might itself be a useful fiction, one that disguises more contemporary forms of corruption, abuses of power, and collusion among the political elite, as the collaborators in *CT o la Cultura de la Transición: Crítica a 35 años de cultura española* (CT or the Culture of the Transition: Critique of 35 Years of Spanish Culture) suggest. Amador Fernández-Savater thus asserts that, in the CT, "se escenifica un conflicto permanente en el que estamos invitados a tomar partido: PSOE o PP, izquierda o derecha, ... 'las dos Españas'" (a permanent conflict is staged in which we're invited to take sides: PSOE or PP, left or right, "the two Spains") precisely to avoid discussion of other themes: economic precarity, mortgage rates, forced evictions, and so forth.

Our discussion of globalized capitalism, the posthuman, and the postsecular may also remind us that the unrecovered victims of Francoist state terror were not the only invisible bodies in 2004. Gays and lesbians. as well as migrants from Eastern Europe, Latin America, and Africa, often post-colonial and racialized subjects, barely register in 11-M discourse, anthologies, or poetry. In "Tu amigo invisible" (Your Invisible Friend), an anonymous author on the website of the Asociación 11-M Afectados del Terrorismo laments the impossibility of mourning his gay lover. María Victoria Reyzábal's elegiac *M11M* figures Madrid as the poet's lesbian lover, and the text also mentions the cities of origin of many of the immigrant victims, but it does not give them a voice. The hip-hop song "El último tren" by the group Arma Blanca, which I discussed in chapter 2, evokes the Afro-origins of the genre in 1980s Madrid, but the genre's metrical innovations have not found their way into Spanish poetry. There are poems in the archives by Ecuatorians (DP-1725) and Dominicans (DP-135), along with texts by Moroccans, but in the mainstream anthologies there are no poems by Romanians, Sahrawis, or Nigerians, and only one by a Moroccan, along with a sprinkling of Latin Americans.

The political analysis of 11-M also largely neglects feminist issues, disregarded as somehow irrelevant or secondary to more "pressing" or "serious" concerns, generally articulated as a kind of geopolitics that abstracts away gender. Such arguments ignore the instrumentalization of feminism as one of the democratic values that the West claims to defend in the "War on Terror" (see, e.g., Riley, Mohanty, and Pratt; Taylor and Zine; Bhattacharyya), at the same time that violence against women is downplayed and women's rights are curtailed at home (see, e.g.,

Delphy and Broder; Hammer; Cvetkovich). Indeed, women are targets of violent discourses and practices – including domestic violence, femicide, laws regulating women's bodies, infanticide, unequal pay and other forms of workplace discrimination, trolling, and so forth – throughout the world and in the West, not only in Islamist states. The most prominent example from 11-M would be the treatment of Pilar Manjón, the founder and president of the Asociación 11-M Afectados del Terrorismo, who has been the target of violent gender-specific attacks on her Twitter account.[1] Although article 578 of the Spanish Criminal Code forbids insults to the victims of terrorism, the judiciary refused to investigate the incidents involving Manjón until 2014 (Pérez).[2] Still, women like her have played an important role in contesting state violence worldwide. Indeed, the Asociación 11-M Afectados del Terrorismo was the only one of the victims' groups that fought for rights and recognition for all of those *afectados* (affected), rather than just the *víctimas* (victims), in order to circumvent laws that restricted the family members in the latter category to a very narrow group of husbands and wives, children, and parents.

It is notable that the spontaneous shrines contained few texts by contemporary poets; rather, musicians provided the lyrics for the time. This suggests that, in contrast to the more public role of poets in the 1930s, most contemporary writers and their poems were not effectively circulating in the public sphere or responding to the concerns of peripheral populations, those who were most impacted by both this terrorist act and the systemic violence of neoliberal urban and social policies. As we have seen, some 11-M poems reflect specifically on feminist issues – Ana Rossetti's "Ciudad profanada," Julia Piera's "Atlas de muerte," Pedro Provencio's *Onda expansiva* – but the debates among Spanish poets regarding the social role of poetry at the time of the attacks largely elided questions of gender, sexuality, and race.

Much of this would later change as a result of 11-M. The impulse toward socially engaged poetry would strengthen, and many poets would seek direct interaction with marginalized people through performance in the public sphere. The election of a Partido Socialista Obrero Español government on 14-M would facilitate the passage of legislation criminalizing gender violence and recognizing it as an expression of systemic discrimination against women (December 2004), and establishing marriage rights for gay and lesbian partners (July 2005). It would not be until 2011, after the next crisis – the economic collapse in 2008 – that a splintering of identities and a new form of networked politics would fully emerge, in the form of the 15-M and Orgullo Indignado (Indignant Pride) movements, endeavouring to harness both new media technologies and affective relationality to critique neoliberalism, create broad networks of solidarity that included migrants, as well as queer and transgendered people, and effect social change. The 15-M movement seemed to be the culmination of a certain poetics of affective engagement that would replace traditional political organizations and their cultural adherents. Still, Leticia Sabsay has remarked that "we might want to be cautious not to definitely celebrate the affective force of the happening itself when such a celebration's focus on the affective dimension of experience serves to dismiss the necessary transience of such moments and to disavow the current difficulty for articulating effective and sustainable political alternatives to neoliberal policies" (296). Indeed, subsequent events have reminded us that the mass media are both potentializing and inhibiting, subject to control and usurpation by the capitalist modes of power, authoritarian forces, extremists of all sorts, criminal individuals and organizations, and traditional political parties.

Poems, of course, can be subject to those same forces, subsumed into ideological causes, legitimating practices, or consumerist propaganda, but, like other forms of literary and cultural expression, they can also provide a space for reflection or resistance. Unlike novels, films, or theatrical productions, however, poems can circulate in public spaces in unexpected ways, creating links and relationships that can be ephemeral or binding. They can be inscribed on banners and monuments; musicalized in anthems, protest songs, and ditties; reproduced on manifestoes and blogs; declaimed by politicians; read at graduations, weddings, and funerals; sent by email and text; scribbled on scraps of paper and posted on walls; painted as graffiti. They can remain forgotten or hidden like a written trace in an archive or book, until they are liberated by a reader. Thus, although 11-M poetry reflects in many senses the fleeting sensibility of a particular juncture in Spanish history, its performative qualities and slippery elusiveness may allow it, like affect and memory, to resist capture and endure.

Notes

Introduction

1 Fernando Reinares explains that the attacks were planned and carried out by three clusters of people: "a very important al-Qaeda cell that had been established in Spain a decade before the 3/11 attacks and was dismantled as a result of the major antiterrorist operation launched in November 2001"; a group linked to the Moroccan Islamic Combatant Group; and "a bunch of former delinquents active throughout Spain who specialized in trafficking in illegal drugs and stolen vehicles" (2).

2 Another victim of the attacks was a member of the Grupo Especial de Operaciones (GEO, the SWAT unit), who was killed in the suicide explosion of four terrorist suspects in Leganés on 3 April 2004.

3 Antony Rowland notes that this was the case for 9/11 as well: "it is clear that the prosaic accounts of newspaper reports, magazine articles, and TV bulletins were not felt to be commensurate with the advent of 9/11" (108).

4 The irony is that it was the first PSOE president, Felipe González, who created extralegal death squads – Grupos Antiterroristas de Liberación (Antiterrorist Liberation Groups, GAL) – to pursue ETA in both Spain and France during his presidency, which lasted from 1982 until 1996.

5 See Vives and Rullan, 392.

6 All translations are my own.

7 Žižek writes in *Origins of Violence* that, "Therein resides the fundamental systemic violence of capitalism, much more uncanny than any direct pre-capitalist socio-ideological violence: this violence is no longer attributable to concrete individuals and their 'evil' intentions, but is purely 'objective,' systemic, anonymous" (11).

8 The Red represents a loose yet dynamic web of connections among survivors, families and friends of the dead, social and health workers, political

organizers, victims of other acts of political violence, and so on, who informally elaborate responses to the catastrophe, including, but not limited to, political action and emotional support. The network began with a group of social workers and activists who hoped to organize a response to 11-M, but it grew through word of mouth and through Internet posts, and eventually the professionals dropped out, leaving only those affected by the tragedy (Desdedentro 26–8).

9 See, for example, my 2003 article on this topic.

10 Antony Rowland writes that

> After recounting how people "scrawled poems in the ash that covered everything" in their introduction to Poetry after 9/11, Dennis Loy Johnson and Valerie Merians note, "Prose wasn't enough. There was something more to be said that only poetry could say. Everybody, apparently, knew this" (Johnson and Merians ix). As a form of heightened rhetoric and memorable speech, as well as signalling cultural continuity, poetry – unlike prosaic prose – assuaged what Butler termed the new "precariousness" of US life ... This glut of poetry readings and poetic production was not without its detractors, however. Johnson and Merians note that poems were so dispersed in downtown Manhattan behind "mountains of flowers" and photographs of the dead, that a fire chief issued a statement: "Thank you for the food and the blankets and the flowers but please – no more poetry." (108)

11 Sánchez-Carretero also notes the tone of the graffiti in contrast to that of texts written on paper, with the former expressing more virulent political and antiterrorist emotions ("La vida social" 143). We will see this dichotomy as well in the musical texts associated with those forms of writing: hip hop and ballads.

12 Freud notes that "many emotions which are essentially painful may become a source of enjoyment to the spectators and hearers of a poet's work" (Freud 125).

13 Jung criticizes what he sees as Freud's reductive characterization of the poet as neurotic, a procedure that exposes the humanity of the artist but does not explain the brilliance of artistic creation: "If a work of art is explained in the same way as a neurosis, then either the work of art is a neurosis or a neurosis is a work of art" (Jung para. 100). In similar fashion, he points out that "a work of art is not a human being, but is something supra-personal. It is a thing and not a personality; hence it cannot be judged by personal criteria" (para. 107). The work of creation comes from a supreme act of will on the part of the artist or from a nearly unconscious process of inspiration in which the poet is distanced from "the creative process than moves him" (para. 112).

14 Sánchez-Carretero later published an edited book, *El Archivo del Duelo: Análisis de la respuesta ciudadana ante los atentados del 11 de marzo en*

Madrid, about the meanings of the memorials, the process and implications of dismantling them, and the interactions of visitors with the *Espacio de Palabras*, among other topics. She also published several articles on the topic, alone and with co-author Carmen Ortiz, including one in Jack Santino's *Spontaneous Shrines and the Public Memorialization of Death*. She also co-edited, with Peter Jan Margry, an English-language volume, *Rethinking Memorialization: The Concept of Grassroots Memorials*, for which they co-authored the introduction. These studies constitute an invaluable resource for understanding the implications of grassroots memorials in general, and the 11-M sites in particular, and I refer to them extensively in this book.

15 There is a similar 9/11 anthology, edited by Dennis Loy Johnson and Valerie Merians, with an introduction by Alicia Ostriker, *Poetry after 9/11: An Anthology of New York Poets* (2002).

16 For more details, see the association's website.

17 Crumbaugh writes that

> the discourse of victimhood is so ubiquitous that a reasonable response to Manjón would be that, nowadays, one can only enter the political sphere by speaking through the victim of one form of political violence or another. For politics in Spain presents itself as an imagined dispute among victims, at times resembling a competition to pile up dead bodies and leave them at an opponent's doorstep, and other times a morbid theatre of ventriloquists, or, in the words of the leader of Spain's right-wing Partido Popular, Mariano Rajoy, a "guerra de esquelas." Competing modes of enshrinement and moral traps built around victims seek to outdo one another in an ongoing negotiation of what Judith Butler, in a different context, recently called a public "hierarchy of grief." (366)

18 Also self-published was Juan Castrillo's 2005 book of verse, *Dolor de luz: A las víctimas del terrorismo 11 de marzo 2004* (Light's Pain: To the Victims of Terrorism, 11 March 2004).

19 See, for example, his description of the 2012 piece *Los encargados* (Those in Charge) by artists Santiago Sierra and Jorge Galindo (Snyder 116–24).

20 Jorge Riechmann articulates this concept again in his 2006 essay about Joan Brossa: "El realismo es una actitud frente a lo real y no un catálogo de procedimientos; la indagación realista tiene que ver con un compromiso moral más que con la búsqueda de efectos. Realismo: una obra abierta a la irrupción de lo contingente" (Realism is an attitude toward the real and not a catalogue of procedures; realist inquiry has to do with a moral commitment more than a search for effects. Realism: a work open to the eruption of contingency) (Por un realismo 2). See also the discussion in Iravedra (54–6).

21 In his 2011 book, *Ahí es nada,* Jorge Riechmann defines this kind of engagement with the physical world as a Spanish poetic version of "dirty realism," which attempts to bring the body into poetry and politics in an "authentic" way: "Realidad: aquello que te da ganas de tocar y morder, porque estás seguro de que el tacto, el sabor y el aroma van a ser únicos e incomparables" (Reality: that which gives you the desire to touch and bite because you are sure that the touch, flavour and aroma will be unique and incomparable) (75).

22 "Ciudad profanada" first appeared in February 2004, in the journal *Ciscus,* before the 11-M attacks. Like Clara Janés's "La rosa de Hal.lach" (one of four long poems in her 2005 *Huellas sobre una corteza*), it was intended as a protest against the destruction of Baghdad. Nonetheless, the timing of its publication and its representation of holy war make it an apt text for 11-M as well, as Rossetti confirmed to me in a personal interview, 15 November 2015.

23 By "scopic regime," Feldman refers to "the agendas and techniques of political visualization: the regimens that prescribe modes of seeing and object visibility and that proscribe or render untenable other modes and objects of perception. A scopic regime is an ensemble of practices and discourses that establish the truth claims, typicality, and credibility of visual acts and objects and politically correct modes of seeing" (30).

Part 1. Poetry, Politics, Performance

1 Flesher Fominaya notes that already on 14 March, "the newspaper *Metro Directo* reported that the foreign press in Madrid had filed a complaint against the government for engaging in 'inadmissible behaviour' by pressuring and tricking them into supporting the ETA thesis. Other accusations and evidence of partisan manipulation of news were reported ("Madrid Bombings and Popular Protest" 296).

2 Available at https://elpais.com/diario/2004/03/12/

3 *ABC* showed the black body bags lined up beside the train.

4 See http://hemeroteca.lavanguardia.com/preview/2004/03/12/pagina-1/33654145/pdf.html

5 For a detailed analysis of the relationship between labour unions and the government in the post-Franco era, see Burgess.

1. Rhetoric and Ideology in Grassroots Memorials and Official Monuments

1 See, for example, José María Pemán's highly influential epic poem, "Poema de la bestia y el ángel" (Poem of the Beast and the Angel, 1938], and its prologue.

2 Sánchez-Carretero calls black ribbons "the most important antiterrorist symbols in Spain" (Madrid Train Bombings 256). She continues: "Blue ribbons were used in demonstrations demanding the release of people kidnapped by ETA. The blue ribbon turned into black as a mourning symbol to indicate an assassination committed by ETA. After the March 11 attacks, black ribbons could be found on facades and cars, and at offices, stores, banks, and the railway stations. Black ribbons were stuck to various supporting fabrics: sewed on curtains, painted on tablecloths, or pinned to towels" (257). Significantly, black ribbons were also drawn next to the text of many of the poems left at the grassroots memorials.

3 All texts with accession numbers are from the Archivo del Duelo in the Archivo Histórico Ferroviario del Museo del Ferrocarril de Madrid.

4 Agamben discusses at length the

> ambiguity inherent in the nature and function of the concept of *people* in Western politics. It is as if, in other words, what we call people was actually not a unitary subject but rather a dialectical oscillation between two opposite poles: on the one hand, the *People* as a whole and as an integral body politic, and, on the other hand, the *people* as a subset and as fragmentary multiplicity of needy and excluded bodies; on the one hand, an inclusive concept that pretends to be without remainder while, on the other hand, an exclusive concept known to afford no hope; at one pole, the total state of the sovereign and integrated citizens and, at the other pole, the banishment ... of the wretched, the oppressed and the vanquished. (31)

5 This observation could certainly apply to the growing encroachment of fundamentalist, and sometimes undemocratic, Christian religious beliefs on public institutions in the United States today.

6 See, for example, Gutmaro Gómez Blanco, who writes about the practical economic benefits of the "redemption" of prisoners through work.

7 Miguel Ángel Perfecto sums it up:

> El modelo económico iniciado por Ramiro Ledesma y Onésimo Redondo, continuado por José Antonio y Franco se estructuraba en torno a tres grandes ideas: El rechazo absoluto del liberalismo económico y del marxismo y la defensa de un nacionalismo económico extremo de tipo autárquico. En segundo lugar, la ideología agrarista y su proyecto de colonización del campo. En tercer lugar, como instrumento esencial para el desarrollo del nacionalismo económico y el control social de trabajadores y campesinos, la creación de un sindicato obligatorio para empresarios y trabajadores que acabara con el conflicto social y la lucha de clases y lo sustituyera por un régimen de armonía social. (137)
>
> (The economic model initiated by Ramiro Ledesma and Onésimo Redondo, continued by José Antonio [Primo de Rivera] and [Francisco] Franco, was structured around three grand ideas: the absolute rejection of economic liberalism

and Marxism and the defence of an extreme economic nationalism based on autarky. Second came an agrarian ideology, with its project of colonizing the countryside. Third, as an essential tool for developing both economic nationalism and the social control of workers and peasants, came the creation of an obligatory syndicate for business owners and workers to eliminate social conflict and class warfare, putting in their place a regime of social harmony.)

8 Antonio Cea Gutiérrez notes that "subyace un espíritu un tanto oficialista de la Iglesia Católica madrileña, comprometida con un catolicismo al mismo tiempo tradicional y combativo" (there is underlying a rather officialist spirit of Madrid's Catholic Church, committed to a Catholicism that is at the same time traditional and combative) (185).

9 Indeed, the PP has fought relentlessly to undermine the court's findings following the conviction of the Moroccan defendants and sentencing of twenty-one Islamist defendants on 31 October 2007. Their motivations, however, may have had more to do with defending party members from prosecution in other arenas than with elucidating the truth about 11-M, as the trials coincided with important initiatives aimed at unearthing the Franco-era injustices perpetrated by the right and prosecuting the corruption of PP politicians in the present day. The most important of these were the approval of Law 52/2007, commonly known as the *Ley de Memoria Histórica* (Law of Historical Memory), by the Congress of Deputies on 31 October 2007; the continued recovery efforts by the ARMH; and the case brought by the Spanish judge Baltasar Garzón against perpetrators of state crimes under Franco in 2008. Garzón had cited the doctrine of universal jurisdiction for grave human rights violations, to pursue legal judgments against world leaders responsible for the disappearance, torture, and murder of their citizens – among them, the Chilean dictator Augusto Pinochet (1998) and members of the Argentine military junta (2005). After he turned his lens toward the Franco dictatorship, Garzón himself became the object of investigation, accused of abusing his power, as well as violating the Constitution and the 1977 amnesty law. Although he was cleared of those charges, he was removed from the bench following his conviction in 2012 for ordering the illegal wiretapping of prisoners and lawyers in the Gürtel case, which involves a vast corruption network composed primarily of PP politicians and business leaders. A whistle-blower came forward with the first accusations in the case in 2007; the charges were initially brought by Garzón in 2009; despite his removal in 2012, thirteen defendants were convicted in Valencia in February 2017; Ángel Acebes testified in June 2017; and President Rajoy was summoned to testify before Congress in August 2017.

10 The historian Paul Preston suggests that the reorganization of the Guerrilleros de Cristo Rey in the late 1960s, along with the "addition of

paid thugs," was "probably masterminded by Admiral Carrero Blanco's more or less private intelligence service, the Servicio de Documentación de la Presidencia del Gobierno" (162).

11 The poem appears in Neruda's book about the Civil War, *España en el corazón: Himno a las glorias del pueblo en guerra* (Spain in My Heart: A Hymn to the Glories of the People in Arms), published in 1937.

12 I have transcribed the items from the Archivo del Duelo exactly as they are, with all spelling and grammatical errors intact. I have not added "*sic*" after such errors, in order to avoid overuse of the term.

13 There are clear echoes of Franklin Delano Roosevelt's Pearl Harbor speech – in which he called 7 December 1941 "a date which will live in infamy" – in the discourse of then-president José María Aznar, who declared on the day of the attacks that "[e]l 11 de marzo de 2004 ocupa ya su lugar en la historia de la infamia" (11 March 2004 now occupies a place in the history of infamy) (Romero), symbolically connecting Madrid with Pearl Harbor, Nagasaki, and Hiroshima as a kind of "ground zero." In the context of the 2015 national elections, Esperanza Aguirre, then spokesperson for the PP in Madrid, claimed that Spain had never actually participated in the Iraq War. Aguirre was forced to resign in 2016 due to corruption charges linked to the Gürtel scandal.

14 Another was dedicated in Leganés to the SWAT officer who died when several members of the terrorist cell responsible for the attacks immolated themselves in their apartment in that city.

15 King Juan Carlos and Queen Sofía presided over the inauguration of the memorial, "in which they laid a Spanish flag draped wreath at the monument followed by three minutes of silence and a cello recital" (Flesher Fominaya, "Madrid 2004 Bombings" 417) of Pau Casals's "El canto de los pájaros" (Birdsong) on 11 March 2007, in the presence of President Zapatero, Mariano Rajoy (the head of the PP and president of Spain), Esperanza Aguirre (the PP president of the Community of Madrid), Alberto Ruiz-Gallardón (the PP major of Madrid), and representatives of the three major 11-M victims' groups.

16 The names of the Alcalá victims are also inscribed at the site I describe below. An interactive page on the website of the newspaper *El Mundo* offers another approach to the memorialization of individuals: a virtual wall of images, which, when clicked, bring up that individual's biography, another way of evoking bodies and lives.

17 A 2015 article published in *El País*, for example, references a document from February of that year revealing that the PP City Council had not financed maintenance since 2009, when the first structural problems surfaced; the air conditioning system did not work because no one had the codes to turn it on; and the structure had leaks, but there were no funds to

repair them (Gualtieri and Olaya). The progressive news site ElPlural.com reported on 17 November 2015 that the administration of the new mayor, Manuela Carmena, planned to repair the monument (El Ayuntamiento). On 31 August 2016, however, the conservative newspaper *ABC* reported the complaints by the PP and its political ally Ciudadanos (Citizens Party) that the city was disrespecting the victims of terrorism by not repairing the memorial (Domingo). Before Carmena's election in June 2015, the PP had controlled the Madrid government for twenty-four years.

18 Masterson-Algar also discusses the museum Andén 0 (Platform 0), inaugurated in 2008 in the Chamberí station, which purports to tell the story of the Madrid metro but does not mention the migrant workers from other regions in Spain who actually built it (55).

19 As I explain in the following chapter, some of these pieces also appear in the collaborative book edited by the Comisiones Obreras, *Homenaje a las víctimas 11-M* (Homage to the 11-M Victims), along with texts by well-known writers, including Ramón Mayrata, Luis Antonio de Villena, Moncho Alpuente, and Luis del Val.

2. Circulation and Performance in Memorial and Media Sites

1 Stephanie Sieburth makes a different argument about the ways in which the lyrics, music, and performance of a series of *coplas* by Conchita Piquer provided healing benefits for those most oppressed by a vengeful regime, who suffered from psychological trauma brought on by incomplete mourning, stress, dehumanization, and loss. Although Piquer herself identified with the victors in the Spanish Civil War, the characters in the songs she sang largely came from the margins of society, where the *vencidos* (vanquished) found themselves throughout the Franco dictatorship, and especially for the first decades. The *vencidos* identified with those characters, Sieburth argues, and, as they sang the songs themselves, they were able to give voice to their woes in a camouflaged fashion.

2 "Elements of the canon are marked by three qualities: selection, value, and duration. Selection presupposes decisions and power struggles; ascription of value endows these objects with an aura and a sacrosanct status; duration in cultural memory is the central aim of the procedure" (A. Assmann, "Canon" 100).

3 The phenomenon of the *movida* is far too complex to address in these pages. For an introduction, see the volume edited by Nichols et al.

4 We discussed the performance of Flores's "No dudaría" at the Santa Eugenia memorial in the previous chapter.

5 Paloma Díaz-Mas studies these texts alongside the other literary objects in the shrines in her article (110–11).

6 Broza's website explains that his music is

> a fusion of three different countries in which he was raised: Israel, Spain, and England, filling concert halls with famous guitar playing, ranging from flamenco-flavored rhythmic and percussive techniques, to whirlwind finger picking, to a signature rock 'n' roll sound. Broza unites the three worlds by ... featuring lyrics of the worlds' greatest poets. More than a singer/songwriter, David Broza is also well known for his commitment and dedication to several humanitarian causes, predominantly, the Israeli-Palestinian conflict. ... In the year 2006 David Broza received the "In Search for Common Ground" award along with Palestinian musician/composer Said Murad, and in 2009 the Spanish King, Juan Carlos I, decorated him with the Spanish Royal Medal of Honor for his longtime contribution to Israel-Spain relations, and his dedication to promotion of tolerance and conflict resolution." ("About: Bio of David Broza")

7 Garofalo writes that, in the "America: A Tribute to the Heroes" concert, "the tribute was not about desire or celebrity; it was about people, community, and rebuilding America. The notion of 'celebrity' was frustrated in the tribute in order to foreground a unified community that included both the performers and the audience members at their TV sets. This was accomplished through a number of important means: the concert lacked a live audience and the familiar introductions to performers and speakers were noticeably absent throughout. Tom Hanks, in fact, made explicit reference to the common status of the speakers and performers" (96).

8 Gurruchaga is a Spanish celebrity who rose to fame in the years of the *movida madrileña*. A television personality and founder of the Orquesta Mondragón, with which he has recorded numerous albums, he has also appeared in some thirty films.

9 Reina is a poet, novelist, and playwright from Cádiz. He is best known for his novel about Federico García Lorca's last lover, titled *Los amores oscuros* (The Dark Loves, 2012). He later adapted that work into a flamenco-infused musical theatrical piece, titled *Lorca, muerto de amor* (Lorca Madly in Love), which had its premiere in Jerez de la Frontera in 2014 and was performed at Carnegie Hall on 25 November 2015.

10 "One of the most common objections [to considering song lyrics as poetry], voiced best by the critic Simon Frith, is that musical lyrics do not need to generate the highly sophisticated poetic effects that create the 'music' of verse written for the page. Indeed, the argument goes, if a lyric is too poetically developed it will likely distract from the music itself" (Bradley n.p.).

11 Marwan, another young artist and poet who composed an original song about 11-M for the album, also went on to a successful musical career. On *No os olvidamos*, the title of the song is "Madrid 11 de marzo," but he later

changed the title to "Jueves 7.36h" (Thursday 7:36 a.m.) on his 2008 album, *El trapecista* (Trapeze Artist). In contrast to the texts I have described so far, Marwan's song links the Iraq War to 11-M and rejects easy patriotism: "Y yo que hoy tenía que repartir flores, / Estoy llorando en Madrid como en Bagdad / ... / Y mi patria es la piel que me recubre, / Mi bandera nunca me llegó a importar" (And today I had to spread flowers, / I am crying in Madrid as in Baghdad / ... / And my patria is the skin that covers me / I never cared for my flag).

12 La Oreja de Van Gogh performed the song with the previously mentioned Israeli singer David Broza (singing in Hebrew) and the Arabic singer Mira Awad (singing in Arabic) during the group's 2009 concert in Israel (La Oreja).

13 Elena Bugedo's "De Madrid a cielo" video had some 96,600 hits as of October 2018.

14 El Pozo station is located between those of Vallecas and Entrevías, home to the schoolchildren who published poems in the anthology put together by the neighbourhood association.

15 Hip hop is a culture dominated by young men, and the lyrics of the songs can be quite misogynistic, but there are also important women rappers in Spain, the most famous of whom is the Romani-Dominican singer María "La Mala" Rodríguez.

16 An MC (master of ceremonies or mic controller) is the main rapper.

17 Jazz also impacted American poetry, of course, from Langston Hughes to the Beat Generation.

18 A hip-hop group.

19 Hip-hop DJ Murat Hendes.

20 In the ingenious futuristic 11-M novel *La vida antes de marzo* (Life before March, 2009) by Manuel Gutiérrez Aragón, the two protagonists travel in an infinitely looping transcontinental train, recounting their pasts. The train never stops – passengers board via satellite, and when one approaches, the passengers are alerted with a similar sound, described repeatedly as notes from a musical composition whose title eludes us. It is represented in the text as "Tiro, tariro, roró. Tiro."

3. Archives and Grassroots Anthologies

1 One of the most memorable was a retired man, who spent hours each day informally investigating the history of public transportation and its social impact.

2 Mayrata is now principally known as a novelist, most famous for his book about the Western Sahara, *El imperio desierto* (Desert Empire, 1992), a novel that combines elements of autobiography, anthropology, history,

and fiction. He began his career, however, as a poet, and his fiction remains quite lyrical. He explained to me that he does not generally write poetry immediately in response to traumatic experiences, preferring to return to them from a reflective distance, but that the poems in this text came upon him almost unheeded, out of necessity, much as the oscillation between prose and verse implies (personal interview, 13 November 2015).

3 These interactions were filmed over the course of several months and then studied by the anthropologist Gérôme Truc. In his article, he focuses primarily on the age and gender of the participants and the dynamics of the various groups that visited the site and inscribed texts there.

4 For an anthropological study of visitors' interaction with the site, see the article by Gérôme Truc.

5 The narrator of the novel, named Ángel, is a survivor of 11-M who was disabled in the attacks and forms a relationship with another disabled survivor. He becomes a kind of visionary, able to see the stories, not only of the other 11-M victims, figured as angels as well, but also the homeless of Madrid and a prisoner in Guantánamo.

6 The artworks were all donated to the Asociación 11-M, and digital reproductions are available on the association's website: http://asociacion11m.org/que-hacemos/trazos-y-puntadas-para-el-recuerdo/cuadros/.

7 See, for example, the article in *El País*, dated 29 May 1986 (Fresneda).

8 "Alma ausente," the last text in Lorca's four-part elegy, ends thus: "Yo canto su elegancia con palabras que gimen / y recuerdo una brisa triste por los olivos" (I sing his elegance with words that moan / and remember a sad breeze through the olive trees). The website of this school explains that Entrevías, a neighbourhood in the district of Puente de Vallecas, was populated by the waves of immigrants who came to Madrid fleeing the poverty of Extremadura and Andalusia, and it is now also the home to a growing population of Asian, Moroccan, Eastern European, and Latin American immigrants ("Quiénes Somos | C.E.I.P. 'Padre Mariana' | EducaMadrid").

9 The poem appears as well in *11-M: Poemas contra el olvido*, which I discuss in the second part of this book.

10 For Paz's blog, see http://11mcartasaldirector.blogspot.com.es/

Part 2. Poets, Cultural Politics, and Crisis

1 It received glowing reviews in the *New Yorker* on 31 October 2011 and the *New York Review of Books* on 8 December 2011, as well as on National Public Radio's *Fresh Air* on 9 November 2011, but also a critical one in the *Chicago Review* in 2012.

2 He remarks, in particular, on his inability to feel much about poetry, although he is a poet himself, claiming that "I tended to find lines of poetry

beautiful only when I encountered them quoted in prose, in the essays my professors had assigned in college, where the line breaks were replaced with slashes, so that what was communicated was less a particular poem than the echo of poetic possibility" (Lerner 8–9).

3 At times, they even provoke heartbreaking experiences so they will have something to write about. For example, Adam's friend Cyrus and his girlfriend Jane encourage a young woman to swim in a river in Xalapa, and she drowns. When Adam asks how Jane is reacting to the tragedy, Cyrus responds, "She's probably writing a novel now" (Lerner 77).

4 The Moroccan response also appeared in the grassroots memorials, as Virtudes Téllez explains.

5 As Raquel Medina puts it, "La misma forma y estructura de toda antología enfatiza la descentralización, la fragmentación y el collage en nombre de una supuesta totalidad" (the very form and structure of every anthology emphasizes decentralization, fragmentation, and collage in the name of a supposed totality) (524).

6 There were no poems solicited, for example, from the members in Madrid of the Western Saharan poetic group La Generación de la Amistad (Friendship Generation).

7 "Los trenes heridos" (Juan Lamillar, "11 de marzo: Tríptico," in Jordá and Mateos 86); "una pierna sola en un andén" (Pedro Sevilla, "Madrid, once de marzo," ibid. 158); "una plaza compartida" (García Montero, "Soneto herido" [Wounded Sonnet], in *11-M* 71); "Íbamos todos / en los trenes" (Jesús Munárriz, "Pocas palabras" [Few Words], in Jordá and Mateos 119); "en todos los paraguas del dolor repicaba / la piedad de la lluvia" (Eloy Sánchez Robayna "Madrid, para una elegía" [An Elegy for Madrid], in Jordá and Mateos 161).

8 Marta Ferrari traces the poetics articulated in Spanish poetry anthologies in the 1990s, "de la tranquilidad a la ferocidad: experiencia, conciencia, diferencia" (from tranquility to ferocity: experience, conscience, difference) (31).

4. Body, Affect, Flesh

1 I also explained in part 1 the ethical implications of the photo.

2 Sonsoles Ónega Salcedo provides a graphic description of this process in her 2007 novel, *Donde Dios no estuvo* (Where God Was Not, 103–5, 108.).

3 Melissa Gregg and Gregory J. Seigworth identify eight different orientations of affect theory. Likewise, Sara Ahmed claims that affect is not a coherent object of study: "Instead, I would begin with the messiness of the experiential, the unfolding of bodies into worlds, and the drama of contingency, how we are touched by what we are near" ("Happy" 30).

4 In many senses, the contrast I suggest here corresponds with the cogent and even-handed analysis by Araceli Iravedra of the debates between proponents of the poetics of "normality" (poets of experience, the other sentimentality), and "extrañeza" (strangeness or estrangement) (the group "Alicia Bajo Zero" [Alicia Below Zero], dirty realism, etc.), which consists in "una negación a aceptar moralmente la realidad" (a refusal to morally accept reality) (50). Iravedra does not, however, discuss questions of the sacred, the feminine, or the vulnerable body. My analysis also seeks to link these to the broader social practices of relationality and communication that emerge after 11-M.

5 In the documentary *Antonio Gamoneda: Escritura y alquimia*, Gamoneda notes that his own political orientation came not from ideology but from his own lived experience of poverty (Cortí and Rendueles).

6 This appears to be a Petrarchan sonnet, divided into two quatrains (ABBA CDDC) and two tercets (EFE FEF), but it clearly functions more like an English one, with three quatrains and a couplet.

7 Contrast this form of address with Jaime Gil de Biedma's "Piazza del Popolo," for example, where the distance between self and other is both established (the exiled philosopher María Zambrano is on the balcony, observing the multitude below in the piazza in Rome) and attenuated through attentive silence, a common heartbeat, a common song, common hopes and questions in the plazas of Italy and Spain, and even the ballad form, which echoes popular song. The speaker does not preach but listens, joins the singing, and interiorizes the experience.

8 Born in Barcelona in 1926, Gatell became an important voice in Spanish social poetry beginning in the 1950s, and she participated in Madrid's literary circles along with Carmen Conde, Félix Grande, Francisco Brines, Luis Rosales, Ángel González, Ángela Figuera Aymerich, and Vicent Gaos. In 1969, she abruptly stopped publishing, but not writing, and in 2001, Bartleby published her unpublished work from that period. She continued publishing thereafter, until her death on 7 January 2017 (Rico). Her edited book *Con Vietnam* (With Vietnam), which had been suppressed by Francoist censors in 1968, was published posthumously in March 2017.

9 Gatell, as a witness, is not removed from the suffering of the people in El Pozo; when she received in 2015 an homage at the twenty-sixth annual book festival of Vallecas (where El Pozo is located), she commented that she knew the neighbourhood well, having been friends with Father Llanos, whom we discussed in chapter 3, at whose home she participated in clandestine meetings (La primera vez).

10 The poem was subsequently published in the 2008 book *Razón de más* (Reason Enough). Méndez Rubio articulates the conception of the non-subject

subject that I describe here, as well as the non-figurative language and rejection of logic, in his 2002 article in *Ínsula*.

11 Like García Montero's "Soneto herido," the poem appeared in *Babelia*, the cultural supplement of *El País*, on 15 May 2004. However, although Janés comes from a literary family – her father, Josep Janés, founded the Plaza y Janés press – and has been recently inducted into the Spanish Royal Academy, she belongs to no Spanish literary group. She is best known not only for her engagement with a variety of cultural, philosophical, scientific, religious, artistic, and linguistic traditions in her own creative work, but also for her considerable portfolio as a translator. The broad interculturalism of her work also engages with philosophical and religious concepts of perception that question dominant Western understandings of reality and meaning, and of violence and death.

12 For more on this topic, see the essays in my edited book, *P/Herversions: Critical Studies of Ana Rossetti*, which includes an extensive bibliography about Rossetti's work.

13 When 11-M anthologists requested a poem from her, Rossetti had just published this poem, in February 2004, to protest the bombing of Baghdad in the Iraq War, so she did not send it to them (personal interview, 15 November 2015). Nonetheless, she agrees that it serves as her 11-M text, asserting the parallelism of the events. The poem also appears in her 2016 book *Deudas contraídas* (Debts Owed), her first foray into social poetry. Rossetti has participated in 15-M political activities, as well as solidarity work with the Western Saharan, or Sahrawi, poets of the Generación de la Amistad (Friendship Generation).

14 Piera studied economics at the Complutense University in Madrid. She lived in Cambridge, Massachussetts, for four years, completing postgraduate work in Romance languages and literature at Harvard University. She has also lived in Dublin, Ireland, where she directed the Cervantes Institute. Her best-known book to date is *Puerto Rico Digital* (2009).

15 In this sense, the poem is reminiscent of Bill Viola's video portraits.

16 These techniques, as well as the intimacy of the mother-daughter relationship, might also bring to mind Akerman's films.

17 Certainly the poetry of Antonio Gamoneda does so as well, and his work is an important source of inspiration for these poets. In fact, Piera co-authored with Amalia Iglesias the script for a 2009 documentary about Gamoneda: *Antonio Gamoneda: Escritura y alquimia*, directed by Enrique Cortí and César Rendueles. Daniel Aguirre Oteiza writes that "el testimonio gamonediano resulta 'incomprensible' porque aspira a dar fe de ausencias, pérdidas y silencios cuanto tales" (Gamoneda's style of testimony is "incomprehensible" because it aspires to attest to absences, losses, and

silences as such) (26). Gamoneda's 11-M poem, "El 11 ensangrentado" (Bloody 11th], however, is a direct and transparent condemnation of Bush and Aznar, and I have therefore not included it in this study.

5. Pixel, Bar Code, Algorithm

1 For more on the history of this group and the production of affect in the Nocilla novels, see the article by Jesse Barker.
2 There are, however, numerous references to cellphones.
3 Prigogine applied the second law of thermodynamics to complex systems, showing how ordered structures can develop from disorder. Clara Janés also dialogues with Prigogine in her 1999 book *El libro de los pájaros* (The Book of Birds), and several of her books engage with the physical sciences, including *Fractales* (Fractals, 2005), *Los números oscuros* (The Obscure Numbers, 2006), and *Variables ocultos* (Hidden Variables, 2010).
4 Again, I will point out that all of the interlocutors are men.
5 See http://www.uvm.edu/~tescaja/htm_cdb/quiet.htm
6 This was my initial sense, and Provencio confirmed to me in a personal interview (2 November 2015) that Bach's music helped him give order to his emotions and thoughts. From my description of the book, it should be clear that it is not only the sacred nature of Bach's music that offered comfort; it is also what John Eliot Gardner describes in his musical biography *Bach: Music in the Castle of Heaven*:

> The music gives us shafts of insight into the harrowing experiences he must have suffered as an orphan, as a lone teenager, and as a grieving husband and father. They show us his fierce dislike of hypocrisy and his impatience with falsification of any sort; but they also reveal the profound sympathy he felt toward those who grieve or suffer in one way or another, or who struggle with their consciences or beliefs. His music exemplifies this, and it is in part what gives it its authenticity and colossal force. But most of all we hear his joy and sense of delight in celebrating the wonders of the universe and the mysteries of existence – as well as in the thrill of his own creative athleticism. (n.p.)

7 Guillem Martínez and his collaborators also show how, as in the United States, ultraconservative religious precepts on morality are often used in Spain to justify neoliberal or "free market" policies and explain away their deleterious impact on the poor, both local and global. They argue that, taking its cue from Reaganism and Thatcherism in the 1980s, the right wing has disguised the authoritarian, Catholic, Francoist, and neoliberal concepts underpinning their schemes to limit political, economic, and cultural agency by co-opting democratic, progressive words – freedom, peace, stability, and modernity – to describe their goals.
8 Interview with the author, 2 November 2015.

Conclusions

1 She has been called, among other misogynistic slurs, "golfa" (slut), a "puta prototerrorista" (proto-terrorist whore), and "una puta zorra oportunista subsidiada por la izquierda etarra que brinda con quienes desmembraron a tu hijo" (a fucking opportunistic whore subsidized by the pro-ETA left who raises a glass with those who dismembered your son) (Pérez).

2 According to an article published in *eldiario.com* under the pseudonym "Barbijaputa," when writer Laura Freixas tweeted after the November 2015 Paris attack that it was another example of masculinist violence, the comments posted to her Twitter account were equally violent: "'Implantaría sin dudar la pena de muerte para ti,' '¿por qué no ejecutamos a Laura Freixas?', 'que las liquiden a ustedes feminazis de mierda hijas de puta'" ("I would use the death penalty on you without a doubt," "Why don't we execute Laura Freixas?," "I hope they liquidate all of you fucking feminazi daughters of bitches") (Barbijaputa).

Works Cited

11-M: Poemas contra el olvido. Madrid: Bartleby, 2004. Print.

"About: Bio of David Broza." N.p., n.d. Web. Accessed 11 November 2015. http://www.davidbroza.net/en/about/#

Agamben, Giorgio. *Means without End: Notes on Politics*. Trans. Vincenzo Binetti and Cesare Casarino, U of Minnesota P, 2000. Print.

Agencia de Noticias de Información Alternativa. "Gays y lesbianas se suman al homenaje y solidaridad a Las víctimas del 11-M." *Colegas*, 3 October 2005. Reprinted in ANIA, Agencia de Noticias de Información Alternativa. Web. Accessed 7 November 2014. http://ania.urcm.net/spip.php?article12793

Aguilera Díaz, Juan Antonio. *PáZsalo: Multitud en rebelión*. Madrid: Fundamentos, 2004. Print.

Aguirre Oteiza, Daniel. *El canto de la desaparición: Memoria, historia y testimonio en la poesía de Antonio Gamoneda*. Madrid: Devenir Ensayo, 2015. Print.

Ahmed, Sara. "Happy Objects." *The Affect Theory Reader*. Ed. Melissa Gregg and Gregory J. Seigworth. Durham and London: Duke UP, 2010. 29–51. Print.

– *The Cultural Politics of Emotion*. New York: Routledge, 2004. Print.

Aigor. "Las calles de Venecia: Onda Expansiva." *Las Calles de Venecia*. 14 March 2014. Weblog. Accessed 16 November 2015. http://larevistademuga.blogspot.com.es/2014/03/onda-expansiva.html

Alexander, Jeffrey C. *Trauma: A Social Theory*. Cambridge: Polity, 2012. E-book.

Álvarez de Toledo, Consuelo. *4 días de marzo: De las mochilas de la muerte al vuelco electoral*. Barcelona: Editorial Planeta, 2004. Print.

Amorós, Amparo. "El espacio en la poesía de José Ángel Valente." *Ínsula* 412 (1981): 1, 10. Print.

Aparicio, Sonia. "'No os olvidamos': El homenaje del mundo de la música a todas las víctimas del terrorismo." *Elmundo.Es*, 3 March 2005. Web. Accessed 10 November 2015. http://www.elmundo.es/elmundo/2005/03/03/cultura/1109855386.html.

Arís, Ricardo. *El escándalo de la comisión del 11-M*. Barcelona: Carroggio, 2005. Print.

Arma Blanca. "El último tren." *Autodidactas*. Boa Musica, 2007. CD.

Artal, Rosa María. *11-M/14-M. Onda expansiva: Un libro para la memoria*. Madrid: Ediciones Espejo de Tinta, 2004. Print.

Asociación de Vecinos y Amigos del Pozo del Tío Raimundo, ed. *11-M: Palabras para el recuerdo*. Madrid: Suma de Letras, 2004. Print.

Assmann, Aleida. "Canon and Archive." *A Companion to Cultural Memory Studies*. Ed. Astrid Erll and Ansgar Nünning. New York: De Gruyter, 2010. 97–107. Print.

– *Cultural Memory and Western Civilization: Functions, Media, Archives*. Cambridge: Cambridge UP, 2011. Print.

Assmann, Jan. "Communicative and Cultural Memory." *A Companion to Cultural Memory Studies*. Ed. Astrid Erll and Ansgar Nünning. New York: De Gruyter, 2010. 109–18. Print.

Baeza, Álvaro. *ETA, 11-M, la conjura de la Goma 2: Historia ETA, 1958–2006*. Madrid: ABL, 2006. Print.

Barbadillo, Pedro, et al. *Madrid 11-M: Todos íbamos en ese tren*. Docus Madrid. October 2004. Film. Web. Accessed 20 October 2015. https://www.youtube.com/watch?v=hl4bDcyfE9I

Barbijaputa. "Eso no. Ahora no. Tú no." *Eldiario.es*. 16 November 2015. Web. Accessed 20 November 2015. http://www.eldiario.es/zonacritica/barbijaputa-isis-machismo-violencia_masculina-laura_freixas_6_452914721.html

Barker, Jesse. "Agustín Fernández Mallo's Nocilla Project: Seeking Affective Engagement in the World City." *Arizona Journal of Hispanic Cultural Studies* 18 (2014): 31–52. Print.

Belau, Linda. "Trauma and the Material Signifier." *Postmodern Culture* 11.2 (2001): N.p. Print.

Benítez Reyes, Felipe. "Una mañana." *11-M: Poemas contra el olvido*. Madrid: Bartleby, 2004. 26–7. Print.

Bernard-Donals, Michael, and Richard Glejzer. *Between Witness and Testimony: The Holocaust and the Limits of Representation*. Albany: SUNY P, 2001. Print.

Bhattacharyya, Gargi. *Dangerous Brown Men: Exploiting Sex, Violence, and Feminism in the War on Terror*. London: Zed, 2008. Print.

Blair, Carole. "Reflections on Criticism and Bodies: Parables from Public Places." *Western Journal of Communication* 65.3 (2001): 271–94. Print.

Bodhi, Bhikkhu. "Introduction." *Abhidhamma Studies: Buddhist Explorations of Consciousness and Time*. 3rd ed. Boston: Wisdom Publications, 1998. Print.

Bourdieu, Pierre. *The Rules of Art: Genesis and Structure of the Literary Field*. Trans. Susan Emanuel. Stanford: Stanford UP, 1996. Print.

Bracegirdle, Christina. "Writing Poetry: Recovery and Growth Following Trauma." *Journal of Poetry Therapy* 24.2 (2011): 79–91. Web. Accessed 5 November 2015. DOI: 10.1080/08893675.2011.573285

Bradley, Adam. *Book of Rhymes: The Poetics of Hip Hop*. New York: Basic Civitas Books, 2009. E-book.

Braidotti, Rosi. *Nomadic Theory: The Portable Rosi Braidotti*. New York: Columbia UP, 2011. Print.

– *The Posthuman*. Cambridge: Polity, 2013. Print.

Bray, Patrick M. "Aesthetics in the Shadow of No Towers: Reading Virilio in the Twenty-First Century." *Yale French Studies* 114 (2008): 4–17. Print.

Brenner, Neil. "Global Cities, 'Glocal' States: Global City Formation and State Territorial Restructuring in Contemporary Europe." *The Global Cities Reader*. Ed. Neil Brenner and Roger Kell. London: Routledge, 2006. 259–66. Print.

Burgess, Katrina. *Parties and Unions in the New Global Economy*. Pittsburgh, PA: U of Pittsburgh P, 2004. Print.

Burgo, Jaime Ignacio del. *11-M: Demasiadas preguntas sin respuesta*. Madrid: La Esfera de los Libros, 2006. Print.

Butler, Judith. *Frames of War: When Is Life Grievable?* London: Verso, 2009. Print.

– *Gender Trouble: Feminism and the Subversion of Identity*. New York: Routledge, 1990. Print.

– *Precarious Life: The Powers of Mourning and Violence*. London: Verso, 2004. Print.

– "Rethinking Vulnerability and Resistance." *Vulnerability in Resistance*. Ed. Judith Butler, Zeynep Gambetti, and Leticia Sabsay. Durham, NC: Duke UP, 2016. Print.

Cañada, Javier. "Pásalo: Redes y dispositivos en la víspera electoral." N.p., n.d. Web. Accessed 27 October 2014. http://www.terremoto.net/x/archivos/000080.html

Cantelli, Marcos. *Del parpadeo: 7 poéticas*. Madrid: Libros de la Resistencia, 2014. Print.

Cardeñosa, Bruno. *11-M: Claves de una conspiración: Las pruebas del engaño*. Madrid: Espejo de Tinta, 2004. Print.

Caruth, Cathy. *Unclaimed Experience: Trauma, Narrative, and History*. Baltimore: Johns Hopkins UP, 1996. Print.

Castilla, Amelia. "Manuel Francisco Reina: 'Ya es hora de descorrer este velo de silencio.'" *El País*, 11 May 2012. Web. Accessed 12 November 2015. http://cultura.elpais.com/cultura/2012/05/10/actualidad/1336676221_353822.html

Castrillo, Juan. *Dolor de luz: A las víctimas del terrorismo 11 de marzo 2004*. Madrid: Gráficas Almeida, 2005. Print.

Cea Gutiérrez, Antonio. "Sistema y mentalidad devocional en las estampas eel 11 de marzo: Imágenes, palabras, tiempos, lágrimas." *El Archivo del Duelo: Análisis de la respuesta ciudadana ante los atentados del 11-M en Madrid*. Madrid: Consejo Superior de Investigaciones Científicas, 2011. 175–206. Print.

Chalvidant, Jean. *11-M: La manipulación*. Madrid: Fernández Ciudad, 2004. Print.

Chamarette, Jenny. "Between Women: Gesture, Intermediality and Intersubjectivity in the Installations of Agnès Varda and Chantal Akerman." *Studies in European Cinema* 10.1 (2013): 45–57. Print.

Clough, Patricia. "The Affective Turn: Political Economy, Biomedia, and Bodies." *The Affect Theory Reader*. Ed. Melissa Gregg and Gregory J. Seigworth. Durham, NC: Duke UP, 2010. 206–25. Print.

Cole, Sarah. "Enchantment, Disenchantment, War, Literature." *PMLA* 124.5 (2009): 1632–47. Print.

Coleman, Renita. "The Effect of Visuals on Ethical Reasoning: What's a Photograph Worth to Journalists Making Moral Decisions?" *Journalism and Mass Communication Quarterly* 83.4 (2007): 835–50. Print.

Comisiones Obreras Unión Sindical de Madrid-Región. *Homenaje a las víctimas 11-M*. Madrid: Ediciones GPS, 2005. Print.

Coronil, Fernando, and Julie Skurski. "Introduction: States of Violence and the Violence of States." *States of Violence*. Ed. Fernando Coronil and Julie Skurski. Ann Arbor: U of Michigan P, 2005. 1–31. Print.

Corti, Enrique, and César Rendueles, dir. *Antonio Gamoneda: Escritura y alquimia*. Interviews by Amalia Iglesias and Julia Piera. Produced by the Círculo de Bellas Artes, the Universidad Nacional de San Martín (Argentina), and the Sociedad Estatal de Conmemoraciones Culturales. 2009. Web. Accessed 27 October 2017. https://www.circulobellasartes.com/ediciones-audiovisuales/antonio-gamoneda-escritura-y-alquimia-cba-unsam-secc-2009–46/

Crumbaugh, Justin. "Are We All (Still) Miguel Ángel Blanco? Victimhood, the Media Afterlife, and the Challenge for Historical Memory." *Hispanic Review* 75.4 (2007): 365–84. Print.

Cvetkovich, Ann. *An Archive of Feelings: Trauma, Sexuality, and Lesbian Public Cultures*. Durham, NC: Duke UP, 2003. Print.

Davies, Ann. *Spanish Spaces: Landscape, Space, and Place in Contemporary Spanish Culture*. Liverpool: Liverpool UP, 2012. Print.

Delgado, Maria M, and Robin W Fiddian. *Spanish Cinema 1973–2010: Auteurism, Politics, Landscape, and Memory*. Manchester: Manchester UP, 2013. Print.

Delphy, Christine, and David Broder. *Separate and Dominate: Feminism and Racism after the War on Terror*. London: Verso, 2015. Print.

Derrida, Jacques. "Archive Fever: A Freudian Impression." Trans. Eric Prenowitz. *Diacritics* 25.2 (1995): 9–63. Print.

Desdedentro. *Red ciudadana tras el 11-M: Cuando el sufrimiento no impide pensar ni actuar*. Madrid: Acuarela, 2008. Print.

Díaz de Castro, Francisco. "Atocha." *Madrid, once de marzo: Poemas para el recuerdo*. Ed. Eduardo Jordá and José Mateos. Valencia: Pre-Textos, 2004. 47. Print.

Díaz-Mas, Paloma. "Literatura para la vida: Textos en los santuarios del 11 de marzo." *El Archivo del Duelo: Análisis de la respuesta ciudadana ante los atentados del 11 de marzo en Madrid*. Ed. Cristina Sánchez-Carretero. Madrid: Consejo Superior de Investigaciones Científicas, 2011. 85–131. Print.

Dickinson, Greg, Carole Blair, and Brian L. Ott. "Introduction." *Places of Public Memory: The Rhetoric of Museums and Memorials*. Ed. Greg Dickinson, Carole Blair, and Brian L. Ott. Tuscaloosa: U of Alabama P, 2010. 1–54. Print.

Domingo, Marta. "PP y Ciudadanos, 'indignados por el abandono' del Monumento del 11-M." *ABC*, 13 August 2016. Web. Accessed 14 November 2017. https://www.abc.es/espana/madrid/abci-pp-y-ciudadanos-indignados-abandono-monumento-11-m-201608310047_noticia.html

Dos platos y un micrófono: 30 años de hip hop en España. RTVE. es. 23 February 2015. Film. Web. Accessed 12 November 2015. http://www.rtve.es/alacarta/videos/otros-documentales/dos-platos-microfono-30-anos-hip-hop-espana/3011578/

Duque Colino, Francisco, María Mallo Caño, and Mar Álvarez Segura. *Superando el trauma: La vida tras el 11-M*. Barcelona: La Liebre de Marzo, 2007. Print.

Efe. "Un monumento como un 'grito' recuerda en El Pozo a las víctimas del 11-M." *El Correo*, 11 March 2011. Web. Accessed 30 October 2015. http://www.elcorreo.com/vizcaya/20110311/mas-actualidad/sociedad/monumento-como-grito-recuerda-201103111237.html.

"El Ayuntamiento espera reabrir, en diciembre, el monumento a las Víctimas del 11-M." *El Plural*, 17 November 2015. Web. Accessed 15 November 2017. https://www.elplural.com/politica/el-ayuntamiento-espera-reabrir-en-diciembre-el-monumento-a-las-victimas-del-11-m_25295102

El blog del Guernica. "Homenaje al 11- M." 9 March 2012. Web. Accessed 20 October 2015. http://elblogdelguernica.blogspot.com/2012/03/homenaje-al-11-m.html

Elola, Joseba. "La base americana contagió el 'Rap.'" *El País*, 25 May 2008. Web. Accessed 13 November 2015. http://elpais.com/diario/2008/05/25/cultura/1211666402_850215.html

Ennis, Juan Antonio. "El idioma de la herida: La lengua del vencido y la escena del perdón en *Los girasoles ciegos*, de Alberto Méndez." *Entre la memoria propia y la ajena: Tendencias y debates en la narrativa española actual*. Ed. Raquel Macciuci and María Teresa Pochat. La Plata, AR: Ediciones del Lado de Acá, 2010. 153–74. Print.

Epps, Bradley S, and Luis Fernández Cifuentes. *Spain beyond Spain: Modernity, Literary History, and National Identity*. Lewisburg, PA: Bucknell UP, 2005. Print.

Erll, Astrid. *Memory in Culture*. Trans. Sarah B. Young. New York: Palgrave Macmillan, 2011. Print.

Escaja, Tina. *Código de barras*. Salamanca: Celya, 2007. Print.

– *Código de Barras*. 2006. Video. Accessed 26 October 2017. http://www.uvm.edu/~tescaja/htm_cdb/

– "Quiet Zone / Lugar de silencio." 2006. Video. Accessed 26 October 2017. http://www.uvm.edu/~tescaja/htm_cdb/quiet.htm

Europa Press. "Declaración íntegra de Aznar." Elmundo.es. 11 March 2004. Web. Accessed 11 November 2015. https://www.elmundo.es/elmundo/2004/03/11/espana/1079016264.html

Evaluación del plan urbanístico de 1997. Web. Accessed 1 November 2014. https://www.madrid.es/revisionplangeneral.

Falcón, Enrique, ed. *Once poetas críticos en la poesía española reciente*. Tenerife: Baile de Sol, (2007) 2009. Web. Accessed 4 December 2017. https://www.nodo50.org/mlrs/Biblioteca/oncemlrs.pdf

–, ed. *Once poéticas críticas*. Tenerife: Baile de Sol, 2007. Web. Accessed 20 November 2017. https://www.nodo50.org/mlrs/Biblioteca/falcon/onpocri.pdf

– "Vientres de Madrid y de Baghdad." Asociación de Vecinos y Amigos del Pozo del Tío Raimundo, ed. *11-M: Palabras para el recuerdo*. Madrid: Suma de Letras, 2004. 160–1. Print.

Feldman, Allen. "Violence and Vision: The Prosthetics and Aesthetics of Terror." *Public Culture* 10.1 (1997): 24–60. Print.

Fernández Mallo, Agustín. *Postpoesía: Hacia un nuevo paradigma*. Barcelona: Anagrama, 2009. Print.

– Untitled poem. *11-M: Poemas contra el olvido*. Madrid: Bartleby, 2004. 61–3. Print.

Fernández-Savater, Amador. "Emborronar la CT (del 'No a La Guerra' al 15-M)." *CT o La Cultura de la Transición: Crítica a 35 Años de Cultura Española*. Ed. Guillem Martínez. Barcelona: Debolsillo, 2012. E-book.

Ferrán, Ofelia. *Working through Memory: Writing and Remembrance in Contemporary Spanish Narrative*. Lewisburg, PA: Bucknell UP, 2007. Print.

Ferrari, Marta. "Un error necesario: Sobre las antologías poéticas españolas de la década de los 90." *Los usos del poema: Poéticas españolas últimas*. Ed. Laura Scarano. Granada: Diputación de Granada, 2008. 25–38. Print.

Fishman, Jessica M., and Carolyn Marvin. "Portrayals of Violence and Group Difference in Newspaper Photographs: Nationalism and Media." *Journal of Communication* 53.1 (2003): 32–44. Web. Accessed 9 August 2008. https://doi.org/10.1111/j.1460-2466.2003.tb03003.x

Flesher Fominaya, Cristina. "The Madrid 2004 Bombing: Understanding the Puzzle of 11-M's Flawed Commemorative Process." *Routledge International Handbook of Memory Studies*. Ed. Anna Lisa Tota and Trever Hagen. New York: Routledge, 2016. 414–27. Web. Accessed 16 November 2017. http://www.myilibrary.com?ID=830647

– "The Madrid Bombings and Popular Protest: Misinformation, Counterinformation, Mobilization, and Elections after '11-M.'" *Contemporary Social Science* 6.3 (2011): 289–307. Print.

Flesler, Daniela. *The Return of the Moor: Spanish Responses to Contemporary Moroccan Immigration*. West Lafayette, IN: Purdue UP, 2008.

Fraenkel, Béatrice. "Street Shrines and the Writing of Disaster: 9/11." *Grassroots Memorials: The Politics of Memorializing*. Ed. Cristina Sánchez-Carretero and Peter Jan Margry. New York: Berghahn Books. 229–43. Print.

Fraser, Benjamin. "Madrid's Retiro Park as Publicly Private Space and the Spatial Problems of Spatial Theory." *Social and Cultural Geography* 8.5 (2007): 673–700. Print.

Fresneda, Carlos. "El Pozo del Tío Raimundo dice adiós a las chabolas." *El País*, 29 May 1986. Web. Accessed 1 November 2014. http://elpais.com/diario/1986/05/29/madrid/517749860_850215.html

Freud, Sigmund. "The Relation of the Poet to Daydreaming." *Twentieth Century Theories of Art*. Ed. James M. Thompson. Ottawa: Carleton UP, 1990. 124–31. Print.

Galeano, Eduardo. *Amares*. Madrid: Alianza, 1993. Print.

Gamoneda, Antonio. "El once ensangrentado." *11-M: Poemas contra el olvido*. Madrid: Bartleby, 2004. 65–6. Print.

García Casado, Pablo. "Las cosas que llevaban." *11-M: Poemas contra el olvido*. Madrid: Bartleby, 2004. 68. Print.

García Fernández, Carlos Javier. *Tres días que conmovieron España: Tres periódicos y el 11-M*. San Lorenzo de El Escorial, Madrid: Langre, 2008. Print.

García Montero, Luis. *La puerta de la calle*. Valencia: Pre-Textos, 1997. Print.

– "Soneto herido." *11-M: Poemas contra el olvido*. Madrid: Bartleby, 2004. 71. Print.

García Ortega, Adolfo. *El mapa de la vida*. Barcelona: Seix Barral, 2009. Print.

Gardiner, John Eliot. *Bach: Music in the Castle of Heaven*. New York: Knopf, 2013. Ebook.

Garofalo, Reebee. "Pop Goes to War, 2001–2004: US Popular Music after 9/11." *Music in the Post-9/11 World*. Ed. Jonathan Ritter and J. Martin Daughtry. New York: Taylor and Francis, 2013. 49–89. Print.

Garton Ash, Timothy. "Nuestro nuevo 'Guernica.'" *El País*, 13 March 2005. Web. Accessed 18 October 2015. http://elpais.com/diario/2005/03/13/domingo/1110688231_850215.html

Gatell, Angelina. "11 de marzo de 2004." *11-M: Poemas contra el olvido*. Madrid: Bartleby, 2004. 72. Print.

Gil Calvo, Enrique. *11/14-M, el cambio trágico: De la masacre al vuelco electoral*. Las Rozas (Madrid): Adhara, 2005. Print.

Glazier, Loss Pequeño. *Digital Poetics: The Making of E-Poetries*. Tuscaloosa: U of Alabama P, 2002. Print.

Gómez Blanco, Gutmaro. "La política penitenciaria del franquismo y la consolidación del Nuevo Estado." *Anuario de derecho penal y ciencias penales*. 2008. Web. Accessed 10 November 2017. https://www.boe.es/publicaciones/anuarios_derecho/abrir_pdf.

php?id=ANU-P-2008-10016500198_ANUARIO_DE_DERECHO_PENAL_Y_CIENCIAS_PENALES_La_pol%EDtica_penitenciaria_del_franquismo_en_la_consolidaci%F3n_del_Nuevo_Estado

Gonick, Sophie. "From Occupation to Recuperation: Property, Politics, and Provincialization in Contemporary Madrid." *International Journal of Urban and Regional Research* 40.4 (2016): 833–48. Print.

González, David. "En el cielo como en la tierra." *11-M: Poemas contra el olvido.* Madrid: Bartleby, 2004. 76. Print.

Gordon, Avery F. *Ghostly Matters: Haunting and the Sociological Imagination.* 2nd ed. Minneapolis: U of Minnesota P, 2008. Print.

Gray, Jeffrey. "Precocious Testimony: Poetry and the Uncommemorable." *Literature after 9/11.* Ed. Ann Keniston and Jeanne Follansbee Quinn. New York: Routledge, 2008. 261–84. Print.

Gray, Richard. *After the Fall: American Literature since 9/11.* Madden, MA: John Wiley and Sons, 2011. Print.

Gregg, Melissa, and Gregory J. Seigworth. "An Inventory of Shimmers." *The Affect Theory Reader.* Ed. Melissa Gregg and Gregory J. Seigworth. Durham, NC: Duke UP, 2010. 1–25. Print.

Gualtieri, Thomas, and Vicente G. Olaya. " El monumento al 11-M, hundido por la pelea entre administraciones. " *El País,* 19 November 2015. Web. Accessed 14 November 2015. https://elpais.com/ccaa/2015/11/18/madrid/1447876948_546161.html

Gutiérrez Aragón, Manuel. *La vida antes de marzo.* Barcelona: Anagrama, 2009. Print.

Hammer, Rhonda. *Antifeminism and Family Terrorism: A Critical Feminist Perspective.* Lanham, MD: Rowman & Littlefield, 2002. Print.

Haraway, Donna J. *Simians, Cyborgs, and Women: The Reinvention of Nature.* New York: Routledge, 1991. Print.

Hayles, N. Katherine. *How We Became Posthuman: Virtual Bodies in Cibernetics, Literature, and Informatics.* Chicago: U of Chicago P, 1999. Print.

Iravedra, Araceli. "De la 'normalidad' a la 'extrañeza': Sobre vinculaciones y diferencias en las nuevas poéticas del compromiso." *Los usos del poema: Poéticas españolas últimas.* Ed. Laura Scarano. Granada: Diputación de Granada, 2008. 41–57. Print.

Janés, Clara. "La rosa de Hal.lach." *Huellas sobre una corteza.* Valladolid, ES: Fundación Jorge Guillén, 2005. 32–42. Print.

– "Todo es muerte en el aire. " *11-M: Poemas contra el olvido.* Madrid: Bartleby, 2004. 85. Print.

Jenkins, Henry. *Convergence Culture: Where Old and New Media Collide.* New York: New York UP, 2008. Print.

Jerez-Farrán, Carlos, and Samuel Amago, eds. *Unearthing Franco's Legacy: Mass Graves and the Recovery of Historical Memory in Spain.* Notre Dame, IN: U of Notre Dame P, 2010. Print.

Johnson, Dennis Loy, and Valerie Merians. *Poetry after 9/11: An Anthology of New York Poets*. Hoboken, NJ: Melville House, 2002. Print.

Joralemon, Donald. "Ordering Chaos: The Process of Remembering Mass Murder." *Mortality* 20.2 (April 2015): 178–91. Print.

Jordá, Eduardo, and José Mateos, eds. *Madrid, once de marzo: Poemas para el recuerdo*. Valencia: Pre-Textos, 2004. Print.

Juarasti, Felipe. "Txorien aberria / La patria de los pájaros." *Madrid, once de marzo: Poemas para el recuerdo*. Ed. Eduardo Jordá and José Mateos. Valencia: Pre-Textos, 2004. 82–3. Print.

Jung, Carl Gustav. "On the Relation of Analytical Psychology to Poetry." In *The Spirit in Man, Art and Literature*. Princeton, NJ: Princeton UP, 1971. E-book.

Kaplan, Ann E. *Trauma Culture: The Politics of Terror and Loss in Media and Literature*. New Brunswick, NJ: Rutgers UP, 2005. Print.

"La goma 2 ECO incautada a trashorras en su garaje en 2001 también tenía DNT." *ABC*, 15 February 2007. Web. Accessed 20 November 2015. http://www.abc.es/hemeroteca/historico-15-02-2007/Nacional/la-goma-2-eco-incautada-a-trashorras-en-su-garaje-en-2001-tambien-tenia-dnt_1631485525196.html

"La inauguración del monumento del 11-M." *20minutos.Es*. 11 March 2007. Web. Accessed 6 November 2014. http://www.20minutos.es/fotos/actualidad/la-inauguracion-del-monumento-del-11-m-2173/

"La Oreja de Van Gogh Ha Grabado una Película en Israel – Qué.es –." N.p., n.d. Web. Accessed 12 November 2015. http://www.que.es/musica/200912301535-oreja-van-gogh-grabado-pelicula.html

"La primera vez que supe de la existencia de Vallecas fue durante la Guerra Civil." *Vallecasweb*. 21 April 2015. Web. Accessed 28 November 2017. http://vallecasweb.com/ocio-y-cultura/item/vallecas-angelina-gatell-la-primera-vez-que-supe-de-vallecas-fue-en-la-guerra-civil-150421

Labanyi, Jo. "Doing Things: Emotion, Affect, and Materiality." *Journal of Spanish Cultural Studies* 11:3–4 (2011): 223–33. DOI: 10.1080/14636204.2010.538244

– *Rescuing the Living Dead from the Dustbin of History: Popular Memory and Postwar Trauma in Contemporary Spanish Film and Fiction*. Bristol: U of Bristol P, 1998. Print.

Labari, Nuria. *Cosas que brillan cuando están rotas*. Madrid: Círculo de Tiza, 2016. Print.

Lamillar, Juan. "11 de marzo: Tríptico." *Madrid, once de marzo: Poemas para el recuerdo*. Ed. Eduardo Jordá and José Mateos. Valencia: Pre-Textos, 2004. 86–7. Print.

Lamo de Espinosa, Emilio. "El 11-S y el Nuevo Escenario Estratégico." *Cuadernos de pensamiento político* (2007): 9–36. Print.

Langenohl, Andreas. "Memory in Post-Authoritarian Societies." *A Companion to Cultural Memory Studies*. Ed. Astrid Erll and Ansgar Nünning. New York: De Gruyter, 2010. 163–72. Print.

Lebow, Alisa. "Memory Once Removed: Indirect Memory and Transitive Autobiography in Chantal Akerman's *D'Est*." *Camera Obscura* 18.1 (2003): 35–82. Print.

Leggott, Sarah. *Memory, War, and Dictatorship in Recent Spanish Fiction by Women*. Lewisburg, PA: Bucknell UP, 2015. Print.

Lerner, Ben. *Leaving the Atocha Station*. Minneapolis, MN: Coffee House Press, 2011. Print.

"Letra de 'El Ultimo Tren de Arma Blanca.'" MUSICA.COM. N.p., n.d. Web. Accessed 14 November 2015. https://www.musica.com/letras.asp?letra=1057752

Lezra, Jacques. *Wild Materialism: The Ethic of Terror and the Modern Republic*. New York: Fordham UP, 2010. Print.

"Life without Plot in 'Leaving the Atocha Station.'" National Public Radio, *Fresh Air*, 9 November 2011. From Literature Resource Center. Accessed 23 November 2017. go.galegroup.com/ps/i.do?p=LitRC&sw=w&u=ucmerced&v=2.1&it=r&id=GALE%7CA272365625&asid=0fb1f6ec33b599a047e29c64f99463b8.

Llorente, Marina. "La memoria histórica en la poesía de Isabel Pérez Montalbán y David González." *Hispanic Review* 81.2 (2013): 181–200. Print.

López Fernández, Laura. "El esencialismo poético en José Angel Valente." *Espéculo* 16 (2000): Web. Accessed 4 November 2015. https://pendientedemigracion.ucm.es/info/especulo/numero16/valente.html.

López Raso, Pablo. "La aplicación del método iconológico en el análisis de la imagen fotoperiodística." *La comunicación en situaciones de crisis: Del 11-M al 14-M*. Actas Del XIX Congreso Internacional de Comunicación. Ed. Alonso Vara Miguel. Pamplona: EUNSA, 2006. 75–84. Print.

Macciuci, Raquel. "La memoria traumática de la novela del Siglo XXI: Esbozo de un Itinerario." *Entre la memoria propia y la ajena: Tendencias y debates en la narrativa española actual*. Ed. Raquel Macciuci and María Teresa Pochat. La Plata, AR: Ediciones del Lado de Acá, 2010. 17–49. Print.

Macías, C.S. "A mazazos contra el monumento a las víctimas del 11-M de El Pozo." *LaRazon.es*, 20 November 2015. Web. Accessed 16 November 2017. http://www.larazon.es/local/madrid/a-mazazos-contra-el-monumento-a-las-victimas-del-11-m-de-el-pozo-CG11241276

Maeso, María Ángeles. *Basura Mundi*. Madrid: Huerga y Fierro, 2008. Print.

Manovich, Lev. *The Language of New Media*. Cambridge, MA: MIT Press, 2001. Print.

Manrique Sabogal, Winston. "Un informe oficial ve 'altamente probable' que Neruda fuera asesinado." *El País*, 9 November 2015. Accessed

18 November 2015. http://cultura.elpais.com/cultura/2015/11/05/actualidad/1446716786_968782.html?id_externo_rsoc=FB_CM

Marcos, Carlos. "El Madrid más 'hip-hopero': Un rapero y un profesor de universidad recorren lugares clave de esta música." *El País*, 24 March 2010. Web. Accessed 11 October 2018. https://elpais.com/diario/2010/03/24/madrid/1269433466_850215.html·

Margry, Peter Jan, and Cristina Sánchez-Carretero. "Introduction." *Rethinking Memorialization: The Concept of Grassroots Memorials*. New York: Berghahn Books, 2011. 1–47. Print.

Marlasca, Manuel, and Luis Rendueles. *Una historia del 11-M que no va a gustar a nadie*. Madrid: Temas de Hoy, 2007. Print.

Maroto Camino, Mercedes. *Film, Memory, and the Legacy of the Spanish Civil War: Resistance and Guerrilla, 1936–2010*. Houndmills, UK: Palgrave Macmillan, 2011. Print.

Marti-López, Elisa. "Autochthonous Conflicts, Foreign Fictions: The Capital as Metaphor for the Nation." *Spain beyond Spain: Modernity, Literary History, and National Identity*. Ed. Bradley S. Epps and Luis Fernández Cifuentes. Lewisburg, PA: Bucknell UP. 148–67. Print.

Martínez, Guillem. "El concepto CT." *CT o la Cultura de la Transición: Crítica a 35 años de cultura española*. Ed. Guillem Martínez. Barcelona: Debolsillo, 2012. E-book.

– *Pásalo*. Barcelona: Debolsillo, 2004. Print.

Massumi, Brian. *Parables for the Virtual: Movement, Affect, Sensation*. Durham, NC: Duke UP, 2002. Print.

Masterson-Algar, Araceli. *Ecuadorians in Madrid: Migrants' Place in Urban History*. New York: Palgrave Macmillan, 2016. Print.

Mayhew, Jonathan. *The Poetics of Self-Consciousness*. Lewisburg, PA: Bucknell UP, 1994. Print.

– *The Twilight of the Avant-Garde: Spanish Poetry, 1980–2000*. Liverpool: Liverpool UP, 2009. Print.

– "Valente/Tàpies: The Poetics of Materiality." *Anales de la literatura española contemporánea* 22.1/2 (1997): 91–102. Print.

– "Valente's Lectura de Paul Celan: Translation and the Heideggerian Tradition in Spain." *Diacritics* 34.3/4 (2004): 73–87. Print.

Mazza, Nicholas. *Poetry Therapy: Theory and Practice*. New York: Routledge, 2004. Print.

McClintock, Anne. "Imperial Ghosting and National Tragedy: Revenants from Hiroshima and Indian Country in the War on Terror." *PMLA* 129.4 (2014): 819–29. Print.

Medina, Raquel. "Poesía y política cultural: Las antologías de poesía en la España democrática." *Hispanic Review* 80.3 (2012): 507–28. Print.

Méndez, Ricardo. "Globalización, neoliberalismo y dinámicas metropolitanas en Madrid." *Documentos y aportes en administración pública y gestión estatal* 19 (2012): 29–49. Print.

Méndez Rubio, Antonio. "Des(a)punte sobre poética, política y figuración." *Once poéticas críticas*. Ed. Enrique Falcón. Tenerife: Baile de Sol, 2007. 42–55. Web. Accessed 20 November 2017. https://www.nodo50.org/mlrs/Biblioteca/falcon/onpocri.pdf

– "La música que oiremos." *11-M: Poemas contra el olvido*. Madrid: Bartleby, 2004. 111. Print.

– "Otra poesía es posible (La cuestión del sujeto y la crítica social en la poesía reciente)." *Ínsula* 671–2 (2002): 42–4. Print.

– *Razón de más*. Tarragona: Igitur, 2008. Print.

Menéndez Salmón, Ricardo. *El corrector*. Barcelona: Seix Barral, 2009. Print.

Meyer-Minnemann, Klaus, Ana Luengo, and Daniela Perez. "'La ponencia colectiva' (1937) de Arturo Serrano Plaja: Una toma de posición literaria y política en la Guerra Civil." *Revista de literatura* (Madrid) 65.130 (2003): 447–70. Print.

Miller, J. Hillis. "What Do Stories about Pictures Want." *Critical Inquiry* 34.5 (2008): S59–S97. Print.

"Monumento a las víctimas del 11 M." *Minube*. N.p., n.d. Web. Accessed 6 November 2014. http://www.minube.com/rincon/monumento-a-las-victimas-del-11-m-a423051

"Monumento homenaje a las víctimas de los atentados de 11-M." *FAM. Estudio de Arquitectura* 2007. Web. Accessed 15 October 2015. http://www.estudiofam.com Accessed 10 October 2018. https://es.wikiarquitectura.com/edificio/monumento-del-11-m/

Moreno, Inmaculada. "Volcán de sangre y hierro." *Madrid, once de marzo: Poemas para el recuerdo*. Ed. Eduardo Jordá and José Mateos. Valencia: Pre-Textos, 2004. 118. Print.

Munárriz, Jesús. "Pocas palabras." *Madrid, once de marzo: Poemas para el recuerdo*. Ed. Eduardo Jordá and José Mateos. Valencia: Pre-Textos, 2004, 119–21. Print.

Nealon, Christopher. "Affect, Performativity, and Actually Existing Poetry." *Textual Practice* 25.2 (2011): 263–80. Print.

Neruda, Pablo. *España en el corazón: Himno a la gloria del pueblo en la guerra*. Santiago de Chile: Ercilla, 1937. Print.

Neumann, Birgit. "The Literary Representation of Memory." *A Companion to Cultural Memory Studies*. Ed. Astrid Erll and Ansgar Nünning. New York: De Gruyter, 2010. 333–43. Print.

Nichols, William J., et al., eds. *Toward a Cultural Archive of La Movida: Back to the Future*. Madison, WI: Fairleigh Dickinson UP, 2014. Print.

No os olvidamos. BMG, 2005. CD.

Noland, Carrie. *Agency and Embodiment: Performing Gestures / Producing Culture*. Cambridge, MA: Harvard UP, 2009. Print.

Nora, Pierre. "Between Memory and History: Les Lieux de Mémoire." *Representations* 26 (1989): 7–24. Print.

Ónega Salcedo, Sonsoles. *Donde Dios no estuvo*. Madrid: Grand Guignol, 2007. Print.

Ordaz, Pablo. *Los tres pies del gato: 11:M. La crónica del juicio*. Madrid: Santillana, 2007. Print.

Orihuela, Antonio. "11-M." *11-M: Poemas contra el olvido*. Madrid: Bartleby, 2004. 131. Print.

– "Voces del mundo posible." *Once poéticas críticas*. Ed. Enrique Falcón. Tenerife: Baile de Sol, 2007. 22–4. Web. Accessed 20 November 2017. https://www.nodo50.org/mlrs/Biblioteca/falcon/onpocri.pdf

Orr, Gregory. *Poetry as Survival*. Athens: U of Georgia P, 2002. Print.

Palmer, Andrew, and Sally Minogue. "Memorial Poems and the Poetics of Memorializing." *Journal of Modern Literature* 34.1 (2010): 162–81. Print.

Partal, Vincent, and Martxelo Otamendi. *11-M: El periodismo en crisis*. Barcelona: Ara Llibres, SL, 2004. Print.

Partido Popular. "Avanzamos Juntos: Programa de gobierno del Partido Popular." 2004. Web. Accessed 11 October 2015. http://www.pp.es/sites/default/files/documentos/1152-20090908162339.pdf

Paz Fernández, Eulogio. *11-M: Palabras para Daniel y Cartas al Director*. Rivas Vaciamadrid, ES: Concejalía de Salud y Consumo, 2006. Print.

Pemán, José María. *Obras completas*. Vol. 1. Madrid: Escelicer, 1947. Print. 5 vols.

Pérez, Fernando J. "El juez Moreno investiga humillaciones en Twitter a Pilar Manjón." *El País*, 10 June 2014. Web. Accessed 20 November 2015. http://politica.elpais.com/politica/2014/06/10/actualidad/1402410634_113119.html

Pérez Montalbán, Isabel. *Animal ma non troppo*. Huelva, Spain Crecida, 2008. Print.

– "Identificación de cadáveres: Madrid, 11 de marzo de 2004." *11-M: Poemas contra el olvido*. Madrid: Bartleby, 2004. 135–6. Print.

Perfecto, Miguel Ángel. "El nacional-sindicalismo español como proyecto económico-social." *Espacio, tiempo y forma* 27 (2015): 131–62. Web. Accessed 4 September 2017. http://dx.doi.org/10.5944/etfv.27.2015

Piera, Julia. "Atlas de muerte." *Madrid, once de marzo: Poemas para el recuerdo*. Ed. Eduardo Jordá and José Mateos. Valencia: Pre-Textos, 2004. 133–4. Print.

Pino González, L.M. del. *Las mentiras del 11-M: 192 falsedades sobre la mayor masacre terrorista que ha sufrido España*. Barcelona: Debolsillo, 2007. Print.

Preston, Paul. *The Politics of Revenge: Fascism and the Military in 20th-Century Spain*. London: Routledge, 2003. Print.

Provencio, Pedro. *Onda expansiva*. Madrid: Amargord, 2012. Print.

"Quiénes Somos: C.E.I.P. 'Padre Mariana.'" EducaMadrid. N.p., n.d. Web. Accessed 28 October 2015. http://www.educa2.madrid.org/web/centro.cp.padremariana.madrid/quienes-somos#main-content

Rancière, Jacques. *The Politics of Aesthetics*. Trans. Gabriel Rockhill. London: Bloomsbury Publishing, 2013. Print.

Redondo, Javier. "Identidades mediáticas y adhesiones políticas." *La comunicación en situaciones de crisis: Del 11-M al 14-M*. Actas Del XIX Congreso Internacional de Comunicación. Ed. Alonso Vara Miguel. Pamplona: EUNSA, 2006. 35–50. Print.

Reina, Manuel Francisco. "Poemas en los andenes." *Asociación 11-M Afectados del Terrorismo* Web. Accessed 12 November 2015. http://asociacion11m.org/poemas-en-los-andenes/

Reinares, Fernando. *Al-Qaeda's Revenge: The 2004 Madrid Train Bombings*. Washington, DC, and New York: Woodrow Wilson Center P and Columbia UP, 2016. Print.

Resina, Joan Ramon. *Disremembering the Dictatorship: The Politics of Memory in the Spanish Transition to Democracy*. Amsterdam: Rodopi, 2000. Print.

Reyes, Ángeles. *Los trenes de marzo (11-M)*. Madrid: SIAL, 2008. Print.

Reyes Mate, Manuel. "From History and Memory – and Back: Factuality, Knowledge, and Morality." *The Holocaust in Spanish Memory: Historical Perceptions and Cultural Discourse*. Ed. Antonio López-Quiñones and Susanne Zepp. Trans. Elena Valdés Luxán. Leipzig, DR: Leipziger Universitätsverlag, 2010. 15–30. Print.

Reyzábal, María Victoria. *M11M*. Málaga: Ayuntamiento de Málaga, 2009. Print.

Ribeiro de Menezes, Alison. *Embodying Memory in Contemporary Spain*. New York: Palgrave Macmillan, 2014. Print.

Richards, Michael. "Grand Narratives, Collective Memory, and Social History: Public Uses of the Past in Postwar Spain." *Unearthing Franco's Legacy: Mass Graves and the Recovery of Historical Memory in Spain*. Notre Dame, IN: U of Notre Dame P, 2010. 121–45. Print.

Rico, Manuel. "Angelina Gatell, Una mujer de la Generación Del 50." *El País*, 9 January 2017. Web. Accessed 28 November 2017. https://elpais.com/cultura/2017/01/09/actualidad/1483963472_268842.html.

Ricoeur, Paul. *Memory, History, Forgetting*. Trans. Kathleen Blamey and David Pellauer. Chicago: U of Chicago P, 2004. Print.

Riechmann, Jorge. *Ahí es nada: Nuevos ensayos sobre el mundo y la poesía y el mundo*. Madrid: El Gallo de Oro, 2013. Print.

– *El día que dejé de leer "El País."* Madrid: Hiperión, 1997. Print.

– "Poesía que no cede a la hipnosis (sobre los tres mundos, los cuatro riesgos y la fractura interior de las palabras). *Once poéticas críticas*. Ed. Enrique

Falcón. Tenerife: Baile de Sol, 2007. 13–21. Web. Accessed 20 November 2017. https://www.nodo50.org/mlrs/Biblioteca/falcon/onpocri.pdf
– "Por un realismo de indagación (homenaje a Joan Brossa)." Alicante, ES: Biblioteca Virtual Miguel de Cervantes, 2006. Web. Accessed 13 December 2017. http://www.cervantesvirtual.com/nd/ark:/59851/bmc5x2q1
– "Un día después del once de marzo." *11-M: Poemas contra el olvido*. Madrid: Bartleby, 2004. 149–50. Print.

Rigney, Ann. "The Dynamics of Remembrance: Texts between Monumentality and Morphing." *A Companion to Cultural Memory Studies*. Ed. Astrid Erll and Ansgar Nünning. New York: De Gruyter, 2010. 345–53. Print.

Riley, Robin L., Chandra T. Mohanty, and Minnie B. Pratt. *Feminism and War: Confronting US Imperialism*. London: Zed, 2008. Print.

Rivera, Mayra. *Poetics of the Flesh*. Durham, NC: Duke UP, 2015. Print.

Robbins, Jill. *Crossing through Chueca: Lesbian Literary Identities in Queer Madrid (1988–2005)*. Minneapolis: U of Minnesota P, 2011. Print.
– Encuentros éticos en la poesía española contemporánea." *La nueva literatura hispánica* 11 (2007): 95–119. Print.
– "Globalization, Publishing, and the Marketing of 'Hispanic' Identities." *Iberoamericana* 3.9 (2003): 89–101. Print.
– "Memorials, Shrines, and Umbrellas in the Rain: Poetry and 11-M." *Studies in 20th/21st Century Literature* 36.2 (2012): 391–408. Print.
–, ed. *P/Herversions: Critical Studies of Ana Rossetti*. Lewisburg, PA: Bucknell UP, 2004. Print.

Rodríguez, Josep M. *Ecosistema*. Valencia: Pre-Textos, 2015. Print.
– "Frente al televisor." *Madrid, once de marzo: Poemas para el recuerdo*. Ed. Eduardo Jordá and José Mateos. Valencia: Pre-Textos, 2004, 151–2. Print.
– "Las semillas del viento." *11-M: Poemas contra el olvido*. Madrid: Bartleby, 2004. 153. Print.
– *Raíz*. Madrid: Visor, 2008. Print.

Rodríguez Jiménez, José L. "The Spanish Extreme Right: From Neo-Francoism to Xenophobic Discourse." *Mapping the Extreme Right in Contemporary Europe: From Local to Transnational*. Ed. Andrea Mammone, Emmanuel Godin, and Brian Jenkins. London: Routledge, 2012. 109–23. Print.

Rodríguez Marcos, Javier. "Solo en casa." *11-M: Poemas contra el olvido*. Madrid: Bartleby, 2004. 156. Print.

Romero, José Manuel. "Cuatro atentados simultáneos causan una matanza en trenes de Madrid." El País Digital, 12 March 2004. Web. Accessed 18 September 2015. https://elpais.com/diario/2004/03/12/espana/1079046001_850215.html

Rossetti, Ana. "Ciudad profanada." *Cercha: Revista de los aparejadores y arquitectos técnicos*. 73 (February 2004): 95. Web. Accessed 9 October 2018. http://www.arquitectura-tecnica.com/cercha/pdf/73.pdf

– *Deudas contraídas*. Madrid: La Bella Varsovia, 2016. Print.

Rothberg, Michael. "Seeing Terror, Feeling Art: Public and Private in Post-9/11 Literature." *Literature after 9/11*. Ed. Ann Keniston and Jeanne Follansbee Quinn. London: Routledge, 2008, 123–42. Print.

– "'There Is No Poetry in This': Writing, Trauma, Home." *Trauma at Home: After 9/11*. Ed. Judith Greenberg. Lincoln: U of Nebraska P, 2003. Print.

Rowland, Antony. *Poetry as Testimony: Witnessing and Memory in Twentieth-Century Poems*. New York. London: Routledge, 2014. Print.

Sabsay, Leticia. "Permeable Bodies: Vulnerability, Affective Powers, Hegemony." *Vulnerability in Resistance*. Ed. Judith Butler et al. Durham, NC: Duke UP, 2016. 278–302. Print.

Salido Andrés, Noelia. "Del 11-M al 14-M: Jornadas de movil-ización social." *La comunicación en situaciones de crisis: Del 11-M al 14-M*. Ed. Alfonso Vara Miguel et al. Pamplona: Ediciones Universidad de Navarra, 2006. 271–84. Print.

Sánchez-Carretero, Cristina, ed.. *El Archivo del Duelo: Análisis de la respuesta ciudadana ante los atentados del 11 de marzo en Madrid*. Madrid: Consejo Superior de Investigación Científicas, 2011. Print.

– "La vida social de las emociones: Ropa y grafiti en los memoriales de los atentados del 11 de marzo." *El Archivo del Duelo: Análisis de la respuesta ciudadana ante los atentados del 11 de marzo en Madrid*. Ed. Cristina Sánchez-Carretero. Madrid: Consejo Superior de Investigaciones Científicas, 2011. 135–53. Print.

– "The Madrid Train Bombings: Enacting the Emotional Body at the March 11 Grassroots Memorials." *Grassroots Memorials: The Politics of Memorializing*. Ed. Cristina Sánchez-Carretero and Peter Jan Margry. New York: Berghahn Books, 2011. 244–61. Print.

– "Trains of Workers, Trains of Death: Some Reflections after the March 11 Attacks in Madrid." *Spontaneous Shrines and the Public Memorialization of Death*. Ed. Jack Santino. New York: Palgrave Macmillan, 2006. 333–47. Print.

Sánchez-Carretero, Cristina, and Carmen Ortiz. "Grassroots Memorials as Sites of Heritage Creation." *Heritage, Memory and Identity*. Ed. Raj Isar Yudhishthir and Helmut K. Anheier. Thousand Oaks, CA: Sage, 2011. 106–13. Print.

Sánchez Rosillo, Eloy. "Inscripción." *Madrid, once de marzo: Poemas para el recuerdo*. Ed. Eduardo Jordá and José Mateos. Valencia: Pre-Textos, 2004. 156. Print.

Santino, Jack, ed. *Spontaneous Shrines and the Public Memorialization of Death*. New York: Palgrave Macmillan, 2006. Print.

Scarano, Laura, ed. *Los usos del poema: Poéticas españolas últimas*. Granada: Diputación de Granada, 2008. Print.

Schwab, Gabriele. *Haunting Legacies: Violent Histories and Transgenerational Trauma*. New York: Columbia UP, 2010. Print.

Sevilla, Pedro. "Madrid, once de marzo." *Madrid, once de marzo: Poemas para el recuerdo*. Ed. Eduardo Jordá and José Mateos. Valencia: Pre-Textos, 2004. 158–9. Print.

Sey, Amanda, and Manuel Castells. "From Media Politics to Networked Politics: The Internet and the Political Process." *The Network Society: A Cross-Cultural Perspective*. Ed. Manuel Castells. Cheltenham, UK: Edward Elgar, 2004. 363–81. Print.

Siebers, Tobin. *Disability Aesthetics*. Ann Arbor: U of Michigan P, 2010. Print.

Sieburth, Stephanie Anne. *Survival Songs: Conchita Piquer's Coplas and Franco's Regime of Terror*. Toronto: U of Toronto P, 2014. Print.

Snyder, Jon. *Poetics of Opposition in Contemporary Spain: Politics and the Work of Urban Culture*. New York: Palgrave Macmillan, 2015. Print.

Sontag, Susan. *Regarding the Pain of Others*. New York: Picador, 2003. Print.

Taylor, Diana. *The Archive and the Repertoire: Performing Cultural Memory in the Americas*. Durham, NC: Duke UP, 2003. Print.

Taylor, Lisa K., and Jasmin Zine. *Muslim Women, Transnational Feminism, and the Ethics of Pedagogy: Contested Imaginaries in Post-9/11 Cultural Practice*. London: Routledge, 2014. Print.

Téllez, Virtudes. "Respuesta de los musulmanes a los atentados del 11 de marzo." *El Archivo del Duelo: Análisis de la respuesta ciudadana ante los atentados del 11 de marzo en Madrid*. Ed. Cristina Sánchez-Carretero. Madrid: Consejo Superior de Investigaciones Científicas, 2011. 159–70. Print.

"Trazos y puntadas para el recuerdo – Asociación 11-M Afectados del Terrorismo." N.p., n.d. Web. Accessed 27 October 2015. http://asociacion11m.org/que-hacemos/trazos-y-puntadas-para-el-recuerdo/

Treglown, Jeremy. *Franco's Crypt: Spanish Culture and Memory since 1936*. New York: Farrar, Straus and Giroux, 2013. Print.

Truc, Gérôme. "*Espacio de Palabras* y rituales de solidaridad en Atocha." *El Archivo del Duelo: Análisis de la respuesta ciudadana ante los atentados del 11 de marzo en Madrid*. Ed. Cristina Sánchez-Carretero. Madrid: Consejo Superior de Investigaciones Científicas, 2011. 209–26. Print.

Vara Miguel, Alfonso, ed. *La comunicación en situaciones de crisis, del 11-M al 14-M*. Actas del XIX Congreso Internacional de Comunicación. Pamplona: EUNSA, 2006. Print.

Velasco, Lola. "El aliento del cazador." *Madrid, once de marzo: Poemas para el recuerdo*. Ed. Eduardo Jordá and José Mateos. Valencia: Pre-Textos, 2004. 175–6. Print.

Villena, Luis Antonio de. *10 menos 30: La ruptura interior en la poesía de la experiencia*. Valencia: Pretextos, 1997. Print.

Vives, Sònia, and Onofre Rullan. "La apropiación de las rentas del suelo en la ciudad neoliberal española." *Boletín de la Asociación de Geógrafos Españoles* 65 (2014): 387–408. Print.

Volcansek, Mary L., and John F. Stack Jr. *Courts and Terrorism: Nine Nations Balance Rights and Security*. Cambridge: Cambridge UP. Print.

Wood, James. "Reality Testing." *New Yorker* 87.34 (31 October 2011): 96. *Music Periodicals Database; Performing Arts Periodicals Database*. Web. Accessed 15 October 2017. https://www.newyorker.com/magazine/2011/10/31/reality-testing

Žižek, Slavoj. *Origin of Violence: Six Sideways Reflections*. Trans. Fabrice Humbert and Frank Wynne. New York: Picador, 2008. Print.

Index

Note: Page numbers in italics indicate illustrations.

Toronto Iberic

1 Anthony J. Cascardi, *Cervantes, Literature, and the Discourse of Politics*
2 Jessica A. Boon, *The Mystical Science of the Soul: Medieval Cognition in Bernardino de Laredo's Recollection Method*
3 Susan Byrne, *Law and History in Cervantes'* Don Quixote
4 Mary E. Barnard and Frederick A. de Armas (eds), *Objects of Culture in the Literature of Imperial Spain*
5 Nil Santiáñez, *Topographies of Fascism: Habitus, Space, and Writing in Twentieth-Century Spain*
6 Nelson Orringer, *Lorca in Tune with Falla: Literary and Musical Interludes*
7 Ana M. Gómez-Bravo, *Textual Agency: Writing Culture and Social Networks in Fifteenth-Century Spain*
8 Javier Irigoyen-García, *The Spanish Arcadia: Sheep Herding, Pastoral Discourse, and Ethnicity in Early Modern Spain*
9 Stephanie Sieburth, *Survival Songs: Conchita Piquer's* Coplas *and Franco's Regime of Terror*
10 Christine Arkinstall, *Spanish Female Writers and the Freethinking Press, 1879–1926*

11 Margaret Boyle, *Unruly Women: Performance, Penitence, and Punishment in Early Modern Spain*
12 Evelina Gužauskytė, *Christopher Columbus's Naming in the* diarios *of the Four Voyages (1492–1504): A Discourse of Negotiation*
13 Mary E. Barnard, *Garcilaso de la Vega and the Material Culture of Renaissance Europe*
14 William Viestenz, *By the Grace of God: Francoist Spain and the Sacred Roots of Political Imagination*
15 Michael Scham, Lector Ludens*: The Representation of Games and Play in Cervantes*
16 Stephen Rupp, *Heroic Forms: Cervantes and the Literature of War*
17 Enrique Fernandez, *Anxieties of Interiority and Dissection in Early Modern Spain*
18 Susan Byrne, *Ficino in Spain*
19 Patricia M. Keller, *Ghostly Landscapes: Film, Photography, and the Aesthetics of Haunting in Contemporary Spanish Culture*
20 Carolyn A. Nadeau, *Food Matters: Alonso Quijano's Diet and the Discourse of Food in Early Modern Spain*
21 Cristian Berco, *From Body to Community: Venereal Disease and Society in Baroque Spain*
22 Elizabeth R. Wright, *The Epic of Juan Latino: Dilemmas of Race and Religion in Renaissance Spain*
23 Ryan D. Giles, *Inscribed Power: Amulets and Magic in Early Spanish Literature*
24 Jorge Pérez, *Confessional Cinema: Religion, Film, and Modernity in Spain's Development Years (1960–1975)*
25 Joan Ramon Resina, *Josep Pla: Seeing the World in the Form of Articles*
26 Javier Irigoyen-García, *"Moors Dressed as Moors": Clothing, Social Distinction, and Ethnicity in Early Modern Iberia*
27 Jean Dangler, *Edging toward Iberia*
28 Ryan D. Giles and Steven Wagschal (eds), *Beyond Sight: Engaging the Senses in Iberian Literatures and Cultures, 1200–1750*
29 Silvia Bermúdez, *Rocking the Boat: Migration and Race in Contemporary Spanish Music*
30 Hilaire Kallendorf, *Ambiguous Antidotes: Virtue as Vaccine for Vice in Early Modern Spain*
31 Leslie Harkema, *Spanish Modernism and the Poetics of Youth: From Miguel de Unamuno to* La Joven Literatura
32 Benjamin Fraser, *Cognitive Disability Aesthetics: Visual Culture, Disability Representations, and the (In)Visibility of Cognitive Difference*
33 Robert Patrick Newcomb, *Iberianism and Crisis: Spain and Portugal at the Turn of the Twentieth Century*

34 Sara J. Brenneis, *Spaniards in Mauthausen: Representations of a Nazi Concentration Camp, 1940–2015*
35 Silvia Bermúdez and Roberta Johnson (eds), *A New History of Iberian Feminisms*
36 Steven Wagschal, *Minding Animals in the Old and New Worlds: A Cognitive Historical Analysis*
37 Heather Bamford, *Cultures of the Fragment: Uses of the Iberian Manuscript, 1100–1600*
38 Enrique Garcia Santo-Tomás (ed), *Science on Stage in Early Modern Spain*
39 Marina Brownlee (ed), *Cervantes'* Persiles *and the Travails of Romance*
40 Sarah Thomas, *Inhabiting the In-Between: Childhood and Cinema in Spain's Long Transition*
41 David A. Wacks, *Medieval Iberian Crusade Fiction and the Mediterranean World*
42 Rosilie Hernández, *Immaculate Conceptions: The Power of the Religious Imagination in Early Modern Spain*
43 Mary Coffey and Margot Versteeg (eds), *Imagined Truths: Realism in Modern Spanish Literature and Culture*
44 Diana Aramburu, *Resisting Invisibility: Detecting the Female Body in Spanish Crime Fiction*
45 Samuel Amago and Matthew J. Marr (eds), *Consequential Art: Comics Culture in Contemporary Spain*
46 Richard P. Kinkade, *Dawn of a Dynasty: The Life and Times of Infante Manuel of Castile*
47 Jill Robbins, *Poetry and Crisis: Cultural Politics and Citizenship in the Wake of the Madrid Bombings*

www.ingramcontent.com/pod-product-compliance
Lightning Source LLC
LaVergne TN
LVHW090200080826
844660LV00013B/885/J

* 9 7 8 1 4 8 7 5 0 4 7 3 1 *